CAR REPAIRS
You Can Make

Edited by Bill Hartford and Joe Daffron

arco

New York

Published by ARCO PUBLISHING COMPANY, Inc.
219 Park Avenue South, New York, N.Y. 10003

Library of Congress Catalog Card Number 66-14067

Arco Catalog Number 1423

Printed in the United States of America

Introduction

An estimated 20% of American car owners now perform their own tune-ups and minor repairs. This represents an increase of 10% from 1957, when there were far fewer cars on the road. One reason, of course, for this phenomenal increase is the fact that more and more car owners have come to realize that the average so-called mechanic often knows less than they do even though he charges exorbitant prices. Cars have been returned to the shop time and time again for the same trouble; each time something else seems to be wrong. Finally the disgusted owner decides to locate and fix the trouble himself — and he usually does it with far greater success than the supposedly expert mechanic.

The main reason for this sorry state of professional service is the fact that there are not enough trained mechanics to go around. One expert estimates that at least 75% of the garage mechanics in the U.S. are insufficiently trained. The cost of having your car repaired is reaching astronomical heights and gas pump jockeys are learning auto repair as they go along — at the customer's expense.

Obviously, then, it not only pays to do your own repairs because of the money you will save, but also because you will be sure that the repair will be done properly. To do this, you don't have to be a professional engineer. All you need is some common sense, patience, and basic knowledge of the workings of an automobile.

In this book we have attempted to show *how* you can make most of the common adjustments and repairs in a professional manner. Detailed how-to photos and drawings help explain the step-by-step instructions of the text and, upon reading this book, it will be quite obvious that there are no secrets to keeping your car in proper tune and running shape. The contents cover most anything the average car owner will want to fix himself. No major tools are required for most of the repairs. The book is broken down into the Engine; Tuning; Ignition; Brakes; Tires; Front End; Cooling System; Body and Interior. There are also several "miscellaneous" chapters dealing with noise, tightening of parts, vapor lock, lubrication, and tools.

This book does not pretend to be a complete manual for all repairs; if it were, it would have to cost ten times as much and you would probably need all types of special tools and equipment in order to make all the repairs shown. You certainly would not want to buy thousands of dollars worth of equipment. What you do want, though, and what this book will help you to achieve, is to make everyday repairs and adjustments — better and more efficiently than the average professional garage mechanic. You will discover that many of these repairs are not difficult, don't require special tools or knowledge, and can even be fun. They certainly will save you money and aggravation and will let you drive a car that is both better running and safer.

Contents

For Topnotch Car Performance—

Take Care of the Engine

At the top, an engine that has been neglected and allowed to become dirty; below it, the same engine cleaned and cared for.

factor—made their car last much longer.

When you get your new car, every unit in it is brand-spanking new, moving parts fit with just the right clearance, the engine quite literally purrs. Then, in time, the engine parts gradually become worn so that clearances between rubbing metal enlarge, components in the ignition system become worn so that timing is late, spark plugs wear out and erosion of the plug electrodes widens the gaps so that plug performance falls off. Other parts loosen or disconnect. Dirt and other foreign matter impedes the operation of the fuel, lubrica-

YOUR car's driving power starts with its engine, and just so long as cars continue to utilize internal combustion engines, engines will continue to receive the greater share of car maintenance. This is so because the engine, in addition to its own mechanical structure—block, head, oil pan, oil pump, crankshaft, pistons, rods, bearings, flywheel and timing gears—takes in the all-important ignition, carburetion, and cooling systems.

If each of these individual units is kept up to standard, your engine will perform substantially as it did when new, even after thousands of miles of operation. But car owners usually become somewhat careless; when the thrill of new-car ownership has worn off they tend to take their car and its engine for granted. Only when trouble shows up do they realize that a little attention at the right time would have forestalled trouble, saved them repair costs and—as a plus

tion and cooling systems, the power and zip of the engine falls off: in short, the engine ceases to purr. . . . Periodic attention could have prevented all of this.

Keep Your Engine Clean. It doesn't take a "mechanically minded" person to keep the outside of the engine clean. And keeping the outside of the engine clean is the first step toward getting the longest possible life from your engine.

Excess operating heat from your engine is dissipated by being passed to the atmosphere through the radiator core, the engine oil pan, and to some extent through other surfaces such as block, cylinder head, and manifold. If you keep the outside of your engine clean, its operating temperature will have a better chance of remaining normal at all times. A dirt-caked oil pan, on the other hand, will not permit excess heat to escape and the bearings, crankshaft, pistons, rods and other parts will operate at higher

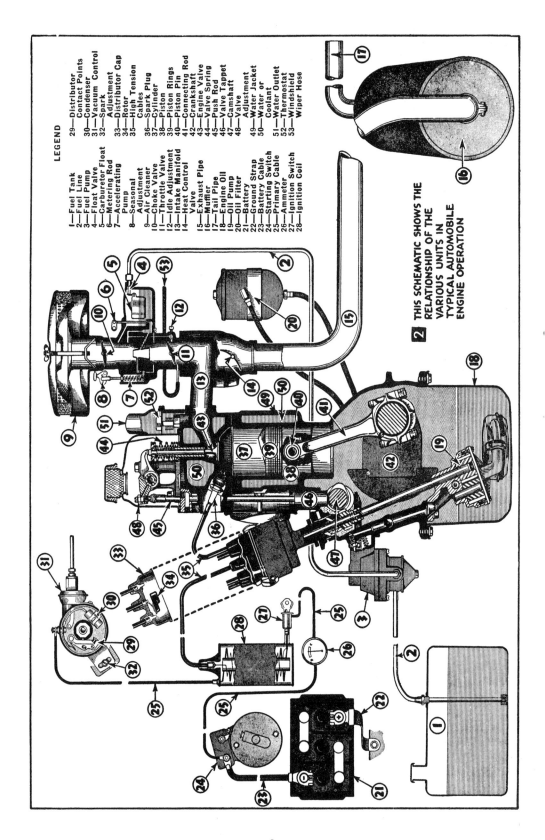

LEGEND

1—Fuel Tank	29—Distributor
2—Fuel Line	30—Condenser
3—Fuel Pump	31—Vacuum Control
4—Float Valve	32—Spark
5—Carburetor Float	Adjustment
6—Metering Rod	33—Distributor Cap
7—Accelerating	34—Rotor
Pump	35—High Tension
8—Seasonal	Cables
Adjustment	36—Spark Plug
9—Air Cleaner	37—Cylinder
10—Choke Valve	38—Piston
11—Throttle Valve	39—Piston Rings
12—Idle Adjustment	40—Piston Pin
13—Intake Manifold	41—Connecting Rod
14—Heat Control	42—Crankshaft
Valve	43—Engine Valve
15—Exhaust Pipe	44—Valve Spring
16—Muffler	45—Push Rod
17—Tail Pipe	46—Valve Tappet
18—Engine Oil	47—Camshaft
19—Oil Pump	48—Valve
20—Oil Filter	Adjustment
21—Battery	49—Water Jacket
22—Ground Strap	50—Water or
23—Battery Cable	Coolant
24—Starting Switch	51—Water Outlet
25—Primary Cable	52—Thermostat
26—Ammeter	53—Windshield
27—Ignition Switch	Wiper Hose
28—Ignition Coil	

2 THIS SCHEMATIC SHOWS THE RELATIONSHIP OF THE VARIOUS UNITS IN TYPICAL AUTOMOBILE ENGINE OPERATION

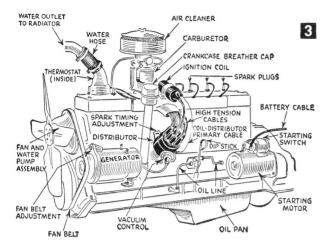

WATER OUTLET TO RADIATOR
WATER HOSE
AIR CLEANER
CARBURETOR
CRANKCASE BREATHER CAP
IGNITION COIL
SPARK PLUGS
THERMOSTAT (INSIDE)
BATTERY CABLE
HIGH TENSION CABLES
SPARK TIMING ADJUSTMENT
COIL-DISTRIBUTOR PRIMARY CABLE
DISTRIBUTOR
STARTING SWITCH
FAN AND WATER PUMP ASSEMBLY
GENERATOR
DIP STICK
OIL LINE
FAN BELT ADJUSTMENT
VACUUM CONTROL
STARTING MOTOR
FAN BELT
OIL PAN

3 clean engine is easier to start, to tune up and to keep in proper adjustment. It enables you to see parts better, and adjustment screws are easier to regulate.

Keeping the engine clean means keeping *all* of it clean, including such parts as the ignition distributor, the carburetor, the fuel pump, the oil filler cap, and the air cleaner. Pay particular attention to the electrical units; keeping them clean gives you a chance to inspect terminals and connections and it also prevents seepage of electrical current and deterioration of cables and wires. Brush out well around the spark plugs so that when the plugs are taken out no foreign matter will fall into the plug hole. Such foreign matter could lodge under a valve head to prevent its seating and it would take but a very short time for the valve and seat to burn, a condition which could only be corrected by removal of the cylinder head to replace the damaged valve.

Some Other Simple Steps. Over the miles, engine performance falls off gradually—but few engines ever have to have all adjustments and tune-up work done at one time. If your engine

than normal temperatures. The oil itself may overheat, oxidize, become black and lose much of its lubricating value.

If you start keeping your engine clean the day you take your new car home it is much easier to keep it clean throughout its life. All you need to keep it clean is a can of solvent or kerosene, an old brush and a plentiful supply of rags. A

NORMAL. If engine is in good condition the vacuum gage hand will remain steady between 18 and 21 (see variations with altitude, Table B). However, later model V-8's should read 14 or 15.

STICKY VALVES. Pointer drops back intermittently when sticky valve or valves come into operation. This condition can be checked further by injecting gum solvent into the manifold through carburetor air horn, freeing valve or valves and subsequently showing normal condition on gage.

BURNT VALVES. If pointer shows a constant drop it indicates a burnt valve or valves. Such a reading may also indicate insufficient valve tappet clearance.

WEAK VALVE SPRINGS. If pointer vibrates excessively it may be an indication of weak valve springs. Check this by spreading two adjacent coils of each valve spring by inserting a large screw driver blade while the engine is running.

WORN VALVE STEM GUIDES. A fast vibration of pointer at idling speed may be an indication of worn valve stem guides. Fast vibration usually disappears with increase of engine speed.

LATE VALVE TIMING. If the engine valve timing is late (due to worn timing gears or chain) the pointer will remain at approximately 16 and a higher reading cannot be obtained. However, later model V-8's should read considerably lower.

RESTRICTED EXHAUST. To check muffler and exhaust line conditions, speed up the engine several times in rapid succession. A clear exhaust is indicated by a quick drop of the pointer to zero. A choked exhaust is indicated by a slow drop.

CARBURETOR IDLE. If at idling speed the pointer moves slowly over a range of two or three divisions, adjustment of the carburetor idling mixture will usually steady the reading.

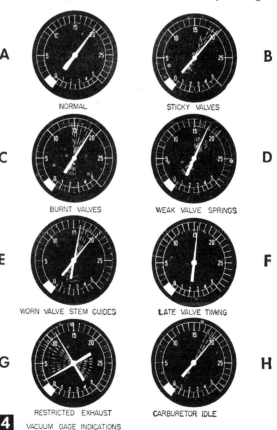

A — NORMAL

B — STICKY VALVES

C — BURNT VALVES

D — WEAK VALVE SPRINGS

E — WORN VALVE STEM GUIDES

F — LATE VALVE TIMING

G — RESTRICTED EXHAUST

H — CARBURETOR IDLE

4 VACUUM GAGE INDICATIONS

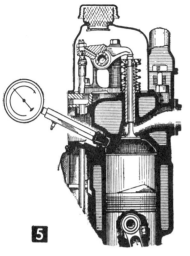

VALVE

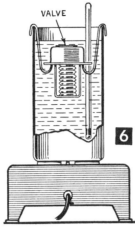

5

Compression gage is held firmly in spark plug hole while starter cranks engine.

Checking temperature at which thermostat opens.

ening done there. And, since the car can be elevated on a lift, the mechanic has ample room to manipulate the wrenches. If you want to do the work yourself, however, better have on hand a couple of strong sawhorses to put under each end of the car after jacking it up to a convenient height. As far as the tightening itself is concerned, you can do just as good a job as the mechanic.

So long as you want to get the most possible good from your engine for the longest possible period, your best plan as far as fuel is concerned is to use any good gas with anti-knock value to prevent ping. Modern higher compression engines give more power and economy and also operate cooler on premium gasoline if timing is adjusted to take advantage of the higher octane.

seems to be ailing, look first for one of the relatively simple sources of troubles listed in Table A, "Simple Engine Troubleshooting."

With the possible exception of bringing the ignition distributor up to standard specifications, you can, with no special equipment, easily make all of the adjustments and repairs listed in Table A. Frequent reference to Fig. 3, which shows the relationship of the various engine parts, will show you how to get at the various parts and will also help to give you a better understanding of your car's operation.

You will be helped considerably in your efforts to keep the engine at its best by buying a set of socket and open end wrenches. If you cannot get these at a hardware store, you can at an automotive parts and equipment jobber. With a set of such wrenches you can go over all the various nuts in the engine, tightening those at such parts as intake and exhaust manifolds, carburetor joints, valve cover plates, timing gear cover, oil filter brackets, fuel lines, oil lines, oil pan—in fact, wherever the nuts are accessible. Be careful of the nuts on the cylinder head. These should be tightened with a torque wrench (a wrench which shows the exact amount of tension being placed on the stud upon which the nut is being tightened). Tightening a cylinder head is a job for the expert who also has available the specifications as to the "in.-lbs." or "lbs.-ft." of torque to which the nuts should be set up.

The attendant at the service station where you have the engine oil changed generally sees to it that the oil pan drain plug is securely tightened. But if you detect oil leaking from your engine onto the garage floor, better take a look underneath; the plug may need tightening.

Some car dealers and service stations have a flat charge for a lubrication and tightening job. You can save a lot of work if you have the tight-

Premium (high octane) fuel allows greater spark advance in your engine timing and the more you can advance the spark the better the engine performance—up to a certain limit, of course.

Using a Vacuum Gage. A vacuum gage is a handy and inexpensive instrument that can tell you much about engine condition. It gives you an approximation of valve conditions and shows leakage tending to lower the vacuum or "suction" within the intake manifold.

Connect the vacuum gage hose to the manifold by slipping off the windshield wiper hose and in its place connect the gage hose. (Or, if there's a small pipe plug screwed into the manifold, remove it, screw on an adapter fitting—usually furnished with the gage—and connect the gage hose to the fitting.)

With the engine at normal operating temperature, allow it to idle and observe the pointer on the vacuum gage. The indications shown in Fig. 4 are sea level readings. These indications will vary with altitude as shown in Table B. They may vary also on some of the latest model cars due to the greater "overlap" in valve timing.

Testing Compression. Good operation of your engine depends to a great extent upon having uniform compression in all the cylinders. A compression gage tests for this. Before removing spark plugs from all cylinders to make such a test, the engine should be operated long enough to bring it to its normal operating temperature. Next, loosen all plugs two turns to crack internal carbon, then start and "gun" engine to blow out this carbon. Then remove the spark plugs, open the carburetor throttle valve wide and block the accelerator pedal if necessary to hold it in this position. Also make sure that the carburetor choke valve is wide open. Place the compression gage in the plug hole of the first cylinder (hold it firmly in place), and with ignition off have someone operate the starting motor (see Fig. 5). Watch the pointer of the compression gage and count the number of revolutions necessary to bring the hand to its highest indication. Actually, you do not count the engine revolutions, but rather the *whrr, whrr,* of the starting motor. Jot down the reading and do the same with the remaining cylinders.

If you have the correct grade and amount of oil in the engine and if pistons, rings, cylinders, valves and gaskets are in good condition the highest readings on all cylinders should be uniform within 6 or 8 lbs. per sq. in. pressure as indicated on the compression gage.

The important thing to watch for in this test is the action of the compression gage pointer. For example, if the pointer does not climb steadily, but remains at rest during the cranking process, indications are that the valve of the cylinder on test is holding open. Or, if on the first turn of the starting motor the hand goes to 35, for example, then remains at 35 on the next turn but

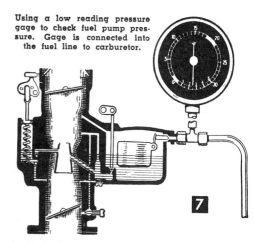

Using a low reading pressure gage to check fuel pump pressure. Gage is connected into the fuel line to carburetor.

climbs higher on succeeding strokes it is likely that the cylinder has a sticky valve. Such a valve condition will show up on the first few revolutions during the test.

Head gasket leakage is generally indicated by low compression readings on adjacent cylinders. If the readings you have jotted down show definite lack of uniformity between cylinders you can often restore normal conditions by using a special gum solvent or similar preparation sold by service stations for this purpose. Valves and piston rings freed in this way may again seat firmly to restore compression, but if the valves are burnt the obvious remedy is replacement of the old valves with new.

The Cooling System dissipates the excess heat from the engine. It must always be kept in the best of condition, that is, it should be serviced at least twice a year (in the spring and fall, or after and before using anti-freeze).

Clean the system with any of the preparations usually sold by gasoline service stations, following the manufacturer's recommendation. It is wise to use an inhibitor in the coolant during the time anti-freeze is not used (almost all anti-freeze preparations have an inhibitor in them). Other

TABLE A—SIMPLE ENGINE TROUBLESHOOTING

If This Is Happening—	Look for This Trouble—	And Fix It Like This—
Low gas mileage.	Dirty air cleaner (9 in Fig. 2).	Remove and clean unit with kerosene, gasoline or a cleaning fluid.
Engine starts hard; idles too fast.	Broken windshield wiper line (53 in Fig. 2).	Slip wiper hose over vacuum tube on carburetor or replace hose with a new one.
Starter works too slow; lights almost go out when starting; engine does not start; lights brighten when engine speeds up.	Battery at low charge (21 in Fig. 2).	Have battery charged and tested for condition of cells.
Sluggish starting motor; engine starts hard, lights dim with engine not running.	Loose, corroded, frayed or broken battery cable or ground strap (22 & 23 in Fig. 2).	Tighten terminals or replace old cable and ground strap with new ones.
Water dripping when car is at rest.	Leaking water hose connection (Fig. 3).	Tighten hose clamps or replace hose with new one.
Engine overheats; water in cooling system boils.	Loose or broken fan belt (Fig. 3).	Adjust tension of belt or install a new belt.
Engine starts hard or fails to start; poor gasoline mileage; fuel drips from carburetor.	Choke sticking partly closed (10 in Fig. 2).	Remove air cleaner and free up choke valve or linkage with kerosene or gum solvent.
Engine oil very dirty.	Clogged oil filter (20 in Fig. 2).	Remove oil filter element and replace with new unit.
Erratic engine operation; engine starts hard.	Loose cable in primary ignition circuit (25 in Fig. 2).	Tighten cable connections on switches, coil and distributor.
Slow acceleration when "stepping on gas."	Wrong seasonal setting of carburetor (8 in Fig. 2).	Make correct setting of seasonal adjustment for cold, hot or normal temperature.
Misfiring; rough operation; poor gasoline mileage; hard starting.	Worn out or wrong type of spark plugs (36 in Fig. 2).	Replace plugs with a new set of correct type and heat range.
Flooding carburetor.	Dirt or chip stuck under carburetor float valve (4 in Fig. 2).	Remove carburetor float bowl cover, remove float and float valve. Watch for foreign matter on valve or its seat.
Rough engine operation; misfiring; hard starting.	Pitted or wrongly spaced distributor contact points (29 in Fig. 2).	Clean, file and adjust gaps with round feeler gauge. Install new points if old are badly worn.
Low gasoline mileage; engine lacks power and pick-up.	Heat control valve sticking (14 in Fig. 2).	Squirt oil and graphite on shaft and tap lightly with hammer.

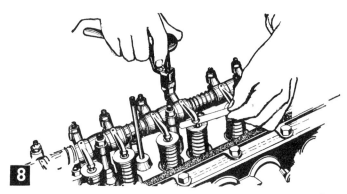

Adjusting valve tappet clearance on an overhead valve type engine. Instead of the special tool shown (used by garage mechanics), an open-end wrench and screwdriver can be used.

warm weather a slightly lower opening temperature compensates for hot weather operation. Your car dealer or service station can give you the specifications on the thermostat in your car. If your car has one thermostat for warm-weather driving and one for cold-weather driving, these are tested to specifications for them in the same manner.

The Fuel Pump forces gasoline from the main tank to the carburetor. It is a highly efficient unit and usually functions for a long time—often 20,000 to 30,000 miles—before any trouble is encountered. Eventually, however, the diaphragm may become punctured or worn to the point where insufficient fuel is pumped to the carburetor. And over a period of time, rocker arm linkage wear also takes place. Further, all fuel pumps have a removable sediment bowl which should be periodically removed and cleaned.

If you have a low reading pressure gage (usually most vacuum gages are so provided), you can check the pressure of the fuel pump by connecting the gage into the line running from the fuel pump to the carburetor (see Fig. 7). Operate the engine and fuel pump pressure will register on the gage. This pressure varies with different makes of fuel pumps and engines but usually runs from about 4 to 7 lbs. If pressure checks okay, make a volume or flow test. The pump on an average car should pump a pint in 30 seconds with engine idling on fuel in the carburetor.

things to check in the cooling system are the tightness and condition of the hose connections, evidence of leakage at the water pump, and the condition and adjustment of the fan belt. Fan belts which also drive the water pump and generator have adjustment devices provided; to get the correct belt tension it is usually only necessary to shift the hinge-mounted generator slightly.

Check the thermostat in the cooling system at least once a year, more often if there are any indications of over-heating. The thermostat is usually located in the water outlet of the engine block and by removing the outer casting (usually held in place by cap screws), you can remove the thermostat for test. To test it, suspend it in a container of water whose level covers the top of the thermostat (see Fig. 6). Heat the water in the container and hold a thermometer in the water to check the temperature at which the thermostat valve opens. The temperature at which low range thermostats start to open is about 150° F.—high range or winter thermostats begin to open at about 180° F. Increase the water temperature until the thermostat valve is completely open. This will be about 30° or 35° F., above the temperature at which the valve started to open. If the thermostat does not open within a reasonable range (5° or 6° F.) of specified opening temperature, it should be replaced with a new one.

Some thermostats are adjustable and these are usually stamped showing the degrees of heat at which the valve opens when set to any of the adjustable positions. Such an adjustable thermostat can be tested as you did the non-adjustable type. If valve does not open within a reasonable range (5° or 6° F.) of specified opening temperature, replace thermostat with a new one. In cold weather a slightly higher opening temperature increases car heater efficiency, while in

TABLE B		
VACUUM GAGE INDICATIONS		
Altitude above Sea Level (in ft.)	Atmospheric Pressure	Vacuum Gage Reading
Sea Level	14.7	19.5
1000	14.1	18.5
2000	13.6	17.5
3000	13.1	16.5
4000	12.5	15.5
5000	12.3	14.5
6000	11.6	13.5
7000	11.2	12.5
8000	10.8	11.5
9000	10.4	10.5
10000	10.0	9.5

After these tests, reconnect the fuel line to the carburetor using a pair of open-end wrenches to tighten the connections. Tightening fuel lines should be carefully done not only to prevent leakage but also to insure ample fuel pump pressure.

The Carburetor. Modern carburetors are complicated units; so far as possible they should be serviced and tuned only at a service station which has the checking equipment, specifications and necessary parts that may be required. You can, however, do some carburetor service work yourself. You can remove the air cleaner and (with the engine idling) look down into the carburetor to see if the tip of the main fuel nozzle is dry. If fuel is coming from this nozzle (2 nozzles, in the case of a double-barrel carburetor) it is probable that the fuel level is too high in the carburetor bowl. On some carburetors a fuel level sight-plug is screwed into the side of the bore. Remove this plug and see if the fuel is level with the bottom of the hole. If fuel comes out, the level is too high. Setting the fuel level requires special gages and should be done at a service station.

If you think your engine has lost some of its zip, make the following tests: With the engine not running, open and close the throttle several times while looking into the carburetor to see if gasoline is squirting from the accelerating pump hole. If the carburetor accelerating pump is working correctly, you will see a solid stream of fuel coming from the pump discharge nozzle. It is this fuel that gives your engine pep during acceleration. Also check to see that the pump arm (on the outside of carburetor) is in the correct hole for seasonal adjustment. In cold weather the pump must have its longest stroke; in warm, its shortest.

Modern carburetors are equipped with automatic chokes, thermostats, fast idle mechanisms, unloaders, etc., which are best left for adjustment to the service station.

On the exhaust manifold of most engines there is a heat control valve which plays an important part in carburetion (14 in Fig. 2). On the outside of the manifold you will see a small lever or weight operated by a thermostat in the shape of a coiled spring. Normally the valve inside the manifold will be in such a position that

9

Distributor with cap removed to show rotor, cam, points and other operating parts.

most of the exhaust heat is passed directly into the exhaust pipe. On a cold engine, however, this valve is closed to direct heat to the intake manifold for better vaporization of the fuel. As the engine warms up, the thermostat comes into action to open the valve. Check this valve for freeness and if it sticks tap the outside weight slightly and squirt a little oil and graphite around the shaft passing into the manifold. This heat control must work freely for good engine performance.

Valve Adjustment. The valves in your engine —if equipped with mechanical lifters instead of hydraulic—have what is called "lash" or clearance between the bottom of each valve stem and the top of the tappet which pushes the valve open (L-head engines) or between the face of the rocker arm and end of the valve stem (overhead valve engines). Many modern engines are equipped with hydraulically operated valve lifters or tappets and the clearance is automatically taken care of. In engines with mechanical tappets it becomes necessary occasionally to adjust the

valve tappet clearance with a pair of special tappet wrenches and feeler gages. The clearance on present day engines varies from .005 in. to .018 in. You must also know for your particular engine whether the clearance specified is for a hot or cold engine. Tappet adjustment on many L-head engines is rather involved because modern engines are fairly well down in the frame and somewhat difficult to get at. If your engine is of this type and develops considerable valve clicking, leave adjustment of clearances to the service station mechanic.

If your engine is of the overhead type and not equipped with hydraulic lifters you can—if you are careful—adjust the clearances between the rockers and valve stems yourself (see Fig. 8). Usually you will find a lock nut and slotted screw on the end of the rocker arm. In making the adjustment, the valve must be fully closed or seated and then—by loosening the lock nut on the rocker arm—you adjust the slotted screw for the necessary clearance. This clearance is established by placing the feeler gage between the end of the valve stem and the contacting face of the rocker arm. Hold the adjustment with a screw driver and tighten the lock nut. Avoid making the adjustments too close or there will be danger of the valves not seating fully with resultant quick burning, compression pressure upset, and poor engine operation.

The Ignition System. Periodic checking and replacement of the spark plugs will not only prolong engine life, but will help you to get maximum fuel mileage. Spark plugs when correctly chosen for the engine operate for a long period, but eventually combustion flame and heat cause gradual deterioration. The insulators literally wear out and oxidation takes place, often causing the spark to jump across the insulator up inside the plug rather than across the intended gap (see Fig. 10). The electrodes, too, become eaten away so that the gap becomes wider than the normal setting called for.

In adjusting electrode gap, always bend the outer, never the center, electrode. Gaps vary from .022 to .040 in., the average being about .025 in. Spark plug makers and service stations have specifications listing all makes of cars and the correct gap setting for each model. Use new gaskets when replacing plugs to insure correct heat transfer. When the plugs are installed, tighten them only enough to compress the gas-

13

ket. If you tighten them too much, the gap setting may be distorted. When buying a new set of plugs be sure that they are of the correct heat range for your engine. Plugs are classified "hot" and "cold," depending upon the length of the insulator.

So far as· the ignition distributor itself is concerned, it is best to have this serviced by your dealer or at the service station equipped with a distributor testing machine which shows actual operating conditions of the distributor. Every 2000 or 3000 miles you can, however, check the distributor with a low reading voltmeter. With the distributor contact points closed and ignition on, connect the meter across the contact points; there should be not more than a 0.2 v. reading. If there is more, it shows excessive resistance between the points which should be cleaned with a thin point file. Do *not* use emery cloth to clean the points.

When the distributor shaft and cam are in a position so that the contact points are open, you can check this opening with a feeler gage. Contact point gaps usually range from .012 to .020 in., with about .018 in., as average. The correct gap is usually specified in the owner's manual or it can be obtained from specification charts at service stations. All distributors have means for adjusting this gap—either with a screw driver or small open end wrench—to move the stationary point closer to or away from the movable or hinged point.

Loosen the clamps which hold the distributor cap in place, wipe out the cap and carefully check it for cracks and corroded electrodes. Scrape any foreign matter off the electrodes with a knife. Slip off the rotor on the end of the distributor shaft and examine it for cracks and condition of the metallic tip. Clean the edge with a knife or fine file and pull the high tension cables out one by one from the cap and clean the sockets and terminals.

After many thousand miles of use the spark plug cables may become chafed, cracked, and oil soaked. If they no longer feel pliable and soft it will pay you to replace them with a new set.

Each time the distributor contact points are replaced with a new set or adjusted for the correct gap opening you must re-time the spark to the engine. You will find timing marks either on the engine flywheel (look through small hole on the front of the flywheel housing on the right hand side of the engine) or on the rim of the vibration dampener or pulley mounted on the end of the crankshaft (look over the top of the radiator, bringing into view the dampener or pulley on the front end of the crankshaft). The easiest way to set the timing is with a neon "timing light," usually connected to No. 1 spark plug and to ground. Usually the mark UDC (Upper Dead Center), or TDC (Top Dead Center), or IGN is placed on the flywheel or dampener to show the point where ignition should **take** place. Some cars have a bright steel ball

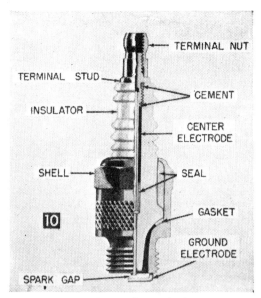

Principal parts of a spark plug.

fastened on the flywheel to indicate this point; otherwise, using white chalk or quick drying white enamel, make a ⅛-in. wide mark directly on this ignition mark and also put a white mark on the end of the pointer or at the center of the inspection hole if there is no pointer there.

With timing light connected, start the engine and allow it to warm up. The neon light flashes regularly every time the spark takes place in the cylinder to which it is connected. Hold the timing light as close as possible to the flywheel or dampener. *Watch out for the fan!* The effect of the timing light is to make the white mark on 'the dampener of flywheel appear to stand still so that you can readily see if it lines up with the mark you made on the stationary pointer. If the timing mark does not line up with the stationary pointer, loosen the lock screw on the distributor and move the distributor to the right or left until the white mark appears exactly at the center of pointer over the dampener or on the flywheel housing. Then tighten the lock screw on the distributor. (Your work will be more accurate if the vacuum line to the distributor is disconnected while setting the distributor.)

To check the action of the automatic spark advance, keep the light on the timing marks and slowly open carburetor throttle valve by pushing or pulling on the rod connected to it. The white mark on the flywheel or dampener should then move away from the center line in a direction opposite to that of the flywheel rotation. Slight variations in timing compensate for different grades of fuel, and differences in altitude or operating conditions.

Muffler and Tail Pipe. A badly corroded muffler, broken or disarranged baffle plates, together with a kinked tailpipe, may produce enough back pressure to offset all of your other good work.

Engine Tuning for Power

For fine performance, try this four-hour job
from compression check to final road test

Remove the battery cable clamps and clean both clamps and terminals well. A bit of steel wool to shine the terminals and interior of the clamps will improve the flow of electricity. Retighten the clamps and battery hold-down brackets.

EVERY mechanic has a special way of tuning engines. It is not necessarily the way the factory intended the job be done. However, no matter how you do it, the results should always be improved performance.

Initial Checks. To gain performance by tuning, the best place to begin is with a compression test. Borrow a compression gauge and press it against spark plug holes of the engine, while the latter is being turned by the starter. This will measure the efficiency of each cylinder. About 5 lbs. pressure difference between the cylinders is allowable for peak performance. Ten pounds difference is satisfactory if you're not going to be particular about the results.

Once in a while two next-door cylinders will read lower than others. This may well be caused by a loose head bolt between them. Tighten it.

If you find low-reading cylinders, give them a further check by squirting a tablespoonful of engine oil into the spark plug hole. If this brings the pressure reading up to normal, you've probably found a set of leaking rings. If it does not change the compression reading, the low-reading cylinder may have a couple of sticking valves.

With a manual transmission car, and no compression gauge, you can check compression with aid of a moderate hill. Run the car to the top, put it in High and allow it to slowly lurch down hill against compression. If all cylinders hold the car back equally, you can be sure they're in equally good (or bad) condition. If one or more cylinders allow the car to lurch forward, they are leaking.

Automatic transmission-equipped engines can be partially checked by spinning the engine, with the starter, while all plugs are in place. If there's no speed change, the cylinders are equal. But if starter speed rises and

15

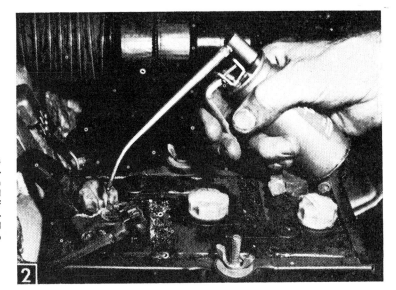

Vaseline, or several drops of fresh engine oil, on terminals will slow the growth of corrosion. Clamps and bolt fittings not kept free of corrosion may "weld" themselves to the terminal and become almost impossible to remove.

Simple voltmeter makes quick check of voltage at low tension terminals of the coil. There should not be more than half a volt drop between battery and coil when ignition is turned on.

falls as the engine turns, it's a fair sign that one or more cylinders has low compression.

The whole point of all this initial checking is: Don't expect too much from the best of tuning, unless the cylinders all have close to the same compression. Period.

Inspect the Electrical Circuits. Clean and tighten all the battery terminals as in Figs. 1 and 2 and fill battery with distilled water. Then follow the ground and starter cables and

tighten the other ends. This makes sure your ignition is getting all the current it requires for perfect performance. A number of domestic and imported cars have more than one ground strap connecting the engine to the frame or body. It's well worth your time to check these out for tightness and electrical conductivity.

Turn on the ignition and use a voltmeter to check current available at the coil as in

16

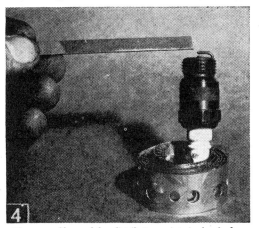

The same file used for distributor points is dandy for filing plugs. Lightly work on the center electrode until it is square, and the end as flat as when it was new. Clean the file afterward to remove any grease.

Electrode in center of the left hand plug has been filed to "like new" condition. That on the right is burned to a rounded end. Square ends require less current to fire, and reduce load on ignition system.

Fig. 3. There should not be more than a ½-volt drop. If more, check wiring all the way back to the battery until you find the connection which is reducing current for the coil. While you're at it, clean the commutator of the starter and generator with carbon tetrachloride and tighten all connections. The only thing we suggest you do with the voltage regulator is tighten the wiring connections and leave the rest alone. If you suspect it requires adjustment, have someone else do it. They're touchy little devils and if out of order, cause everything from dead batteries to burned wiring.

Nuts and Bolts are next. Use a good set of wrenches to tighten all the head, manifold (both intake and exhaust), carburetor attachment, and other odds and ends of hex-headed objects you can find. After thousands of miles of vibration they loosen. Leaking intake manifolds could burn plugs or valves, as well as destroy efficiency of the fuel mixture.

As you well know, exhaust fumes are both dangerous and stinky; which makes a tight exhaust manifold a blessing and a necessity. Best reason for checking head bolts to is to make sure you don't blow a gasket, when making repairs would be the wrong thing to do.

Wiring. From the coil to distributor, and from distributor to spark plugs is a mare's nest of most important wiring. These high tension wires should be firmly soft. If they are hard, cracked, or gooey with oil, replace them all. Cost is low for a new set of high tension wiring, and the results are well worth your trouble. A little cleaning fluid on a clean rag does a good job of wiping off the top of the coil, so electricity can't sneak out of the wires and lose itself to ground.

Inside the Distributor. Removing the distributor cap is only a matter of popping off two spring clips on the side, or loosening two screws through the top. Once off, inspect the inside carefully. If any of the metal tips inside are broken or missing, or the carbon button in the center is gone, buy a new cap. Next check for cracks in the plastic. Find any? Buy a new cap.

Once the buying hurdles are skimmed, you can use a dull knife to scrape the metal contacts clean; but leave the carbon button alone. Then use cleaning fluid and a clean rag to make the inside of the cap spotless. This is most important, as oil or metal particles on the inside bleed valuable current away from the spark plugs, and materially reduce high speed performance. Clean the outside of the cap and lay it to one side.

In the center of the distributor is the rotor, which lifts off after you overcome stiff spring pressure which holds it in place. Use the dull knife to clean the metal and cleaning fluid to wipe off your greasy fingerprints. Points are next. Spread them gently apart with a screwdriver and inspect the little disks which do all the work. If they're not pitted, only a slight touch-up with a breaker point file (Fig. 4) is required. (Never, but never, use sandpaper around a distributor. The bits of sand get in the works and wear things out in a hurry.) Then adjust the points to the engine maker's specifications. This is easily done by loosening the screw in the oval-shaped hole, moving the points open or closed while the rubbing block is on a high point of the central cam, then tightening the breaker screw to hold them where you set them.

Should distributor points be badly pitted or burned, replace them: not to pass the buck, but you'll find complete instructions for point replacement with most point kits. Follow in-

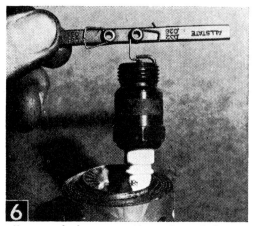

Use a spark plug gauge with round wire feelers to obtain the most accurate setting. Bend only the electrode attached to the metal shell of the plug. If you bend the center electrode you'll break the insulator.

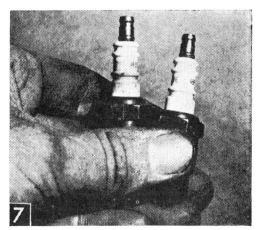

Insulator of plug on right has been cleaned, that on left is in the "as removed" dirty condition. Use cleaning solvent. Gasoline leaves a gummy residue which attracts and holds grimy dirt.

structions carefully; they're written for your specific car. [Editor's note: Also see p. 90, "Is Your Breaker Plate OK?"]

If you do not have access to professional test equipment such as in Fig. 10, a careful inspection of points can tell you plenty about the condenser. Where there are no pits on the points, or only small pits after thousands of miles of service, the condenser is OK. Big pits call for replacement.

An easy check of coil efficiency is to idle the engine with one wire off its spark plug. With a wooden stick, hold the wire about ¼ in. from grounding metal. If the spark between terminal and ground is fat, the coil is dandy. Should it be a weak, thin drizzle, suspect the coil but do not replace it until you've checked everything from the battery forward. If everything checks out OK, then perhaps the coil does need replacing.

Spark Plugs are the real tattle-tale of every engine. Pull yours one at a time so you know for sure which cylinder they came out of. Plugs running too hot are almost pure white, or the center tip may appear to be melted to a round knob as in Fig. 5. If this is what you find, ask for a set of colder plugs the next time you buy. A plug well matched to the engine has a modest coating of light tan or brown haze over the end. This is just right, and replacement plugs should be of the same number.

Every now and then an engine produces a set of plugs that appear to have been soaked in oil, or are carboned with sticky black goo. Here's a situation where hotter plugs will improve almost everything. They cost no more, so specify one range hotter when you buy.

If you have racked up several thousands of miles since the little sparkers were cleaned, it's worth taking time to walk to the nearest service station and have them cleaned by sand-blasting. Once done, use the breaker point file to square off electrodes so they look just like new. Surprisingly enough, this final filing and squaring is as important as cleaning. Then gap the plug to the maker's specifications and tighten them into clean plug holes. It's not necessary to over-tighten spark plugs. Good and snug does it. Too much leverage can warp the head or plug, and in some cases strip the threads.

Timing the Distributor is next. Use a neon timing light, clipped to the number one spark plug, pointed at timing marks on the fan belt crankshaft pulley. On vacuum advance distributors be sure to disconnect the vacuum line for this operation to ensure that the distributor is at maximum retard. A dab of white paint on each side of timing marks make them easier to find. Set the car to basic factory specs, as over-advanced timing ruins more plugs, valves and pistons than all the poor fuel in the world. Keep in mind, you cannot hear spark knock that is strong enough to damage your engine, so use factory specs for timing, unless you have access to a dynomometer for a final check out.

One way to improve timing without engine damage is with the aid of a hill. Time yourself, from a standing start, up the steepest portion of the hill. Then modify ignition timing slightly and see if this improves or worsens the performance. It takes time to fine-tune this way, but it's worth the trouble.

Carburetor Adjustment is not a snap, but neither is it impossible. First off, get the engine thoroughly warmed by at least 30 minutes of running. Tighten all the carburetor hold-down nuts and body screws. Turn the idle mixture screws all the way in until they are gently seated. Unwind them exactly one

Here's why a clean insulator is important. Although the high tension cable terminal is equally between the spark plug terminal and metal shell, high tension current is bleeding along the dirty insulator (to the metal shell) instead of traveling the same distance to center terminal.

SPARK LEAK

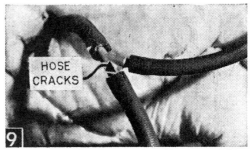

HOSE CRACKS

After 20,000 miles of service, the rubber hoses of this windshield washer line were falling off the connections. A result was added air to the air-fuel mixture which was leaned out during low speed use.

Professional meters, such as this "Allen" unit quickly check coil and condenser of any ignition system.

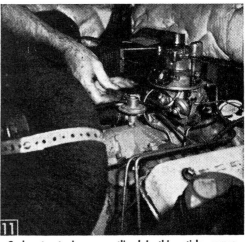

Carburetor tuning, as outlined in this article, comes last. Most carburetors are best left alone, other than tuning. Rebuilding is a time-consuming job that is seldom justified unless the unit is leaking badly, or so old that rebuilding is needed. (Note the cold air tube at left as described on p. 14.)

turn, then set the idle speed adjustment on the throttle linkage to about 450 *rpm* for an automatic transmission car with the trans' in Drive. About 500 *rpm* is right for a manual transmission engine.

If you have no tachometer, the auto transmission engine is adjusted so it won't creep when the unit is in Drive. Manual transmission engines are adjusted to move the car at 5 to 7 *mph* when in high gear.

Once basic settings are made, work with the idle mixture screws until the engine is idling at its smoothest maximum speed. Then readjust the idle adjustment on the throttle lever for the proper *rpm*. Work back and forth until speed and mixture are the smoothest you can get. Then adjust the little button which presses against the dash-pot on automatic transmission cars until there's about $3/16$-in. clearance between the button and the bellows of the dashpot.

A final touch is the high speed idle for the automatic choke. Trace the choke linkage and you'll find a cam-shaped disk against which

an adjustment screw could ride. Set the screw while the engine's warm, so it is about $1/16$ in. away from the cam.

With all adjustments made, have someone else start the car while you watch the automatic choke. If the blades wiggle happily during the start operation, leave it alone. If they seem to bind, use penetrating oil along the linkage to free it. No lubrication though, as lube oil will dry from the heat and make it stick even more than before.

Another item to check is the heat valve on the exhaust manifold. It's that little blob of cast iron, with a flat coil spring behind it. When cold it should wiggle freely. If no wiggle, use penetrating oil and screwdriver leverage to free it. This is most important, as no heat makes for a slow warm-up. Too much heat wastes fuel during normal running.

Last item is the air cleaner. Read the instructions on the outside of the can and do something: Like clean it, replace it, or oil it.

Road Testing the Car is done in the following sequence: In High, run along a level road at some 10 *mph*. The engine should pull evenly, without surge or hesitation. Should it not be smooth, work the idle mixture needles until you have a perfect idle.

Gradual acceleration, resulting from a slow even pressure on the throttle is the next check. During this one, you should have even acceleration, without hesitation or leaping forward. Try this several times, paying close attention to evenness of the speed increase. You'll then notice that between 40 and 60 *mph* there will be a sudden surge forward, though you've not moved your foot that much. Action in the engine room comes from opening of the power valve(s) or secondary throttle blades. All of this is controlled by engine vacuum and position of your foot.

There's more fun to the third check-out. While running 20 to 25 *mph*, floor the throttle. Here you want a smooth, even increase in speed. Again, lack of flat spots is the most important thing. Should the engine seem to gasp once or twice when you floor the throttle, try moving the accelerator pump lever to another hole. This modifies the amount of fuel pumped into the engine and is an adjustment worth making. Make this test several times so you'll have a good idea how well an engine can run. Then as performance changes when the engine ages you'll be in a better position to determine when another tuning is needed.

The last test is to hold the throttle in a steady position at 40 to 50 *mph* on a flat road. Here's where smoothness is the top dog. The engine should keep you rolling at an even pace. If not, the carburetor float level may be off, or the vacuum line to the distributor could be leaking enough to cause spark advance to wander.

One thing sure, after you've spent the necessary four hours making a thorough tune-up, you'll have an engine that outperforms most others of its type. It will also run smoother and be more pleasant to drive; while giving you better fuel mileage than ever before.

How the Idle System Works

THE idle system consists of the idle tubes (5), idle passages (3), idle air bleeds (1), idle adjustment needles (7), and idle discharge holes (6).

In the curb idle speed position, the throttle valve (9), is slightly open, allowing a small amount of air to pass between the wall of the carburetor bore and the edges of the throttle valve.

The idle needle hole (8) is in the high vacuum area below the throttle valves while the fuel bowl is vented to atmospheric pressure.

The fuel is drawn from the bowl through the main metering jets (4) into the main well. The fuel is metered by the idle fuel metering orifice at the lower tip of the idle tube (5) and travels up the idle tube. When the fuel reaches the top of the idle tube, it is mixed with air through two idle air bleed holes (1). This mixture moves through the horizontal idle passage through a restriction (2) and down the vertical idle passage to the four idle discharge holes (6) located just above the throttle valves where more air is added to the mixture. It then passes through the idle needle holes (8) and into the bore of the carburetor.

In addition to this mixture of fuel and air, air enters the bore of the carburetor through the slightly opened throttle valve. For smooth operation, the air from the bore and the air-

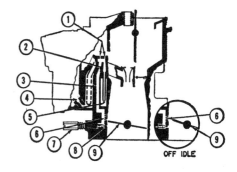

OFF IDLE

fuel mixture from the idle needle hole must combine to form the correct final fixture for curb idle engine speed.

The position of the idle adjusting needle (7) regulates the amount of air fuel mixture admitted to the carburetor bore. Except for this variable at the idle adjustment needle, the idle system is specifically calibrated for low engine speeds.

As the throttle valves are opened, a pressure differential change occurs. Opening of the valve progressively exposes the idle discharge holes (6) to manifold vacuum and the air flow, with the result that they deliver additional air-fuel mixture for off-idle engine requirements.

Pinpointing Ailments With a Vacuum Gage

Save time and money by quickly diagnosing over 30 engine ailments

Using compressed air to keep chips out of manifold while drilling and tapping for gage connection, is a shop job. Compressed air is introduced into a cylinder and the engine is cranked until the intake valve of that cylinder opens, indicated by air rushing out of the carburetor. Then carburetor is plugged with a rag so that when the manifold is drilled any chips that would otherwise fall in are blown out.

NATURE may abhor a vacuum, but the economy-minded motorist is all for it. He knows that high engine vacuum readings indicate superior driving efficiency, excellent engine performance, and more miles to the gallon. And he measures the vacuum of his car's engine with a vacuum gage.

Showing you how to squeeze more mileage from a tankful of gas is not a vacuum gage's only virtue, either. It's also a top-notch troubleshooter —quick to diagnose over 30 engine ailments—all the way from sticking valves, bad carburetor adjustment, worn timing chain, leaky head gasket and clogged muffler, to rings in poor condition, loose valve guides and faulty cylinders.

Figure 3 shows you how the vacuum gage works. You can obtain one of these "engine doctors" for anywhere from $3.85 to $12, from auto accessory stores. It is installed by connecting it to the intake manifold. On cars equipped with a vacuum-operated windshield wiper, you remove the windshield wiper hose and attach the vacuum gage hose. If the car has a vacuum-booster pump, take off the booster line at the manifold and plug the opening.

On most cars without vacuum-type windshield wipers there is a plug in the manifold. Locate this, unscrew it and put in a suitable fitting to take the gage hose. If there isn't such a plug, have a hole drilled and tapped for one (Fig. 1).

Always try to connect the gage as close to the carburetor as possible. The gage you buy should have detailed mounting instructions with it. Follow these carefully.

Vacuum line of shop-type gage has been shortened to show connection to the intake manifold. This gage is calibrated so that range between 18 and 20 indicates a poor vacuum.

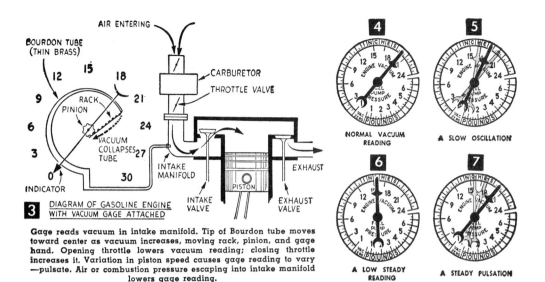

3 DIAGRAM OF GASOLINE ENGINE WITH VACUUM GAGE ATTACHED

Gage reads vacuum in intake manifold. Tip of Bourdon tube moves toward center as vacuum increases, moving rack, pinion, and gage hand. Opening throttle lowers vacuum reading; closing throttle increases it. Variation in piston speed causes gage reading to vary —pulsate. Air or combustion pressure escaping into intake manifold lowers gage reading.

4 NORMAL VACUUM READING

5 A SLOW OSCILLATION

6 A LOW STEADY READING

7 A STEADY PULSATION

Reading a Vacuum Gage. Many automobile engines in good condition show a steady vacuum reading somewhere between 15 and 22 as most gages are calibrated. This reading will drop 1 point for each 1,000 feet that the car is above sea level. Technically, these points on the gage are referred to as "inches of mercury." Originally, vacuum gages were U-shaped glass tubes with mercury at the bottom of the U. The greater the vacuum, the higher the column of mercury. Measured in inches, the standard for vacuum reading became *inches of mercury.*

Let's look at some typical readings. Fig. 4 is a *steady* reading showing 20 inches. But compare this with Fig. 5. Here the needle is slowly swinging back and forth on either side of 18. Something is making the engine speed up and slow down. This something is usually faulty carburetion, though the action may also be due to air leaks between the base of the carburetor and the manifold, or between the manifold and the engine block.

If such oscillation of the hand is noted, tighten the bolts that hold the carburetor to the manifold and those that hold the manifold to the block. Then turn the low-speed mixture, adjusting screws of the carburetor *in* (clockwise), possibly ¼ turn, until the vacuum gage suddenly reduces its reading two or more divisions of the scale. Then turn the mixture screws *out* (counterclockwise) until the gage reading reaches the highest obtainable value.

If the hand still continues to swing, then the carburetor may have a high float level, or the air cleaner may be clogged, or the fuel pump may have high pressure. Any of these conditions could give a rich mixture that would result in the oscillating gage reading seen in Fig. 5. If cleaning the air cleaner does not cure the trouble, try bending the carburetor float *down* 1/16 in. and repeating the test. If no improvement is noted and the carburetor has gone 30,000 to 40,000 miles, try a new or rebuilt carburetor.

Note that the vacuum gage hand in Fig. 6 is steady, but at the *low* end of the acceptable range. This *could* happen on a new engine due to stiffness which necessitates extra throttle opening. Or it could happen on an engine that has not warmed up and is using heavy oil.

The reading in Fig. 6 merely means that the throttle is opened wider—thus admitting more outside air—in order to keep the pistons moving. There are a number of possible causes for this wider throttle opening. It may be because of a new engine, or because valve and ignition timing are late as the result of worn timing gears or timing chain. Or, late ignition alone could cause this low gage reading. Since the ignition is not efficient and full power is not delivered to the piston, the throttle must be opened farther to keep the engine running. And, as we know, opening the throttle lowers the vacuum reading.

Greatest value of the gage results when you check your engine vacuum from time to time. Then if you find the vacuum reading *reducing,* you are on the trail of lost efficiency.

Finally, a totally dead cylinder, blown head gasket, burned distributor contact points, or a leaking intake valve could cause the considerable pulsation at a steady rate indicated in Fig. 7.

Understandably, these vacuum gage indications become even more valuable when followed by compression tests. The average car owner won't have a compression gage, but a garageman usually will. Compression reading in any cylinder should not vary more than 10 pounds from any of the other cylinders in an engine. And *all* should be above 100 pounds in post-war cars. When we have a condition such as that indicated by the vacuum gage in Fig. 7, a compression reading would show whether or not the trouble was due to faulty valves.

Experienced users of the vacuum gage do more than just watch the reading at low idle,

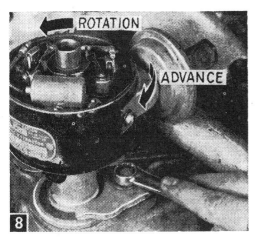

Loosening clamp on engine distributor by turning hold-down bolt allows movement of distributor housing to adjust timing. If rotation of the distributor shaft is counterclockwise, as indicated by arrow, moving the housing clockwise will advance the spark. High steady reading on vacuum gage indicates proper spark advance.

Method of applying gasoline to gaskets between the carburetor and manifold. If gasoline applied here causes fluctuation of the vacuum gage, an air leak is indicated.

however. If the reading is a little low, the operator will open and close the throttle suddenly. If the gage drops to zero and then shoots up between 20 and 22 when this is done, the chances are that the engine needs new rings. A compression test should follow in order to check whether this is the case or not.

If the reading is quite low—between 10 and 15 —loosen the clamp on the ignition distributor (Fig. 8). Turn the distributor *against* the ignition cam rotation while watching the gage. Turning the distributor housing against distribution shaft rotation advances the spark. If this brings the vacuum reading up 1 or 2 or more points it is a sure indication that the car has been running with a retarded spark. Since wear of the

fiber block on the moving arm in the distributor retards the spark, check the condition of the distributor contact points and either adjust them or put in new ones.

Bleeding Air. On old cars, you will often find air bleeding into the intake manifold through a worn carburetor throttle shaft. Air may also get in if the carburetor gasket is broken, or if the carburetor is loose on the manifold. A quick check for these conditions is made by some mechanics by placing a small quantity of gasoline in an oil can and, with the engine idling—and being careful of the fire hazard involved—applying a drop of gasoline at each end of the carburetor throttle shaft. If this causes the vacuum gage reading to vary at all it means that the gasoline is being drawn into the engine. In order to correct this, the carburetor should be overhauled to eliminate air leak.

Make the same kind of test at the base of the carburetor to see if air is being sucked in at the gaskets (Fig. 9). The same check can also be made by dripping gasoline at the exposed edge of each manifold-to-engine gasket.

If any of these other tests show an air leak as indicated by the gage reading varying from 1 to 5 points, tighten the part or replace the gasket.

Sparkplug gaps are often set up to .005 in. wider than specifications call for to give smooth idling and quick starting. Smooth idling from *any* cause gives a steady vacuum gage reading. Sparkplug gaps are also often set .003 to .005 in. closer than specifications call for in order to gain greater top speed. Some individuals may overdo these variations from specifications. If the vacuum gage oscillates over a range of 1 or 2 points, it may be because sparkplugs are set too close. If you get such a swing on your car, check the sparkplug gaps and set them properly to specifications.

When cars overheat or fail to reach expected road speed you may have a restricted exhaust system, from carbon in the exhaust pipe or muffler, or a bent or clogged tail pipe. To test this, run the engine at *about* 2,000 *rpm.* This would be about what would give the car 40-50 *mph* on the road. If the vacuum gage reading reduces gradually from a normal value of between 15 and 22 to almost zero, and then begins to climb slowly, you may be sure that the exhaust system is offering excessive resistance and should be checked.

Power Balance Test. If, because of low or irregular vacuum gage readings you suspect that a cylinder is faulty, how can you tell which one it is? The answer is that you make a *power balance* test, by shorting out certain groups of spark plugs and noting the effect on the gage reading.

For an efficient power balance test, regular automotive trouble shooters often use as many as 6 ground wires attached to a common ground clamp. To avoid electrical shock, attach the common ground clip from the grounding wires to the engine first. Then attach the wires to the sparkplugs. Figure 10 shows an assembly of such

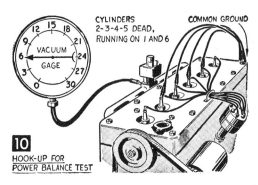

CYLINDERS 2-3-4-5 DEAD, RUNNING ON 1 AND 6

COMMON GROUND

VACUUM GAGE

10 HOOK-UP FOR POWER BALANCE TEST

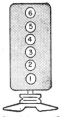

11 ALL 6 CYLINDER ENGINES
FIRING ORDER: 1-5-3-6-2-4
CYL. BAL. ORDER: 1-6, 5-2, 3-4

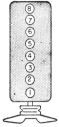

12 ALL 8 CYLINDER IN-LINE ENGINES
FIRING ORDER: 1-6-2-5-8-3-7-4
CYL. BAL. ORDER: 1-8, 2-7, 3-6, 4-5

ground wires attached to a common ground clamp, on a 6-cylinder engine undergoing a power balance test. The engine is running on cylinders 1 and 6, with 2, 3, 4, and 5 dead because their sparkplugs are grounded. The idea is to kill all cylinders except two with the ground wires. This is why most mechanics have the 6-wire assembly so that they can handle both 6- and 8-cylinder engines.

A more scientific test can be made with a tachometer. If you don't have a tachometer, however, try this. Open the carburetor throttle by turning *in* to the right (clockwise) on the throttle stop screw just as much as necessary to keep the engine running on two cylinders. Such a wider throttle opening, will, of course, give a lower vacuum reading. How low this reading will be will vary with the efficiency of the two cylinders under test. When the throttle position that will keep the engine running on only two cylinders is once established it should not be changed during the test; otherwise there will be no standard of comparison between readings for pairs.

Assume a typical firing order is 1, 5, 3, 6, 2, 4 as in Fig. 11. In order to maintain proper balance in testing an engine of this firing order, the pairs of cylinders that operate together are 1-6, 5-2, 3-4. To find the sequence for testing any engine you need only know the firing order. This is generally printed on the engine. When you know the firing order, write it down with the last half of the numbers under the first half. For example, if the firing order is 1, 5, 3, 6, 2, 4 then write down the first half of it as 1 - 5 - 3. Now draw a line beneath these numbers and under the 1 put the 6, under the 5 put the 2, and under the 3 put the 4.

The test is made by running on the pairs of cylinders that line up vertically. In the example given, these would be 1 and 6, then 5 and 2, and then 3 and 4.

If, on this power balance test, the vacuum gage shows a variation greater than 1 inch between *pairs* of cylinders being tested, these cylinders are off balance. (If you used a tachometer, the speed variation should be no greater than 40 *rpm* between pairs of cylinders being tested.) To isolate *one* weak cylinder, short out half of the cylinders in an in-line engine, or an entire bank in a V engine. The bank that gives the lower vacuum gage reading *includes* the weak cylinder.

These, then, are some of the more important of the many applications of the vacuum gage. It can save you money, it can give you the satisfaction of having a smooth-running, efficient car. Unfortunately, it can't remedy the faults it finds. But it can and does simplify that job tremendously.

Installing exchange parts yourself will save you big money.

COIL
DISTRIBUTOR
CARBURETOR
GENERATOR
STARTER SOLENOID
VACUUM BOOSTER END
DOUBLE-DIAPHRAGM FUEL PUMP
STARTER
FUEL PUMP END

Engine accessories which are easily replaced with rebuilt exchange units. Exchange engines include new or reconditioned crankshaft, camshaft, pistons and valves.

Replacing Engine Parts

WHEN your car needs a new generator, carburetor, transmission or engine, you can replace it with an exchange part, doing the tearing down and reinstalling yourself to save the biggest part of a normal repair bill (see the savings on Table A). Exchange parts are completely rebuilt units, guaranteed by the rebuilder to fit and function the same as the original unit. All the work of rebuilding these parts requiring technical skill and expensive shop equipment is done for you. All you do is take the old one off and put a rebuilt one in its place. I'll tell you the exact procedure. Some of the units, distributor and carburetor for example, need to be adjusted to your car's engine, so I'll tell you how to adjust the exchange parts, too.

Take a carburetor, for example. The rebuilder cleans the casting so it's as good as new and puts on brand new jets, nozzles, accelerating pump and linkages. Reputable rebuilders like Wards, Sears and others guarantee them like-new units—at a fraction of the cost for a new assembly. And you get a big allowance on your trade-in. (Of course, you can also buy them without a trade-in.)

Carburetor Replacement. One of the most frequent trouble-makers is the carburetor. Remove the air cleaner and disconnect the throttle, choke linkage and the fuel line from the fuel pump. Two to four studs hold the carburetor body to the flange. Buy an exchange carburetor to fit your car from your rebuilt parts dealer. The carburetor represents a real savings. A new 4-barrel carburetor costs around $70, while the full price of a rebuilt 1957 Ford or Chevy carburetor of this type is $55.95. Sears gives a $33 credit for the old unit, making the price to you only $22.95.

Install the rebuilt carburetor just the reverse of pulling the old one. Install linkage, fuel line and air cleaner, then warm up the engine to operating temperature and you are ready to adjust the carburetor to the engine. A vacuum gage attached to a fitting in the intake manifold on cars with electric wipers (Fig. 3) or to the wiper line in vacuum wiper equipped cars allows you to adjust the mixture and idle controls for peak performance and economy. Turn out the mixture screw (Fig. 4) or the two screws in the case of a two or four barrel carb, until the engine idles smoothly without rolling or galloping. The indicator on the vacuum gage should remain stationary, but if it oscillates in a slow floating motion, keep adjusting the idle-speed screw along with the idle-mixture screws until the gage shows the highest vacuum without vibration. Then adjust the idle-speed screw alone for the best idle speed before the engine warms up thoroughly. On cars with automatic transmissions it may be necessary to readjust the idle speed somewhat lower if the car tends to creep too much at a stoplight.

Distributor. The distributor is another unit likely to cause trouble that can be replaced with a rebuilt one that has all-new working parts. Disconnect spark plug wires at the plugs, the wire harness clamp and the wire from the spark coil. Loosen the screws or bolts that hold the distributor in place, and lift it out with all the harness. If your engine has the

Vacuum gauge being used to adjust carburetor. Vacuum hose is connected to petcock fitted in intake manifold, as car has electric windshield wipers.

TABLE A—REPAIR COSTS YOU CAN SAVE BY USING REPLACEMENT PARTS AND DOING YOUR OWN WORK

Parts	Cars (OHV V-8 except as noted)	Estimated Average Parts and Labor Price	Replacement Parts*	Car Owner Saves
Install brake master cylinder	Chevrolet	$ 15.00	$ 5.00	$ 10.00
	Ford	13.00	5.00	8.00
	Plymouth	15.50	5.70	9.80
Overhaul or install rebuilt carburetor	Chevrolet	25.00	14.00	11.00
	Ford	25.00	14.00	11.00
	Plymouth	25.00	11.00	14.00
Install clutch pressure plate and disk	Chevrolet	43.00	15.50	27.50
	Ford	34.75	14.00	20.75
	Plymouth	24.50	16.00	8.50
Overhaul engine or install exchange engine	Chevrolet 6	225.00	145.00	80.00
	Ford V-8	420.00	320.00	100.00
	Plymouth 6	200.00	160.00	40.00
Install fuel pump	Chevrolet	12.50	3.90	9.50
	Ford	9.25	2.90	6.35
	Plymouth	12.75	4.70	8.05
Install generator	Chevrolet	34.45	12.00	22.45
	Ford	37.50	12.00	25.50
	Plymouth	45.00	12.00	33.00
Install ignition distributor	Chevrolet 6	19.00	7.00	12.00
	Ford V-8	30.50	8.50	22.00
	Plymouth 6	28.00	10.00	18.00
Install one front shock absorber	Chevrolet	12.00	4.00	8.00
	Ford	12.00	4.00	8.00
	Plymouth	9.50	4.00	5.50
Install starting motor	Chevrolet	47.00	14.00	33.00
	Ford	25.00	12.00	13.00
	Plymouth	23.50	12.00	11.50
Overhaul automatic transmission or install exchange unit	Chevrolet	300.00	148.00	152.00
	Ford	212.00	130.00	92.00
	Plymouth	300.00	121.00	179.00
Install standard voltage regulator	Chevrolet	17.00	5.00	12.00
	Ford	12.00	5.00	7.00
	Plymouth	17.50	5.00	12.50
Install water pump	Chevrolet	18.00	6.40	11.60
	Ford	14.00	10.00	4.00
	Plymouth	14.00	8.00	6.00

*Prices are for rebuilt parts and with an exchange, except for brake master cylinder, fuel pump and shock absorber which are new parts not usually exchanged.

plug wires in holders on the valve covers, simply unsnap the distributor cap and push it aside. Remove the distributor and install the new one. The cap can be snapped right back on the new unit unless you also have bought a new cap. In the latter case, position the new distributor as close to that of the removed unit as possible, then pull the wires, one by one, from the old cap and fit each into the new

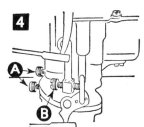

Engines with double-throated carburetor like the Ford V-8 have two idle mixture adjustment screws (a). Other single-throated carburetors have only one screw at about this same location. Idle adjustment screw (b) is usually at end of throttle linkage.

cap. Doing this job one wire at a time will prevent any mistakes in wiring.

A new distributor must be timed to the engine. If you have an inexpensive timing light, simply start the engine and use the light to check the timing mark on the front vibration dampener against the timing arrow on the timing-chain cover. (Chevrolet 6s have a steel ball in the flywheel that can be seen through an opening in the forward side of the flywheel housing. Some other earlier model engines also have timing marks on the flywheel, seen through openings in the housing.) Before starting the engine, turn the timing mark to where you can see it, then mark it with white paint, chalk or soapstone. Hook up your timing light, start the engine, then hold the light as close as possible to the dampener. Caution: Watch that fan, as well as the fan-belt pulleys. You can get your arm badly injured by these whirling units. When timing an engine, have it at operating temperature, so the automatic choke is open and the fast-idle mechanism no longer is keeping the engine running at a faster-than-normal idle. The timing light has a stroboscopic effect, making the timing mark appear to stand still. (The light flashes every time No. 1 plug, to which it is attached, fires.) If the timing mark does not line up with the arrow, loosen the hold-down bolt on the distributor and rotate it slight in one direction or the other until it does align. Tighten the hold-down bolt, then recheck the alignment of the mark. It sometimes happens that tightening the bolt will move the distributor enough to change the timing. Loosen the bolt again, and rotate the distributor enough to compensate for the action when the bolt is tightened.

Other engine parts you can replace that require no adjustment are the *starting motor* and its solenoid switch, the *spark coil* and the *fuel pump*.

Generator and Voltage Regulator. Generator and voltage regulator both can be replaced with rebuilt units, but be sure you know which one is faulty and adjust the regulator to supply the voltage and current your car needs. (A jobber or service station will have a chart showing the required charging rates for various cars. For 6-v. systems, the generator must produce 7.2 v., and about 35 amp., a 12-v. system requires 14.2 v. and from

35 to 38 amp.) This job is best done by a service man with the proper equipment. If the ammeter or indicator light on the instrument panel shows "no charge" have the service man check both the regulator and the generator. Even if you plan on replacing the units yourself, knowing which unit is at fault will save you money. The couple of dollars you pay the service man is a good investment. There are volt-ammeters available for the home mechanic, but they are fairly expensive and only if you plan to do a lot of your own work will they pay for themselves.

When replacing a generator, adjust the

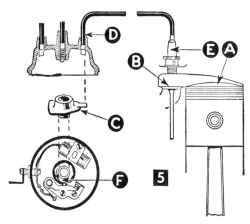

Rough timing distributor to engine. (A) Piston of #1 cylinder at top center of compression stroke, (B) both valves closed, (C) Rotor on distributor shaft directly under #1 cylinder tower (D) with wire leading to #1 spark plug (E). Lobe on cam (F) about to open contact points.

swing arm that adjusts the tension belt (Fig. 7) so the belt does not slip. On modern cars the belt usually is narrow and under a heavy strain. Sometimes simply replacing the belt will repair a non-charging generator. When replacing a voltage regulator, make sure you connect the wires to the same taps—labeling the wires as you disconnect them will help keep them straight.

Don't worry too much about the "genuine" label advertised by car manufacturers. Although car dealers stock parts which assure you of top performance when installed in relatively new cars, with middle-aged cars, replacement or exchange parts can match your car's overall condition without difficulty.

Engine. When the engine in your car needs a complete overhaul including reboring, new pistons, a valve job and new clutch, exchanging it for a rebuilt engine and installing it yourself may be the answer. Besides saving money (a couple of hundred against possibly $600 or more for a new engine) you get the benefit of an assembly-line rebuilt engine that usually carries a 90-day or 4000-mile guarantee—the same as you get with a new car. These engines are tested and aligned before they're approved.

You'll have to buy (or rent) a few tools to exchange the complete engine and to have some means of lifting the heavy block out of the engine compartment. A good set of open-end, box and socket wrenches is minimum. You can add to your tool collection as you go along, knowing that you'll be saving all or nearly all the price of the tools on your first job. After that, all your money savings will be gravy.

To lift out the engine, erect a beam built up from three or four 2x8s nailed together across the top of your garage walls and suspend a chain hoist over the engine compartment (Fig. 9). Don't depend on ordinary bumper or axle jacks designed to help you change tires. You can use these jacks to lift the car, but block it up with short wooden horses or steel supports. If you use common wooden blocks, pile them up in a pyramid so a push on the car won't topple them.

Here's how to systematically remove the engine from its compartment. On a level floor, drain the oil out of the crankcase and replace the plug. Drain out the radiator coolant at the bottom petcock and the plug in the engine block. Remove in turn the battery, hood, air cleaner, radiator (in some cases the grille

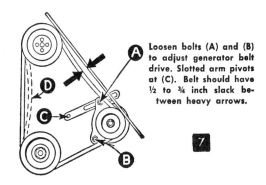

Loosen bolts (A) and (B) to adjust generator belt drive. Slotted arm pivots at (C). Belt should have ½ to ¾ inch slack between heavy arrows.

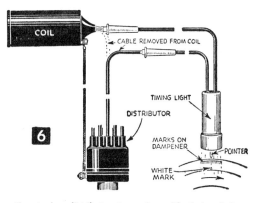

Fine tuning distributor to engine with timing light. Timing marks are on vibration dampener at front end of crankshaft or through hole in flywheel housing.

may have to be removed), ignition distributor, spark coil, carburetor, fan, generator, fuel pump, intake manifold, spark plugs, water pump and any of the other small parts which vary from car to car. The lighter you can make the engine, the easier it will be to handle. As you take off the parts, arrange them systematically on a bench, keeping related parts together and cap screws, nuts, washers and bolts with their respective parts. Write out little tags for all the wires, instrument cables or wires, control linkage, vacuum

and fuel tubing, clutch pedal arms and shift levers. From under the car, disconnect the exhaust pipe at the manifold flange and the flywheel housing from the rear of the engine. On some cars, Ford 1940 to 1948 for example, you must remove the floor boards to get at the upper cap screws. Chevrolets from 1940 to 1948 are detached at the universal joint, removing the engine, clutch and transmission as a unit. Be sure to support the transmission.

There are usually two engine mounts at the front and one or two at the back. Sometimes the rear mounts will be under the transmission rather than the engine block. Pull out the cotter pins and remove the nuts to free the engine. Use a sling chain around the engine at the front and rear where it will not slip off, and hook the ends to the lower pulley of the chain hoist. With a helper working on the chain hoist, move the engine forward and upward. Gradually lift the engine until it is completely free and raise it to a height that allows you to pull it over a clear spot on the floor and lower it beside the car. In some cases it might be easier to take the car off the jacks and roll it back from under the engine, then lower the engine to the floor.

With the engine out, clean the compartment of all grease and mud with a putty knife and rags soaked in solvent. Examine the rubber engine mounts and replace them if they are flattened, broken or uneven. It is inexpensive insurance to replace the mounts, as they will have become worn by the time the engine needs replacing.

Rebuilt engines are supplied stripped of accessories, but including all innards. It's best to equip the rebuilt block with rebuilt carburetor, distributor, fuel pump, generator and other parts subject to wear.

Installing the exchange engine is essentially the reverse of pulling the worn-out engine. As you suspend the rebuilt engine over its compartment, attach those parts which will not interfere with lowering the engine into place. Such parts as the starter, fuel pump, breather pipe are attached low in the engine compartment and are difficult to reach. Make sure that you insert new cotter pins at those

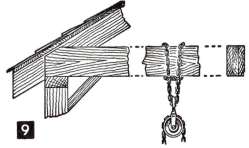

Chain sling over built-up beam across caps of garage walls supports chain hoist to lift out engine.

To remove hood lid on Chevrolet, relieve tension on spring (A) by prying it off at (B). Remove bolts (C).

places where cotter pins were removed. Probably the most difficult spot to wiggle the rebuilt engine in place is at the clutch hub. (You will not have this problem if the transmission first can be bolted to the block and the transmission and engine reinstalled as a unit.) It should slide over the clutch pilot shaft extending from the transmission bell housing. When you assemble the engine to the bell housing, place all capscrews in position and tighten each a little at a time around the rim to draw the assembly together uniformly. Now tighten each a little at a time around the rim to draw the assembly together uniformly. Now tighten the hold-down bolts, and cotter-pin the nuts.

As long as you have a practically new engine use a new fan belt, ignition wiring, battery cables and hose connections to complete the installation. Install new spark plugs of proper heat range and gapped for your engine. (Check with your service station to determine the correct gap for your engine. Most older cars use a .025 in. plug gap, all recent cars use a gap of .035, and most plugs manufactured today are sold with the wider gap.)

Fill the crankcase with No. 10 oil and the radiator with water or antifreeze and you're ready to adjust the carburetor and time the distributor to the engine the same way as noted earlier in this article for replacing only these two units. Make sure the generator and voltage regulator are working, and you're ready for your road test. Treat the engine just like you would on a new car, breaking it in at progressively faster speeds for the first 1000 miles and changing oil after the first 500 miles.

Installing replacement parts is not limited to engine parts. Replacement *transmissions, universal joints, muffler* and *exhaust pipes, brakes, front suspension* parts and *shock absorbers* are available. Some are rebuilt, some new.

Some jobs can be done more quickly and effectively by an automotive repair shop. On a job you might struggle with for half a day and skin your knuckles, a shop equipped with the right equipment can do in a few minutes. For example, take a slipping clutch that pedal adjustment will no longer cure. The clutch cover and pressure plate are under spring tension, so it's quite a job to take it apart and bolt together again. Repair or jobber shops use *clutch rebuilders* to hold the parts in correct position while the repairman bolts the parts together without any strain. Furthermore, clutch covers are steel stampings and can be sprung out of shape if not handled correctly, causing the clutch to chatter when reinstalled.

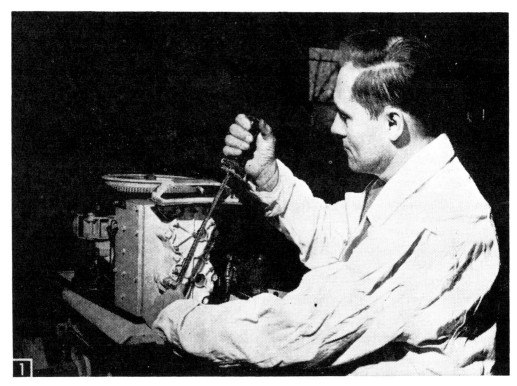

Getting the proper clamping and holding power from any fastener requires that just the right amount of tightening force be applied to the fastener.

How TIGHT Is TIGHT ?

A torque wrench helps you do a quality tightening job and prevents a minor service operation from becoming a major repair bill

EVER-INCREASING use of lighter and softer metal components in automobiles, power mowers, outboard motors, and many household appliances means that homeowners who do their own repairs can no longer rely on hand-tightening nuts and bolts just enough to do the holding job, yet not so tight as to cause damage and premature failure.

Gone are the days when it was permissible to tighten nuts until they squawked or snugged up. To get the proper clamping and holding force from any fastener demands that

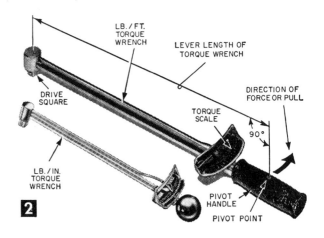

just the right amount of tension be placed on the fastener to stretch it to the predetermined amount of elasticity (Fig. 1).

Too much tightening force can stretch the fastener past the point from which it can snap back into original shape after being stretched, making it unfit for further use. It will also cause the metal component to warp or twist.

On the other hand, too little tension reduces the fastener's ability as a clamping device. Consequently, that part of the assembly will either loosen, fracture, or fail prematurely. General torque tightening specifications are in Table I.

Function of the Torque Wrench is to measure the amount of tightening force applied to the fastener. Today's close-tolerance assemblies require pure precision to establish the correct tightening tension.

All torque wrenches are designed on the principle of the lever. Torque is based on the fundamental law of the lever, which states that force times distance equals the torque about a given point. Force refers to the amount of pull applied to the wrench handle by the operator. Distance is the length of the wrench measured between the centerline of the force being applied to the handle and the centerline of the drive square (Fig. 2). To arrive at torque, multiply force times distance.

Most commonly used torque wrenches are

Never twist the handle of the wrench when applying force, because you can upset the precision calibration and get a false torque reading.

the pound-inch and the pound-foot (Fig. 2). The occasion often arises when it may become necessary to convert lb./in. into lb./ft., or vice versa. To convert a lb./ft. reading on the scale of the wrench to lb./in., multiply the scale reading by 12. To convert lb./in. to lb./ft., merely divide the reading on the lb./ft. scale by 12.

Increase Capacity of the torque wrench by using an extension or adapter to gain access to hidden fasteners (Figs. 3, 6) and nearly double the calibrations on the torque scale (Fig. 4).

A fitting equal to the lever length of the wrench will multiply the torque by two; thus a 100 lb./ft. wrench can be used to tighten bolts up to 200 lb./ft.

There are a number of such fittings available for torque wrenches; in fact, most any socket adapter or extension will fit a torque wrench.

Although these fittings enable you to get maximum utility from the wrench, they also increase the length of the wrench and have the overall effect of increasing the length of the lever so the torque scale will not give an accurate torque reading.

One way to compensate for the length-increasing extension or adapter is to use the formula in Fig. 4. Another way is to

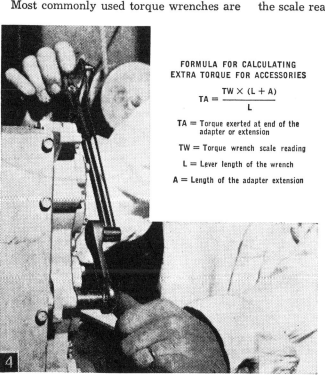

FORMULA FOR CALCULATING EXTRA TORQUE FOR ACCESSORIES

$$TA = \frac{TW \times (L + A)}{L}$$

TA = Torque exerted at end of the adapter or extension

TW = Torque wrench scale reading

L = Lever length of the wrench

A = Length of the adapter extension

Adding extensions or adapters to the basic torque wrench can increase its capacity up to double the calibrations on the scale.

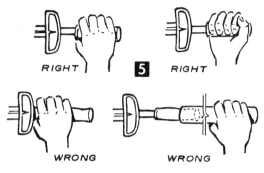

RIGHT 5 RIGHT

WRONG WRONG

This tightening sequence ensures that the holding power of all the fasteners is equally distributed.

send 10¢ and a stamped return envelope to the P. A. Sturtevant Co., 1st and Walnut, Elmhurst, Ill., and request their handy slide rule type of calculator that instantly does the mathematics.

By using the formula in Fig. 4, you can see that a 10-in. torque wrench with a 4-in. adapter or extension will over-torque by 4 lb./ft. even though the scale reads 10 lb./ft.

Using the Torque Wrench is no more difficult than a regular ratchet or pull handle (Fig. 5). There is no hard and fast rule as to whether you should push or pull. The only requirement is that you do not twist or bind the handle.

The pivoted handle, or floating handle as it is sometimes called, is so designed that it conveniently fits the operator's hand and concentrates the pulling force at a fixed point on the torque wrench.

When using the wrench (Fig. 5), the force should be applied to a specific point rather than spreading it out over the entire area of the handle.

Important Points to keep in mind when tightening down threaded fasteners are thread resistance, fastener seizure, and the tightening procedure as in Fig. 6.

Thread resistance is caused by damaged or rusted threads. The rule of thumb to follow when tightening fasteners on such threads is to add the thread resistance to the torque specification for the final torque reading. For instance, if the specification calls for 20 lb./ft. torque for a certain nut, and if it takes 3 lb./ft. to overcome the thread resistance, tighten the nut to a torque of 23 lb./ft.

To determine just what is the amount of thread resistance, note the torque required to pull the nut through its last full turn before exerting any tightening torque. Never check thread resistance anywhere except during the last full turn of the nut.

It is not uncommon for some threads to offer high resistance at the beginning and have little resistance when the nut is run down farther. The leading threads have no effect on the final tightening torque.

Thread seizure shows up as a popping sound that occurs during the final tightening stage of the fastener. To avoid tightening thread seizure instead of the actual elasticity of the fastener, back off at least one-half turn after the popping sound is heard, then apply the final tightening torque with a full sweeping motion. Take the torque reading during this final sweeping motion. Thread seizure can do funny tricks to nuts and bolts, but it can be overcome by the back-off and full-sweep technique.

The tightening sequence in Fig. 6 shows the way to secure a cylinder head. On this particular outboard the recommended torque value is 275 lb./in. Lubricate the fasteners with *Never-Seez,* and tighten the cap screws in the sequence shown to one-third their value, or 90 lb./in. Then to two-thirds the value, followed with a torque at the full value. The fourth step is to apply the full torque counterclockwise.

TABLE I—GENERAL TORQUE TIGHTENING SPECIFICATIONS *

Bolt Size	Cast Iron	Aluminum	Brass
1/4-20	80 lb./in.	60 lb./in.	61 lb./in.
1/4-28	100 lb./in.	84 lb./in.	77 lb./in.
5/16-18	11-12 lb./ft.	8-10 lb./ft.	8-9 lb./ft.
5/16-24	13-14 lb./ft.	10-11 lb./ft.	9-10 lb./ft.
3/8-16	21-23 lb./ft.	17-19 lb./ft.	14-16 lb./ft.
3/8-24	23-25 lb./ft.	19-21 lb./ft.	15-17 lb./ft.
7/16-14	33-35 lb./ft.	27-29 lb./ft.	24-26 lb./ft.
7/16-20	35-37 lb./ft.	30-31 lb./ft.	25-27 lb./ft.
1/2-13	46-48 lb./ft.	37-41 lb./ft.	33-35 lb./ft.
1/2-20	48-50 lb./ft.	42-44 lb./ft.	35-37 lb./ft.
9/16-12	60-62 lb./ft.	57-58 lb./ft.	44-46 lb./ft.
9/16-18	67-69 lb./ft	63-64 lb./ft.	49-51 lb./ft.
5/8-11	104-106 lb./ft.	93-96 lb./ft.	73-75 lb./ft.
5/8-18	116-118 lb./ft.	101-104 lb./ft.	93-95 lb./ft.
3/4-10	144-146 lb./ft.	128-131 lb./ft.	102-104 lb./ft.
3/4-16	140-142 lb./ft.	132-134 lb./ft.	100-102 lb./ft.
7/8-9	218-220 lb./ft.	191-194 lb./ft.	157-159 lb./ft.
7/8-14	217-219 lb./ft.	196-198 lb./ft.	156-158 lb./ft.
1-8	323-325 lb./ft.	293-298 lb./ft.	232-234 lb./ft.
1-14	292-294 lb./ft.	264-266 lb./ft.	210-212 lb./ft.

* These specifications can be followed when specific factory specifications are not available. The many variables of fasteners and materials make the above table useful as a guide only. On especially critical applications, individual manufacturer's specifications must be followed.

correctly tuned, because your carb depends on proper operation of the rest of the engine.

Make No Mistake about one thing, a carburetor would probably function properly forever if it weren't for dirt that is present in the air sucked into it and in the gas. This dirt builds up in the carb and causes the engine to lose power while drinking up an increasing amount of gas. Or, dirt can strike suddenly and cause the engine to stop running without warning. In either case, the results are the same: loss of power, engine sputter, stalling, and wasted gas.

There are several ways to remove this dirt. First, a cleaner can be added to the gas tank. If this cleaner is added three or four times a year from the time the car is new, it does a fairly effective job. The cleaner enters all parts and orifices of the carb and cleans them out while driving.

Put New Life in Your Carburetor

Save yourself a costly repair bill and restore like-new performance to your carb with a gum-chasing treatment and replacement of worn parts

A LIST of malfunctions caused by a sick carburetor reads like a Who's Who of Auto Ailments. It includes hard starting, flooding, delayed acceleration, poor gas mileage, stalling, rough running, fouled spark plugs, and gas leaks at the carburetor.

Not all of these problems, however, result from an ailing carburetor only. For this reason you should make sure spark plugs, ignition parts, compression, and timing are all in good condition before beginning carburetor service. In short, make sure your engine is

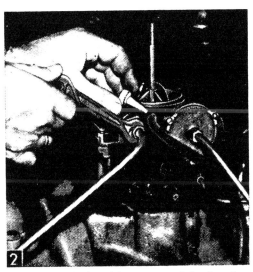

When using the forced-flow process of cleaning, detach gas line and insert tapered plug into the line to prevent gas from flowing.

Another way to keep your carb clean is to introduce the solvent directly into the carb through a forced-flow kit (Fig. 1). One such kit is made by the Gumout Division of Pennsylvania Refining Co. and can be purchased at most auto supply outlets or accessory stores. It contains adapters, a flexible hose line, and a container of cleaner.

To use this cleaner, disconnect the gas line at the carb, then block off the flow of gas through the line with the universal block-off fitting provided with the kit (Fig. 2). Attach the hose to the carb at the gas inlet port, using the adapter that fits the hole. Start the engine and run it at various speeds. Every so often, place the palm of your hand over the carb to block off air and force the cleaner into all gas and air passages.

Most effective method to really clean the carb when the other ways don't correct the ailment is to take it off the intake manifold, disassemble it, and clean each part. This way you can inspect each part, change if necessary, and make internal adjustments.

Replacing Worn Parts need no longer be left up to the rebuilders if you follow a step-by-step approach in tearing down and reassembling the carb. The one in Fig. 4 is a two-barrel Rochester, which is standard on many General Motors engines. Others,

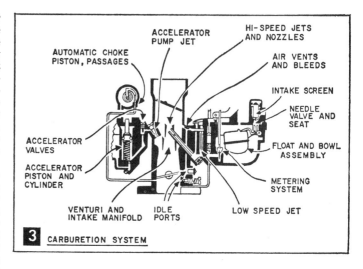

3 CARBURETION SYSTEM

whether single-, two-, or four-barrel, are similar in makeup (Fig. 3) and disassembly, although there are differences in where the parts are located. Literature supplied in the rebuilding kits show where these parts are located in your carb.

A carburetor repair kit contains replacement parts that are most frequently damaged, such as the needle valve assembly, pump plunger and gaskets. Once you tear down a carb you should replace these parts. Kits cost about $4.50 for single- and two-barrel units, and about $6.50 for a four-barrel carb.

When buying your kit, refer to the name and model number of your carb (found on the nomenclature plate attached to it.) If you can't find this plate, give the salesman the

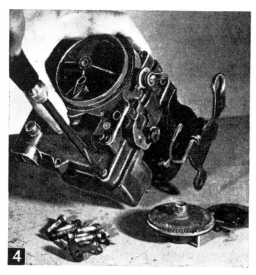

Start disassembly by removing the screws holding the float assembly body to the main body.

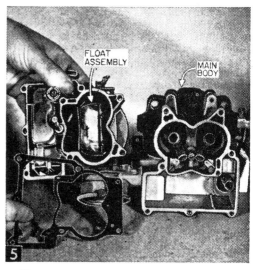

Old gaskets should be discarded and new ones fitted so that holes will match those on the casting.

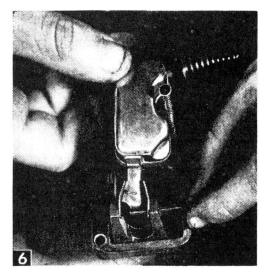

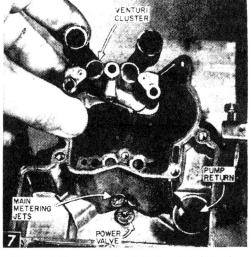

Free the float by pulling out the pin so you can inspect needle valve that controls amount of fuel.

When installing new gasket behind venturi cluster, be sure it is positioned properly under the special screw.

make and year of your car, type of engine (six or eight cylinders), and kind of transmission (manual or automatic).

One tool you'll need—besides various size screwdrivers and a pair of needle-nose pliers —is a float adjustment gauge (Fig. 9). Check to see if the kit you buy has one; if not, then it will cost from 45¢ to $1. Be sure it is the correct one for your carburetor.

To Aid in Diagnosing the cause of your malfunctioning carb, remove it from the engine without draining fuel from the bowl. You can check the bowl for dirt and find out if the float has a hole in it.

Remove the fuel inlet screen retainer nut with an open-end wrench, then use the needle-nose pliers to disconnect the spring clips that hold the throttle linkage. Loosen any vacuum lines, then remove the carb from the engine by taking out the nuts that connect the throttle body to the intake manifold.

Unscrew the cover fasteners (Fig. 4) and lift the cover from the bowl. Discard the gasket separating the two assembly bodies (Fig. 5). Place the upended cover on a clean, flat surface, then disconnect the float by removing the hinge pin (Fig. 6). Use a wide-blade screw-driver to disconnect the float seat, screen, and gasket.

Performance of All Parts of a carb is influenced by the fuel supply in the float bowl. This fuel level must remain constant despite varying speeds of the engine and demands on the carburetor. When the car is driven at high speed, the greater rate of fuel consumption causes the float to lower, the needle valve to open, and more fuel to enter the bowl.

As the throttle closes when the engine idles, thus reducing the demand for fuel, the rising float closes the needle valve, stopping the flow of fuel.

The smallest drop of dirt on the needle valve or a sticky float can cause the carb to flood, resulting in a rich mixture that wastes fuel and causes hard starting.

Check the float by shaking it close to your ear: if there is a sloshing sound, it has a leak and should be replaced. Inspect the lower surfaces of the float bowl to see that the small sealing beads are not damaged, because this can result in air or fuel leaks at that point. Don't try to solder the opening, because it will make the float heavier.

A float that is thrown off balance by anything inside it or any extra weight will lie low in the bowl and keep the needle valve open for a longer period. This lets too much gas into the bowl, resulting in an over-rich mixture.

Free Plunger Assembly (Fig. 8) from the pump arm by removing the small cotter-pin-type retainer on the pump plunger. The pump lever and shaft can be removed by loosening set screws on the inner arm and taking off the outer lever and shaft.

Remove the leather from the bottom of the plunger and clean it with gasoline. If the leather is cracked or creased, replace it. The pump plunger leather must be soft and pliable, so soak it in light oil for 10 minutes. Roll the leather back carefully—more or less turning it inside out—and return it to its normal position. Reshape the leather by rolling it between thumb and forefinger.

Unscrew the venturi cluster and power valve (Fig. 7). Drop the venturi into cleaning solvent. Before doing the same to the power valve, activate the small plunger in the center with your finger. If the plunger

Needle valve should be unscrewed and discarded and the filter screen inside the opening replaced with a new one that is part of the kit.

The gauge should just contact the float in this position for proper adjustment. Be sure to check float alignment after every adjustment.

seems to bind or has friction on it, get a new valve. Unscrew the main metering jets (Fig. 7).

Any restriction in the main metering jets will cause a lean fuel mixture. Never, though, stick a wire in the jet hole to clean out dirt. These are highly machined surfaces, and the least damage to them can cause restricted fuel supply. Let them soak in cleaning solvent, and blow dirt out with compressed air.

In many carbs, metering jets come equipped with a gasket installed on them. In these, a good gas-tight seal between jets and carb body is most important, since leaks around the jet's thread will result in too much gas going into the venturis.

Invert the Carburetor and remove the throttle body attaching screws, then take off the body and gasket. Idle mixture needle screws (Fig. 10) that are dirty or slightly corroded can be cleaned. If, however, they are badly corroded, bent, or damaged in any way, replace them.

No attempt should be made to remove the throttle valves or shaft, because it may be impossible to assemble the valve correctly in relation to the idle discharge orifices.

Thoroughly clean the carburetor castings and metal parts. The choke cover housing and throttle body should not be immersed in solvent. Blow passages in castings and all parts dry with compressed air.

When Reassembling, screw the idle mixture and adjusting needles and springs into the throttle body until finger-tight, then back out 1½ turns as a preliminary idle adjustment. Put a new throttle body gasket in position and tighten screws evenly and securely.

Install the idle air by-pass screw and spring

Make sure the engine is warmed to operating temperature and choke valve completely open before adjusting the throttle and idle screws.

in rear of float bowl until lightly seated, then back the screw out two turns. Replace main metering jets and power valve, and install the pump return spring by pressing it into the well.

After lubricating the pump shaft with a light grease and installing the outer parts in the bowl cover assembly, make sure the float is adjusted properly with your gauge (Fig. 9).

As a carburetor ages, the float level rises naturally. This is due primarily to wear of the float lever pin. As the float rises higher to shut off fuel entering the float bowl, the carb tends to give a richer mixture to the engine. If necessary, adjust the float by bending the tang at the rear of the float, then visually check alignment. Decrease float drop by bending it toward the needle seat, or away from the seat to increase.

All Types of Carburetors—no matter how many barrels—have only one throttle adjusting screw. Two- and four-barrel units, however, have two idle adjustment screws (Fig. 10), one for each idle system.

Warm the engine to operating temperature and have the choke valve completely open when adjusting. Start the engine and let it idle. If it stalls, turn the throttle screw in until the engine is running steady without any foot pressure on the accelerator.

The idle mixture should be adjusted to give a smooth idle. Missing is a sign of too lean an idle mixture while rolling or loping indicates too rich a mixture. Turning the screw in leans the mixture. It may be necessary to readjust the idle speed and mixture after the air cleaner is installed.

Turn the idle adjusting screw in slowly until the engine's about to stall. At this point, turn the screw out about a half-turn. If the engine seems to race, turn the throttle adjusting screw out slowly until the speed comes down. Once you touch the throttle adjusting screw, you must find the best adjustment for the idle adjusting screw.

Best Way to Check Out your work, if you don't have a tachometer, vacuum gauge, and exhaust analyzer, is by sight, sound, and feel.

Listen to the engine to determine if it is operating at an even and smooth speed. The exhaust sound coming from the muffler should sound like the engine is firing steadily. Check for excessive vibration by seeing how the engine rests on the mounts, and feel the fender.

Cars with automatic transmissions should be adjusted with the least pull on the engine. Be sure the handbrake is set and transmission is in DRIVE position when you adjust the idling and throttle screws.

Automatic chokes have a cover adjustment by means of which the choke can be made to open at a lower or higher engine temperature. Loosen the three screws that hold the cover. Then turn the cover one notch either way. Turning the cover to the left will make the choke open at a lower temperature; to the right, at a higher temperature. If you intend to remove the cover for choke repairs, the three screws must be removed.

Keep Your
Automatic Choke
Automatic

**Even a simple device like this can get out of whack.
Here's how it works, and how to adjust and repair it**

WHEN the engine in your car is running at normal temperature, each part of gasoline has to be mixed with about 17 parts air in order to burn in the cylinder combustion chambers. But, when the engine is cold, it needs a richer mixture—more fuel and less air. The choke helps control this mixture.

It is likely, when starting a cold engine, that much of the fuel entering into the carburetor throat is in the form of small drops, and only a small portion of these will be prop-

With the plastic cover removed, you can see the thermostat spring inside the cover. The spring arm fits over the lever which is connected to the shaft.

To change the thermostat spring, lift it out of the cover with needle-nosed pliers. The new thermostat spring should be mounted in the same position.

38

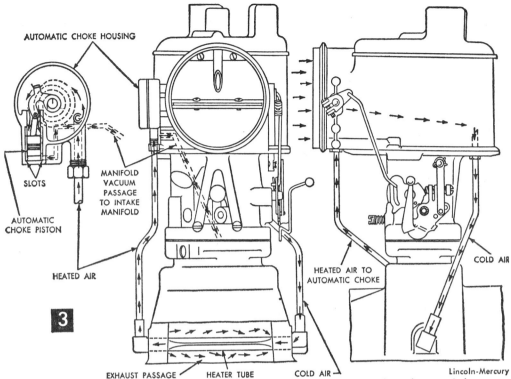

AUTOMATIC CHOKE HOUSING

AUTOMATIC CHOKE PISTON

SLOTS

MANIFOLD VACUUM PASSAGE TO INTAKE MANIFOLD

HEATED AIR

EXHAUST PASSAGE   HEATER TUBE   COLD AIR

HEATED AIR TO AUTOMATIC CHOKE

COLD AIR

Lincoln-Mercury

3

A typical automatic choke system in which the choke is mounted directly to the carburetor air horn.

erly vaporized by the time the mixture reaches the cylinder. By enriching the mixture and increasing the proportion of fuel to the proportion of air, sufficient vaporized gasoline can be delivered to the combustion chamber to start your engine and keep it running until the engine warms up enough to work on a normal fuel-air mixture.

Temporary changes in the fuel-air mixture are regulated by the choke plate in the carburetor throat. As the choke plate is closed, more fuel and less air is allowed down the throat.

The Manual Choke. On most older cars and even many late-model economy cars and

4

Some automatic carburetors, such as this one from Mercury, have a fiber plate cover. Remove this. If the thermostat has a gasket between the cover and plate, remove this also.

5

An emergency repair in case the choke is frozen in closed position. Tie a string to the spring lever to keep it in open position. This avoids running a fuel mixture too rich.

6

To remove the choke, unscrew the two or three screws which release the housing.

4

5

6

7 A Remove the choke plate.

B With the plate off, you can get to the piston.

8 This piston operates the lever, which in turn moves the choke plate. If the piston is burred, it should be replaced.

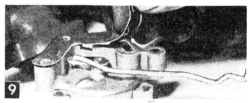

9 There may be two slots in back of the choke housing to provide transfer of vacuum or heat. Some models use tubes. Remove the gasket and make sure that the slots are dry and clean.

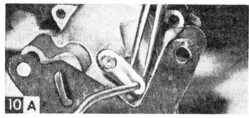

10 A If there is linkage on the choke, it should be checked for alignment. But do not lubricate it, for oil will collect dirt and cause stickiness.

B To replace the linkage, remove the cotter pin.

trucks, temporary choke adjustments are accomplished manually by a pull knob on the dash. Pulling the knob out closes the choke, pushing it in opens the choke.

But manual choking has always been a problem. It is simply too easy to overchoke the carburetor. The threat of overchoking has been removed by the automatic choke, a device which has been put on most cars since the late '40s and early '50s.

The Automatic Choke is a unit which reacts to the engine temperature, either by a temperature-sensitive metal coil or by an electro-magnet coupled to a temperature-sensitive strip, which opens and closes the choke plate in response to the action of the metal.

Most automatic chokes today utilize some variation of the temperature-sensitive metal coil, and many couple a piston to the coil. Until the thermostatic coil becomes warm, its tension is relatively high so that neither the suction effect in the carburetor nor intake manifold is sufficient to overcome the tension, or the tension is high enough to overcome the downward pull of the piston. As the thermostatic metal warms, its tension decreases.

A typical automatic choke is the one illustrated in this article, which is similar to types you will find on cars such as Mercury, most Fords, and many General Motors makes. On this particular version, the choke is actuated by intake manifold vacuum and heated air which is supplied to the choke housing by a tube that runs from a hot spot beneath the intake manifold to the automatic choke cover. The choke plate is normally closed when the engine is off and cold. When the ignition key is turned on, the force of air blowing into the carburetor air horn opens the plate slightly. It can never be completely closed while the engine is running, since this would prevent fuel-air mixture from being delivered to the combustion chamber.

When the engine ignites, the high vacuum in the intake manifold is channeled through a passage in the carburetor to a piston assembly on the automatic choke. The vacuum causes the piston to open the choke plate, but the tension of the thermostat spring is enough to prevent full opening of the choke plate.

As the engine warms, heated air is carried over the thermostat spring. As the spring heats, tension is reduced. When the engine is running at part throttle and the air is not heated enough to affect the spring completely, the piston force opens the choke plate as far as the spring permits. Finally, when the engine is thoroughly heated, the piston overcomes all spring tension, and the choke opens fully.

Problems with an Automatic Choke. An automatic choke is a nearly foolproof item, but there are a few things which can go wrong. The choke can be poorly adjusted; or, as it ages, the spring can become loose or stuck in an open or closed position. If the spring is loose, the choke plate will either open too soon or not close at all, and the car will be difficult to start. If the spring seizes in closed position, the choke plate will close and remain closed. The engine will run with a rich, overchoked mixture.

Overchoking is a very serious problem. Large quantities of raw gasoline enter the combustion chamber and the excess washes the oil from the cylinder walls, creating unnecessary cylinder wall wear. The extra fuel can flow past the rings and dilute the oil in the crankcase. Diluted crankcase oil may cause rapid wear of bearings and other fast-moving engine parts.

If you suspect trouble with the automatic choke, check its operation before you remove or replace it. Remove the air cleaner from the carburetor so you can see the choke plate in the carburetor throat.

When the engine is cold, the choke plate should be closed. Start the engine. The choke plate should open slightly and, as the engine warms, should open gradually. When the engine reaches the proper operating temperature, the choke plate should be fully open.

If the choke plate opens too soon or too slowly, you can compensate by adjusting the position of the thermostat spring cover. If the choke plate seems extremely slow opening, try this check before you remove the automatic choke. Accelerate the engine quickly, then release. The choke plate should remain in full open position. Close the choke plate with your finger, then release it. It should open immediately. If it does not, the trouble may be caused by a bent or sticky choke plate shaft or a vacuum piston rather than the automatic choke.

Adjustment. If the automatic choke opens too soon or too late, you should be able to make an outside adjustment rather than complete repairs. Most automatic chokes are provided with a system of cover adjustments to control the thermostat spring reaction to engine temperature. By loosening three screws enough to move the choke cover, you can turn the cover left or right and change the spring reaction.

On most covers you will find an arrow marked "lean" pointing to the left. If you move the cover to the left, or to lean position, you will cause the choke to open at a lower engine temperature. If you turn the cover to the right, you will cause the choke to open at a higher engine position. The proper adjustment of the choke for your engine should not exceed one cover division, either way from

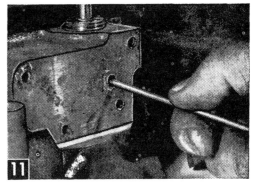

Be sure the vacuum hole is free of dirt. On some engines, you can clean the intake hole with a blunt wire. If it is a tube, you may have to replace it.

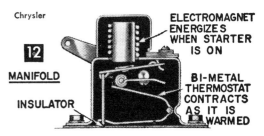

Rare these days, but still around, is the electromagnet type choke such as this one used on a '54 Plymouth.

the mid position. If more adjustment is necessary, the trouble may be in the thermostat or choke rather than in adjustment.

On a few cars, such as pre-'55 Chrysler products, an electromagnet choke is used (Fig. 12). It can be adjusted by inserting a wire into a hole in the shaft. Move the choke lever until the hole in the brass shaft lines up with a slot in the bearings, then insert the wire all the way through the holes in the shaft. Push the wire all the way into the engine manifold until it engages in a notch at the base of the automatic choke. Loosen a clamp screw on the automatic choke lever and push the lever upward until the carburetor choke valve is closed tight. Hold the lever in this position and, with the throttle held about one-third open, tighten the clamp screw. Remove the wire.

All moving parts of any automatic choke should be dry and free of dirt. Do not oil linkages or the shaft. Oil will collect dirt and will cause the parts to stick and eventually bind.

You can clean all parts of common automatic chokes, except the thermostat housing and the coil assembly. Most manufacturers recommend *Metalclene* or its equivalent. Rinse all parts thoroughly in kerosene or white gasoline to remove gummy deposits softened by the solvent. Wipe dry with a clean, soft rag or blow dry with an air hose.

41

FIXING YOUR FUEL PUMP

The simplicity of a fuel pump's operation and design makes troubleshooting and repair procedures correspondingly easy

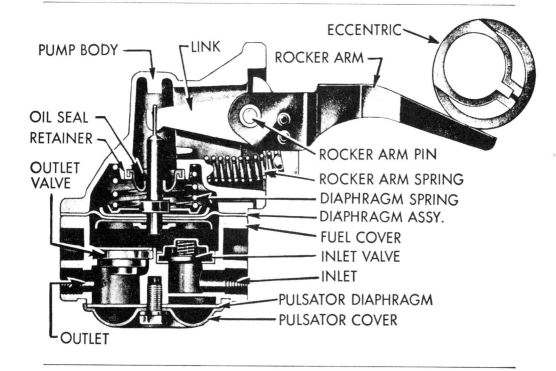

One of the easiest of all parts in your car to understand and troubleshoot is the fuel pump. It is also one of the most important because a faulty pump will cause your engine to run ragged or not at all.

Fuel pumps used in today's cars are of the diaphragm type. This diaphragm, which is an impregnated cloth, creates pressure inside the pump by pulsating back and forth.

The only difference in fuel pumps is that some have a vacuum booster section combined with a fuel pump section, while others consist only of the fuel pump.

In combination pumps, the vacuum booster section has nothing at all to do with the fuel system. Its purpose is to operate the windshield wipers by controlling vacuum pressure from the intake manifold. To do this, it is operated by the same pump arm that controls the fuel portion of the pump.

There is one other difference in fuel pumps used in today's cars. Some have the fuel filter built right in, while others have a separate filter tapped into the fuel line between the pump and the carburetor.

Pump Troubles. Fuel pump troubles are only of two kinds. Either the pump supplies too little gas or too much. Determining when there is trouble is, therefore, an easy job.

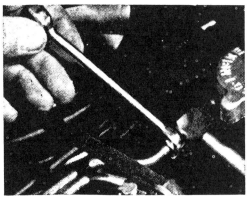

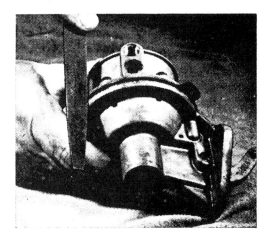

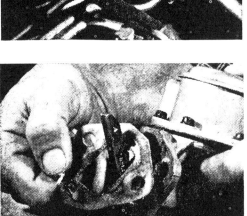

As shown at the top left, the first step in removing the fuel pump from the car is to disconnect the inlet and outlet lines from the pump. Then, once the pump is removed from the engine block (left) discard the old flange gasket. Carefully remove any gasket material that sticks to the machined surfaces. As shown above, file a locating mark on the edges of the valve housing and pump body so you can reassemble it correctly. As shown below, the cap screws were removed to separate the two parts of the pump. Don't pry between two halves with screwdriver, but use a mallet to jar them apart.

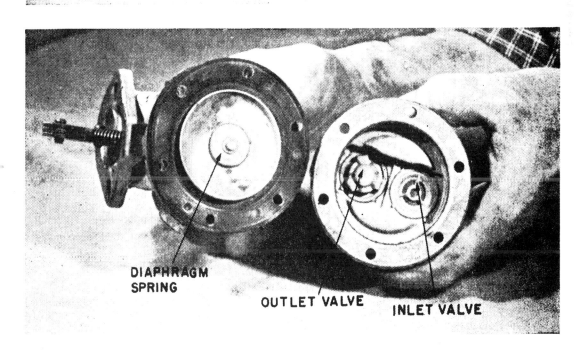

DIAPHRAGM SPRING

OUTLET VALVE

INLET VALVE

If your engine refuses to run, or it coughs and falters, the trouble may be that too little fuel is being supplied to the carburetor by the pump. If, on the other hand, your engine is hard to start, idles rough, or you see gas dripping from the carb, the pump may be supplying too much gas or the diaphragm is ruptured.

Any of these troubles can be caused by any one of a number of other things besides the fuel pump. However, it's a good idea to check the pump first since it is an easy job to do and you can pinpoint the cause of the problem immediately without having to go through a time-consuming inspection of other parts. A bad carburetor, for example, can also cause the kind of trouble just described, but to determine whether it is the cause entails a complete carburetor disassembly.

Test Pressure. A fuel pump is always tested with the pump on the car. The best way to check it is with a fuel pump analyzer (also called a vacuum or pressure tester). This tool records the pressure at which the pump is operating. It costs less than $5 and should be part of your tool kit if you do your own automotive work.

Fuel pumps push a large volume of gas per hour to the carburetor when the engine is operated at normal highway speed. The gas flows at a pressure of from as low as 2½ lbs. per square inch (psi) to as high as 7 lbs. psi, depending on the car. Higher pressure is built up in the pump when the engine is idling, while lower pressure prevails at top engine speed.

To accurately check your fuel pump with the gauge, it is necessary to know the exact pressure limits of the pump; check your car's service manual.

To test the pressure limits of your pump, disconnect the fuel line at the carburetor. Attach the proper-sized T-fitting adapter you will find in your pressure tester kit into the line and then into the carburetor inlet. Screw the pressure gauge hose into the adapter.

Start the engine and let it idle. The gauge should read somewhere within the limits set for your car as outlined in the chart. If so, turn the engine off. The needle on the gauge should remain constant or drift back very slowly toward zero. If it drops back suddenly, something is wrong with the pump.

If the reading is lower than that specified, it means the pump is not pushing out enough gas. If higher, the pump is delivering too much gas.

If pressure is too low, it usually means that one part of the pump is badly worn, several parts are slightly worn, diaphragm is rup-

Disassemble filter by removing retainer nut, then install new filter and bowl gaskets.

tured, valves are dirty, or the valve seats are clogged. If pressure is too high, the trouble is probably a tight fitting diaphragm, one that is too strong, or a pump link which is frozen to the rocker arm.

Replacement Alternatives. Once you've determined that the pump is faulty, you have one of two avenues open to you. If you do your own mechanical work, it would be less expensive to try and rebuild the old pump. If, however, a mechanic does your work, you would be better off installing a new pump since cost of a rebuilt is only a few dollars less than the price of a new one.

There are two types of repair kits available. One is an inexpensive kit which contains a new diaphragm (since this is the most likely part of a pump to go bad), valves, and gaskets. The other is a repair kit which contains all parts for a complete overhaul.

Before purchasing a kit, disassemble the pump to see which part or parts are worn. If it's just the diaphragm, the less expensive diaphragm repair kit should be purchased.

Repair Procedure. To disassemble the pump, proceed as follows:

1. Disconnect the pump-to-carburetor and gas tank-to-pump lines at the pump. Stop gas from flowing from the lines by inserting a stopper into them. If your pump is a combination fuel and vacuum affair, you will have to disconnect the windshield wiper and manifold lines coming into it.

2. Remove the pump from the engine and discard the gasket located between the pump body and engine block. A new gasket is contained in the repair kit.

3. Before taking the pump apart, remove dirt and foreign matter by washing it in gasoline. File a mark across the diaphragm flanges to serve as a guide when reassembling the unit. The two parts of the pump body must be accurately aligned to make sure inlet and outlet holes are correctly positioned.

4. Separate the two parts of the pump body. Note that one part contains the diaphragm and rocker arm assembly, while the other section has the inlet and outlet valves.

5. Remove the rocker arm by prying the rocker arm spring from its seat and driving the rocker arm pin out of its position with a drifting tool.

6. With the rocker arm removed, the diaphragm and its spring will fall from their positions. Inspect the diaphragm for wear and

resiliency. If the part isn't flexible to the touch, it is faulty and needs replacement.

7. Unscrew the retainer which holds the check valves in place. Notice that the valves are facing in opposite directions. The valve with the flat side facing out is the outlet, and the one with the tapered side facing out is the inlet. When replacing the valves, they must be inserted the correct way.

After making the necessary replacements, reassemble the pump in the reverse way in which you disassembled it. Place it back in the engine, making sure you re-insert the new gasket between the pump and the engine block. You must also make sure the cam eccentric engages the rocker arm in the proper way to prevent a broken rocker or link, and, in turn, cause possible engine damage. The pad of the rocker arm, which is the arm's flat surface, must rest against the cam.

Check Fuel Delivery. In addition to the pressure gauge test, you should also make a fuel capacity test to determine if the pump is delivering the correct amount of fuel to the carburetor. More than likely, if the pump pressure records correctly, the amount of fuel it is delivering is okay. But a malfunction other than the fuel pump can cause fuel capacity to be cut down.

Generally, the pump in a passenger car delivers from ¾ to a full pint of fuel to the carburetor every minute. To test for capacity, disconnect the fuel line at the carburetor and hold a pint measuring cup beneath the open end of the line. Let the engine run a minute to determine whether the proper amount of fuel (¾ to 1 pint) is being delivered.

If the pump isn't delivering enough fuel, the cause of the trouble might lie in the gas tank, in the fuel line system, or in the filter, as well as in the pump itself. First make sure there is gas in the tank. If so, look for a leak around the fuel bowl gasket. If there is a leak, the gasket should be replaced.

If the pump is delivering too much gas, look for the cause elsewhere, since it is rare for this trouble to originate in the fuel pump. There are six major causes of too much fuel being delivered to the engine. These are a defective automatic choke, excessive priming with a hand choke, a punctured carburetor float, a defective carburetor needle valve, a loosely connected fuel line or loose carburetor assembly bolts, or an improperly adjusted carburetor.

Prevent and Cure Vapor Lock

To avoid finding yourself in the same predicament as motorist above, see check lists at right and below.

TO PREVENT VAPOR LOCK

A. Clean and flush engine and radiator with a chemical cleaner.

B. Replace fan belt if worn, cracked, or hard.

C. Install low temperature (150°-160°F) thermostats.

D. Remove any winter cover that may be on radiator.

E. Wrap fuel lines under hood with asbestos packing.

F. See that car's original heat deflectors are in place at fuel pump and carburetor.

G. Limber up manifold heat-control valve.

H. Adjust carburetor idle speed to give road speed of about 10 or 12 miles an hour. This will keep air moving better under hood when idling.

I. Add 10% kerosene to gasoline if vapor locking persists. Discontinue use of kerosene when emergency is past.

I F YOUR car has ever stalled on you because of vapor lock, you know what a troublesome nuisance and, in some cases, expense this problem can cause you.

Many a car owner, when confronted with the problem of an engine that has mysteriously died out, calls for help from the motor club or a garage. Usually the serviceman arrives within a half-hour, raises the hood, looks things over in general, tries the starter, and the engine starts immediately. What happened? While the motorist was waiting for the arrival of this expert, things cooled down. Vapor in the lines condensed; the fuel pump was able to draw solid fuel from the tank; and the motorist gave him much credit (plus *cash*) for very little service.

To prevent or cure vapor lock from stalling your car, let's first analyze a car's fuel system to find the cause.

Vapor lock is the vaporization or boiling of the car's gasoline in the car's fuel system before it reaches the carburetor jets. Automobiles are designed to run on gasoline which remains a *liquid* until it passes through the carburetor jets into the incoming air. Then the gasoline becomes a power-producing vapor. But when gasoline vaporizes *before* reaching the jets it completely upsets fuel delivery to the jets. And without fuel the engine stops. So one naturally asks,

TO CURE VAPOR LOCK

A. Raise hood and let engine cool. This may take 20 minutes to half an hour.

B. If cool water is available, pour it on the fuel pump, gasoline lines and carburetor bowl.

C. To remove rich mixture from engine cylinders, hold throttle wide open and use starter at intervals of 10 seconds alternated with a 10-second rest. Do not pump the throttle. It may take 20 seconds to air out the engine and bring fresh solid fuel from the gasoline tank. Then the engine will start.

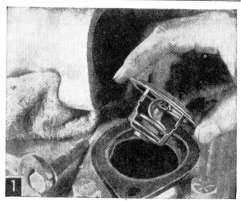

Replacing "hot" Winter thermostat with Summer thermostat that opens between 150° and 160°F will help combat vapor lock.

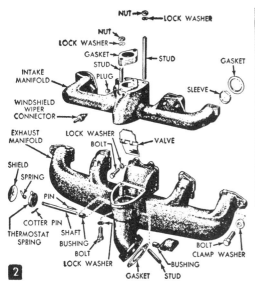

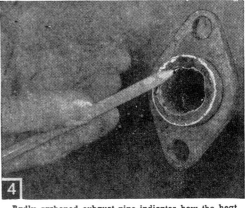

Badly carboned exhaust pipe indicates how the heat valve can get stuck with carbon. This condition is hard to detect without disassembling. It may be suspected when the car loses its normal top speed, and especially if overheating persists. Replacing clogged pipes with new ones is the only cure, and is helpful in correcting "mysterious" cases of vapor lock.

"What causes this gasoline to vaporize in the gas lines, the fuel pump or the carburetor bowl?"

Vapor lock is most severe on the first warm spring day. (And especially at high elevations.) But, later in the season, during weather that is even warmer than the first spring day, little or no vapor lock occurs. The explanation? Gasoline, as produced for use in automobiles, is a *blend*. It includes fuels of many boiling points. During the winter the gasoline refiners produce a fuel that has a higher percentage of *low* boiling-point material than during the summer. The reason for this is that your car engine requires a low boiling-point fuel to vaporize at low winter temperature so as to assure easy starting. So, when you hear or see ads that say "Use *our* gasoline for easy winter starting," you know the refiner is giving you a low-boiling-point winter gasoline.

To picture what blended gasoline is, just think of a person trying to build a fire in a stove. Let's say that he is using coal and chips of wood. Anyone knows that if he has nothing but coal that he would not be likely to get the fire started. On the other hand if he had no coal, but only chips of wood, it would be easy to start the fire;

but it would not last very long. So he uses enough of the easy-to-light chips to get the fire started and then puts on coal to keep it going. Similarly our gasoline is matched to the seasons according to the difficulty of starting. It has enough of the so-called "light ends" or low boiling point material for easy starting and heavy ends or high boiling point material to keep the engine going and give good mileage.

Working as a team with the petroleum refiners are the automotive engineers who furnish automatic chokes and heat-controlled devices to help vaporize gasoline. Actually the carburetor choke does not vaporize the gasoline. It does, however, reduce the amount of air and increase the amount of gasoline so that for any rate of evaporation there is a greater percentage of fuel in the mixture. Thus, starting is improved. But, while it is important when the engine is cold to have this greater percentage of fuel, it is equally important when the engine becomes hot to reduce the amount of fuel and increase the amount of air. This is what the choke is designed to do. So, if when the engine has warmed-up thoroughly the choke-valve does not open all the way, it is inviting an over-rich mixture. And this overly rich mixture when heated can easily create so much fuel vapor that it will not fire. In other words the engine will die.

Thermostatic devices are provided on all engines to make them warm up quickly after starting. The radiator thermostat that controls the cooling system temperature (Fig. 1) and the carburetor heat-control valve in the exhaust manifold (Fig. 2) or exhaust pipe are the two we are concerned about in preventing vapor lock. So let's review the operation and servicing of these two units.

The radiator thermostat controls the freedom with which the cooling liquid in the engine waterjackets passes through the radiator. To as-

OIL HERE ALSO

Applying heavily graphited penetrating oil to the heat control valve shaft. Heat valve must be in "hot" position with the engine cold, and moved to "cold" position with engine hot or vapor lock may result.

REMOVE NUTS AT 4 CORNERS OF HOUSING

HEAT VALVE IS INSIDE ON THIS SHAFT

How exhaust manifold heat valve is reached. Disassembling of the manifold is necessary to scrape out the carbon and limber up the valve.

sure quick warmup the thermostat is closed when the engine is cold. Then, when the engine becomes heated to a pre-determined temperature, the thermostat opens. This lets the cooling liquid (anti-freeze or water) circulate, or circulate more freely, through the radiator and thus limit engine temperature. Two kinds of thermostats are used—so-called "summer" or low-temperature thermostat opening in the range of 150 to 160° F and the "winter" or high temperature thermostat which opens in the neighborhood of 180° F. The low-temperature thermostat must always be used when alcohol serves as an anti-freeze. The high-temperature thermostat is desirable when a so-called "permanent" anti-freeze solution is used, and is particularly valuable in winter because the more quickly an engine warms up the less does the vaporized fuel from the carburetor tend to

condense back into a liquid. When gasoline vapors strike a cold metal surface the effect is much the same as when one exhales or blows on a cold window pane. In each instance a vapor becomes a liquid. But, note that there is a twenty to thirty degree temperature differential between the summer and winter thermostats. Recall that vapor lock is due to the boiling of gasoline in the lines, fuel pump or carburetor bowl. And this boiling is the result of high heat under the hood. So we now have one good reason why many motorists change over to the lower temperature thermostat for the summer months, flush their car's cooling systems clean, and replace worn radiator hoses.

The less known teammate of engine warmup, the carburetor heat-valve, is used to offset the chilling effect of evaporating gasoline. Anyone who ever went swimming on a windy day knows that evaporation creates cold. So picture how much heat the carburetor needs to offset the chilling effect of evaporating the gasoline. Actually, when heat is not directed to the base of the carburetor, there have been many instances where ice formed on the carburetor very much as ice forms on the cooling coils of a refrigerator. So in all cars there is a valve very much like a chimney damper that sends exhaust heat to the base on which the carburetor is mounted (Fig. 2). On V-8 engines this heat is directed through the combined manifold and valve cover casting (Fig. 3). On in-line engines the heat is sent through a double walled chamber on the intake manifold.

While this heat is important for improving the evaporation of the fuel and offsetting the chilling effect of this evaporation, too much heat is bad. For this reason, the exhaust heat is thermostatically controlled with a bi-metallic coil spring. This control gives full heat until the engine warms up. With increasing temperature the weight of a counterbalance on the heat-valve shaft working against the bi-metallic spring slowly closes the valve, thus reducing the amount of heat directed to the base of the carburetor.

A common fault of all these valves is that they carbon-up and stick (Fig. 4). Every time a car is lubricated, penetrating oil with a heavy percentage of graphite should be applied to the heat-control valve shaft (Fig. 5). If this does not keep the shaft free to move, the manifold should be disassembled, the carbon scraped away and the shaft lubricated and limbered up (Fig. 6). Over-heating the base of the carburetor over-expands the fuel charge. In warm weather this reduces engine power and top speed. And where heating is extreme this alone is sufficient to bring on vapor lock.

Many a motorist who knows that his car is subject to vapor lock carries a thermos-bottle of icewater with him. From this he pours just a little water on the outside of the carburetor, some onto the gasolines lines and some onto the fuel pump (Fig. 7). A rag saturated with water to place on hard-to-reach parts will prove help-

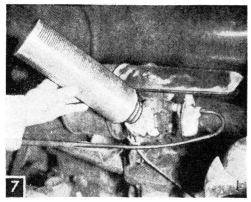

The old standby for curing vapor lock—ice water from a thermos bottle poured over the carburetor. The rag makes the water more effective by holding the water in contact with the carburetor bowl. The same treatment is given to the gasoline filter, fuel pump, and lines. Temporary cure will get you going.

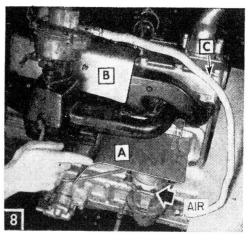

Three means of controlling heat to prevent vapor lock: A—Deflector protecting fuel pump from manifold heat, yet allowing free flow of air from radiator. B—Deflector keeping heat of exhaust manifold from carburetor. C—Asbestos wrapping around fuel line to keep manifold and engine heat from fuel line.

ful. This generally overcomes the trouble, at least for the moment. One commercial organization that was confronted with vapor lock on the first hot days of spring each year cured the problem by creating their own brand of gasoline. Until the refiners could adjust the gasoline and change it over from winter quality to spring or summer grade, this organization put approximately one gallon of kerosene in the fuel tank for each ten gallons of gasoline. This did the trick. Since the cars involved were used in funerals it was extremely important to avoid embarrassing delays.

Successful engine operation requires enough heat to vaporize the fuel completely as it leaves the carburetor. But this heat must not vaporize the fuel while in the carburetor bowl, the lines or the fuel pump. This is why engineers provide radiator thermostats and carburetor heat-control valves to build up the heat. Then they furnish thick gaskets under the carburetors, heat deflectors under or alongside the carburetor, and another heat deflector to keep excessive manifold heat from the fuel pump (Fig. 8). Naturally for good fuel distribution every V-8 has its carburetor well-centered between the cylinders on top of the engine block. But the engine block is more or less like a stove. It is heating up. So long as the car is moving there is a good breeze across the top of the engine and cool gasoline from the tank is keeping the carburetor and fuel temperature under control. But when this car stops, especially when the spring weather turns warm, the gasoline boils. The resulting vapor lock may be so severe as to actually blow all of the liquid gasoline out of the fuel pump,

lines, and carburetor. Now, with the engine full of the gasoline vapor, we are really stalled.

There is the possibility, however, that holding the throttle wide open (do not pump throttle) and using the starter may get this engine going. The gasoline coming from the tank may be cool enough to bring down the temperature of the fuel pump and the carburetor bowl so that the gasoline does not continue to boil. The volume of air introduced by the open throttle may clear the rich mixture from the cylinders. But if this doesn't do it and there is no cool water at hand to pour on the carburetor or the fuel pump, just be patient for twenty minutes or possibly a half-hour. Then by holding the throttle open and using the starter you can do as good a starting job as our friend the garageman would do.

To prevent vapor lock in spring and summer clean your car's cooling system with a commercial radiator cleaner, install a low temperature thermostat, be sure that the carburetor heat-control valve is working freely, check the fan belt to see that it is in good condition and remove any air restricting covers from the radiator. Then to be doubly sure that serious vapor lock from winter-grade gasoline does not tie you up, carry a gallon can of kerosene in the trunk of your car. If vapor lock catches you on the road, just pour this kerosene in the gasoline tank, in the ratio of 1 part kerosene to 10 parts gasoline. This will bring you home with no more trouble from vapor lock.

VACUUM LINE TO WINDSHIELD WIPERS

VACUUM PUMP DIAPHRAGM UNDER THIS COVER

VACUUM LINE TO ENGINE INTAKE MANIFOLD

REMOVE SCREWS AND COVER TO CHECK DIAPHRAGM

Top view of a combination fuel and vacuum booster pump. If your engine is so equipped and using a lot of oil, remove the cover (after disconnecting the lines) and check the diaphragm. If it's ruptured, replace it (Fig. 7).

Stopping Engine Oil Leaks

Before you pay for expensive repairs, why not find out just what is happening to your engine oil

YOU'VE heard the summer month vacationist say the trip was fine but that he "used a lot of oil." But, did he? Perhaps instead of *using* he was *losing* oil. There's a difference. You've seen those familiar dark streaks stretching endlessly along both sides of concrete highways—they are mute evidence of precious engine oil relentlessly dropped from motor vehicles (Fig. 1).

How much can plain everyday oil leakage amount to? Well, if your engine has an external leak which lets a teaspoonful of oil drip from the engine every mile, you'll lose nearly a quart of oil every 200 miles of travel (Fig. 2)! Of course, every normal engine uses oil when operating because some oil naturally is consumed in the combustion process. If this weren't so you wouldn't have to "add a quart" now and then to bring the crankcase oil level to normal. And, like excessive fuel consumption that goes along with sustained high speed driving, oil con-

sumption, too, goes up with high speeds.

But there is such a thing as excessive oil consumption at normal driving speeds. Sometimes the cause may be hard to diagnose, but like a headache, excessive engine oil consumption tells you something's wrong somewhere. If your engine has a lot of miles on it and the exhaust pipe belches blue smoke, the engine may be an oil-hungry "pumper." There isn't much you can do with such an engine outside of a "ring job" or a rebuild job which may end up with reconditioned cylinder walls, new pistons, pins and bearings.

If you think your car's using too much oil, first of all take a look at your garage floor or wherever you normally park the car. The familiar "gooey" spot on the floor under the engine is a dead give-away of dripping oil. Or, try this. Spread some clean newspapers on the floor under the engine

Fig. 1. The dark streak on the highways, especially where bumps occur, shows that many motor vehicles are losing oil through external leakage.

(Fig. 3). Then run the engine at a speed substantially above idling. Allow the engine to run long enough to bring it up to idling temperature and for 5 or 10 minutes thereafter. If oil drips on the paper get under the car and check where it's coming from. Remember that, though the oil drops straight downwards with the car at rest, the source of leakage actually may be farther away with the oil creeping along inside the engine until it finds a convenient spot from which to drip. Also remember that the car's forward motion often makes excess oil show up where a leak is actually not occurring. If you suspect external oil leakage look for "oil washed" areas on the engine; such areas are evidence of leakage *ahead* of the washed areas. While excessive oil consumption also may take place inside the engine, let's first trouble-shoot and correct the external leaks. Fig. 4 shows some of the more common reasons why a typical engine could loose too much oil externally even under normal driving conditions. Very often just tightening a joint, installing a new gasket or tightening the oil pan drain plug stops external leaks.

External oil leakage can also be caused by too much pressure in the engine crankcase. Certain oil washed areas on the crankcase ventilator side of the engine usually indicate oil being forced out of the

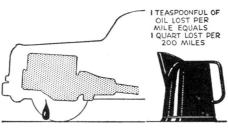

Fig. 2. Here's how a comparatively small amount of leakage will add up on a trip of several hundred miles.

I TEASPOONFUL OF OIL LOST PER MILE EQUALS I QUART LOST PER 200 MILES

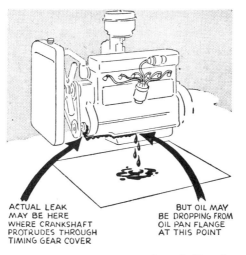

ACTUAL LEAK MAY BE HERE WHERE CRANKSHAFT PROTRUDES THROUGH TIMING GEAR COVER

BUT OIL MAY BE DROPPING FROM OIL PAN FLANGE AT THIS POINT

Fig. 3. If you suspect your engine of leaking oil externally, spread clean paper under the engine and allow it to run awhile. Then watch where the oil is dripping to localize leakage source.

crankcase ventilating tube. Too much crankcase pressure does this. This pressure might be due to excessive "blow-by" from the combustion chambers past the pistons and into the case or oil pan. The customary remedy is a set of new piston rings, but reconditioning the cylinders, new pistons, rings, pins, connecting rod and main bearings may have to be resorted to to overcome blow-by. It's a job for the skilled mechanic and calls for special equipment not usually found in any car owner's shop.

But there's another reason why oil may be blown out through the breather pipe. Too much crankcase pressure may be caused by a clogged outlet or inlet pipe (or both) of the crankcase ventilating system. Removing the pipes and cleaning them may be all that is necessary to bring crankcase pressure back to normal and keep the oil in the case.

Vacuum can also pull the oil out of the crankcase ventilating tube. For example, if the outlet pipe becomes bent, a vacuum may be formed at the open end of the pipe causing oil to be sucked out of the crankcase. So, when you are looking for reasons for high oil consumption, look at the lower venti-

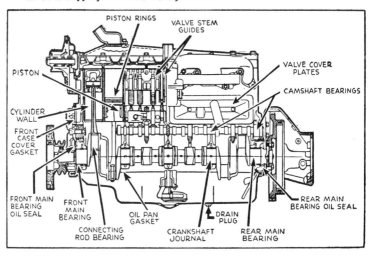

Fig. 4. This illustration shows the engine parts involved in both internal and external oil leaks. Loose joints on such parts as the oil pan and front end timing gear cover do not allow gaskets to seal tightly. Internally, such worn parts as cylinders, rings and bearings, cause excessive oil consumption.

PISTON RINGS

VALVE STEM GUIDES

VALVE COVER PLATES

PISTON

CAMSHAFT BEARINGS

CYLINDER WALL

FRONT CASE COVER GASKET

FRONT MAIN BEARING OIL SEAL

FRONT MAIN BEARING

OIL PAN GASKET

DRAIN PLUG

REAR MAIN BEARING OIL SEAL

CONNECTING ROD BEARING

CRANKSHAFT JOURNAL

REAR MAIN BEARING

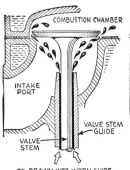

COMBUSTION CHAMBER

INTAKE PORT

VALVE STEM GUIDE

VALVE STEM

OIL DRAWN INTO WORN GUIDE

Fig. 5. Excessive wear of valve stems and their guides causes oil to be drawn into combustion chambers where it is burned with the air-fuel mixture, causing the blue smoke from the exhaust. Worn piston rings will also cause smoke.

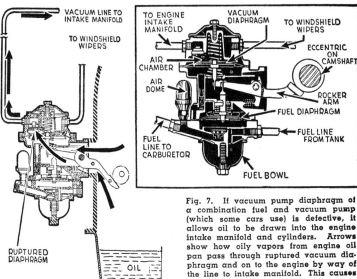

VACUUM LINE TO INTAKE MANIFOLD

TO WINDSHIELD WIPERS

RUPTURED DIAPHRAGM

OIL

TO ENGINE INTAKE MANIFOLD

VACUUM DIAPHRAGM

TO WINDSHIELD WIPERS

ECCENTRIC ON CAMSHAFT

AIR CHAMBER

AIR DOME

ROCKER ARM

FUEL DIAPHRAGM

FUEL LINE TO CARBURETOR

FUEL LINE FROM TANK

FUEL BOWL

Fig. 7. If vacuum pump diaphragm of a combination fuel and vacuum pump (which some cars use) is defective, it allows oil to be drawn into the engine intake manifold and cylinders. Arrows show how oily vapors from engine oil pan pass through ruptured vacuum diaphragm and on to the engine by way of the line to intake manifold. This causes high oil consumption.

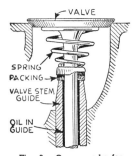

VALVE

SPRING

PACKING

VALVE STEM GUIDE

OIL IN GUIDE

Fig. 6. One remedy for overcoming oil passing through the valve guides is to insert spring-loaded packing on top of the valve guide.

oil, clogged oil passages, dirty oil and similar things invite engine trouble. Such wear is accompanied by high oil consumption. That familiar bluish smoke coming from the tailpipe, especially on acceleration, is an unfailing sign that oil is being burned too lavishly in the engine combustion chambers.

Probably the most prevalent cause of high oil consumption (where oil is actually consumed) is piston ring wear (Fig. 4). Rings have a tough job to do in any engine. They must act as a guide for the piston, must conform to the cylinder walls, and seal against compression and combustion pressures, besides keeping the correct amount of oil on the cylinder walls. They have to constantly battle other hardships like oil dilution, cold weather starting, gum and foreign matter, all of which induce wear or cause sticking and breakage. Worn, broken, or sticking rings (rings that stick in the grooves of the pistons, due to gum, carbon, etc.), when removed and replaced with a new set of rings often bring oil consumption back to normal.

But here's a point to watch. Blue smoke blow-

lator pipe to make sure it's in a normal position.

Now what about the reasons for the engine consuming too much oil internally? Well, wear, heat and corrosives take toll of cylinders, pistons, rings, bearings and other engine parts. Excessive choking (especially in cold weather), dilution of

ing from the exhaust pipe doesn't always mean the rings are to blame. Perhaps the rings are in pretty good shape but not able to handle the excessive oil "throw-off" from the bearings. Remember that bearings, too, have a lot to do with high oil consumption. Engines are fitted with piston rings known as "oil rings" which are there to control the amount of oil for the cylinder walls. The oil rings scrape excess oil back to the crankcase, but when excessive bearing clearance allows too much oil to be thrown on the cylinder walls, the oil rings just can't handle the great volume of oil.

So, when your engine uses a lot of oil and the trouble is traced to "rings," you are in for a job of (a) replacing the old rings with new, (b) reconditioning the cylinders, fitting new pistons, pins, rings, main and connecting rod bearings. Along with this a "valve job" will be done because when an engine is "down" for major work on cylinders, pistons and bearings, the valves are sure to need replacement or reconditioning.

A second way that too much oil gets into the combustion chambers is through worn valve stems and guides (Fig. 5). On L-head type engines the leakage is through the intake valve guides, while on overhead valve type engines, both intake and exhaust valve stem guide leakage can occur. When valve stem guide leakage is responsible, replace the valves and guides with new ones. However, this type of oil leakage and resultant high consumption often can be materially cut down or eliminated by installing valve stem packing under the valve heads (Fig. 6). The coil spring pressure holds the packing against the top of the valve stem guide to keep the oil in the space or "clearance" between the guide and stem. Valve guide packing is made by Burd Piston Ring Co., Eau Claire, Wis.

Typical combination fuel, vacuum pump installation.

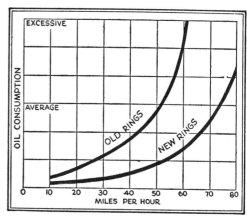

Fig. 9. Curves showing how oil consumption goes up with high road speeds. Consumption is greater with old or worn piston rings.

Here's a note of warning. If only new piston rings are installed, the engine actually may use more oil than before because the new rings increase the manifold vacuum causing more oil to be drawn into the combustion chambers.

Some cars have a combination fuel and vacuum pump—part of the pump being for pumping fuel from the main tank to the carburetor, the other, for producing vacuum for providing uniform operation of the windshield wiper at all engine speeds and loads. If the diaphragm of the vacuum booster portion of the pump is broken or porous it allows oil to be drawn directly into the intake manifold and intake port and you have a condition about the same as with worn valve stems and guides.

Checking for Leakage

To check vacuum pump diaphragm leakage (indicated by sluggish windshield wiper action when the engine is accelerated) have the wiper in operation and disconnect the vacuum pipe at the manifold. Then hold a piece of clean paper

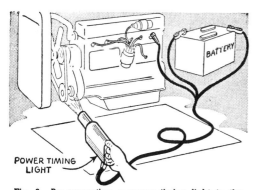

POWER TIMING LIGHT

Fig. 8. By connecting a power timing light to the battery and spark plug, starting the engine, and directing the light on revolving parts, such as the crankshaft front end, the part is "strobed" (stands still), oil can be seen leaking from around shaft.

near the open end of the pipe. If you get an oily discharge, it shows that oil is passing through the vacuum pump requiring replacement of the diaphragm (Fig. 7).

Other reasons why your engine may be using or losing too much oil are: piston rings with too little "end" or "gap" clearance; rings installed upside down in grooves; wrong type rings for the engine; distorted cylinders caused by unequal tightening of cylinder head stud nuts; connecting rods bent or twisted; late valve timing; too much oil pump pressure (can be corrected on some engines by regulating oil pressure relief valve where such a valve is fitted); dirty oil; clogged oil passages; air-fuel mixture too lean (engine may overheat causing rings to stick or break); dirty cooling system, causing local hot spots, distortion and overheating of the engine. In some cases the remedies are obvious; in others, it means a tear-down and rebuild job which should be done by a well-equipped shop.

The more mileage on the engine the more likely it is to use more and more oil. And it usually will take more than just a "ring job" to bring back normal conditions with normal oil consumption. Wear is usually well distributed over the entire engine so that when cylinders have to be reconditioned it's safe to say the valves, bearings, timing chain or gear, camshaft and crankshaft need reconditioning or replacement. The popularity, in recent years, of "rebuilt" or "exchange" engines testifies to the fact that fixing only part of the job certainly won't overcome high oil consumption in a worn engine. Oil consumption also goes up with high road speeds as Fig. 9 shows. As is true with gasoline, moderate speeds will save you money by using less oil.

53

PCV

Positive crankcase ventilation
draws unburned fuel vapors
from crankcase for another
shot at burning and saves
oil's lubricating properties

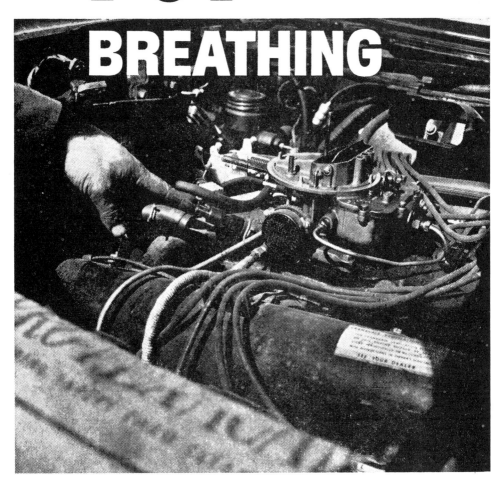

BREATHING

Mention the term engine breathing in your next automotive round table discussion. If there's a hotrodder in the house, you'll hear a discourse on enlarging valve ports and other techniques for getting an engine to inhale more fuel mixture and exhale more exhaust.

But that's only half the story on engine breathing—because an engine has two completely different respiratory systems.

The one that gets the short end of everyone's attention is the crankcase ventilation system, which has the job of purging water and unburned fuel vapors from the crankcase.

The Road Draft Method. As mentioned in the introduction to the Breathing System, until recently, all cars used one simple method of ventilation. A tube, called the road draft tube, was provided at the lower

Fig. 1.

Fig. 2.

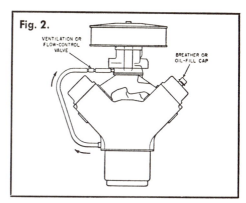

Basic open type of PCV has line that runs from crankcase, tappet chamber or rocker cover to carb base. Has flow-control valve.

◀Clogged breather cap (left) prevents fresh air from blowing contaminating vapors from engine. Keep it clear by soaking in solvent.

Flow control valve is held closed when the engine is off. At idle or part throttle, vacuum pulls valve all the way forward, into nearly closed position. Arrows show flow of air, which is limited by fixed opening in the valve. As vacuum drops the valve settles in mid-chamber, permitting maximum flow. "A" is fixed opening.

Fig. 3.

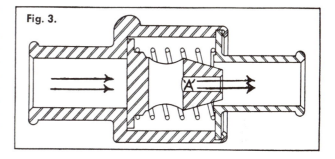

Fig. 4.

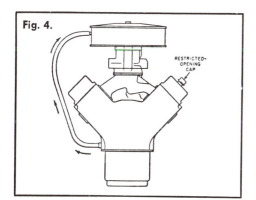

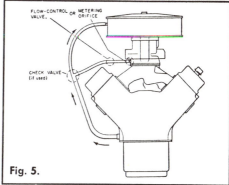

Fig. 5.

This type, where hose runs to air cleaner, uses a restricted inlet breather cap to prevent excessive ventilation at open throttle.

Dual-type is a combination of the basic open and basic air cleaner types. Uses check valve to switch flow from carb to filter.

end of the block or valve tappet chamber.

As the car rolls, air rushing past the tube draws out vapor-contaminated air. This creates a slight vacuum in the crankcase, which is filled by fresh air, admitted through an inlet breather. This breather is an opening, usually containing a filter, and usually built into the oil filler cap.

In some European cars, the inlet breather is simply a tube, with a hose connected to the back of the air filter, so that it also provides filtered fresh air for the crankcase.

The system works reasonably well so long as the engine is warmed up regularly by a sufficiently long trip (15 miles and more). If it isn't, you either change the oil and oil filter more often, or the engine sludges up rather quickly.

Maintenance on the system is simple: the filter in the oil filler cap is cleaned or replaced, with recommended intervals somewhere around twice a year.

If the inlet breather isn't serviced, it clogs, and the vapors that should be exhaled remain in the crankcase to do their worst.

A few years ago, the air pollution problem came to the fore, and smog-troubled California demanded that the car makers do something to keep their products from polluting the air with unburned fuel vapors.

The car makers, in desperation, adopted a system originally designed to keep the road draft tube on military vehicles from providing an entrance for water, when these vehicles were driven across streams, etc.

The system, with several variations on the theme, is commonly called Positive Crankcase Venilation (PCV).

The basic idea of PCV is to run a hose from the road draft tube to the carburetor intake, where manifold vacuum can suck the vapors from the crankcase, back into the combustion chamber for another shot at burning.

The variations fall into four general categories, as follows:

Basic Open Type: A hose from the crankcase, tappet chamber or rocker cover connects to the intake manifold or carburetor base. Additionally, there is a flow control valve (usually installed at either end of the hose, although occasionally somewhere near the middle of it), or an opening of carefully-fixed size in the carburetor base.

The flow control valve or fixed opening is designed to prevent flow of vapor-laden air from reaching the point where it could upset the carburetor fuel mixture.

The flow control valve is actuated by manifold vacuum. At closed or part-throttle, when manifold vacuum is high, the valve is held closed, and vapor bleeds through a small hole in the valve. At open throttle, when manifold vacuum is low, the valve is pushed open by a spring, permitting a greater flow of vapor-laden air.

The air inlet in this system is built into the oil filler cap, as with the conventional road draft tube system.

Air Cleaner Open Type: A hose runs from the crankcase, tappet chamber or rocker cover to the air cleaner, where inrushing air

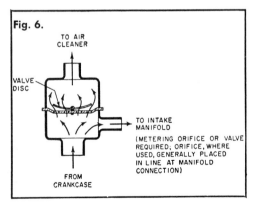

Fig. 6.

TO AIR CLEANER

VALVE DISC

TO INTAKE MANIFOLD (METERING ORIFICE OR VALVE REQUIRED; ORIFICE, WHERE USED, GENERALLY PLACED IN LINE AT MANIFOLD CONNECTION)

FROM CRANKCASE

Flapper valve is used to switch flow from air cleaner to carb with throttle changes. Higher rpm sends flow into air cleaner.

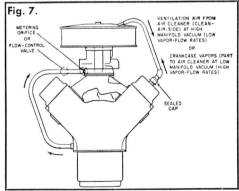

Fig. 7.

METERING ORIFICE OR FLOW-CONTROL VALVE

VENTILATION AIR FROM AIR CLEANER (CLEAN-AIR.SIDE) AT HIGH MANIFOLD VACUUM (LOW VAPOR-FLOW RATES)
OR
CRANKCASE VAPORS (PART TO AIR CLEANER AT LOW MANIFOLD VACUUM (HIGH VAPOR-FLOW RATES)

SEALED CAP

Closed system draws fresh air from air cleaner. Contaminated air expelled at part throttle. Crankcase pressure forces vapor into carb.

pulls vapor-laden air from the hose into the carburetor intake. An advantage of this system is that dirt particles are filtered out of the vapor-laden air immediately before it goes into the engine. Major disadvantage is that air filter element will be clogged more quickly.

To prevent excessive vapor flow at open throttle, the over-all flow of air through the system is limited by use of a restricted inlet air breather cap.

Dual Open System: This is a combination of the first two systems. There is a two-way flapper valve at the rocker cover, connecting to a hose that goes to the air cleaner, and a tube that goes into the carburetor base (the tube to the carburetor base, as in the Basic Open Type, will have a flow control valve or lead into a fixed opening in the carburetor base).

At idle and part throttle, the flapper valve is moved by manifold vacuum to direct contaminated air to the carburetor base. At open throttle, the air flow in the air cleaner, past the hose, moves the flapper valve, and the vapor flows through the air cleaner. The inlet breather cap, as in the Air Cleaner Open Type, is restricted to prevent excessive vapor flow at open throttle.

Closed System: Despite the name, the system isn't really closed. At closed or part throttle (high manifold vacuum), fresh air flows from the air cleaner into the valve cover (and then throughout the engine), becomes contaminated and is drawn into the carburetor by the manifold vacuum.

At open throttle (low manifold vacuum), no ventilating air enters the system, and the system will operate in reverse. That is, the vapor pressure itself forces the vapor from the crankcase, through the hose, into the air cleaner, and also through the tube into the carburetor.

Most of the systems function well on cars in good condition. But they just aren't able to handle high rates of unburned fuel and water blown by worn pistons and rings. Clearly, if the carburetor is designed for a little blowby, the mixture will be upset if a lot is permitted to flow.

Principles of Maintenance. Because of the difference in these systems, it is easiest to learn general principles of maintenance rather than what individual car makers recommend for their particular engine.

To begin, hoses and tubes on all systems should be clear. Check and blow through with compressed air at least twice a year.

Check and service the inlet breather cap on open systems every two months. As in road draft tube systems, if it clogs, fresh air can't enter. To service, soak in solvent and re-oil. Exception is cap on Ford products. Lincoln type should be replaced annually.

If there is a line into the base of the carburetor, there is either a flow control valve in the line or a fixed opening in the carburetor base. The fixed opening should be cleaned twice a year with an appropriate size drill ($\frac{1}{16}$-inch diameter on most cars). Be careful not to enlarge the opening.

The flow control valve can be cleaned in solvent, but this procedure is not sound. The valve is only about a dollar, and should be replaced twice a year.

Dual systems, such as used on some Oldsmobile and Studebaker cars, have a fixed opening in the carburetor base and a flapper valve at the rocker cover. The flapper valve is cleanable in solvent, but should be replaced if there is any question of its operating freely. Service or replace once a year.

Any system that connects to the air cleaner is going to clog the filter element much faster than other types.

The open types, Air Cleaner and Dual Open, are toughest on the air filter, because they permit vapor to flow through it under normal conditions. But the closed type isn't much easier, because it permits partial flow through the filter at open throttle.

Check the filter element every 3000 to 4000 miles. If it is the paper kind, it should be replaced if necessary; wire mesh types can be cleaned in solvent and re-oiled for continued use.

Some systems are equipped with small oil separators, baffled tanks which remove oil droplets from the vapor. The idea is to minimize oil soaking of the air filter and burned oil deposits in the combustion chamber. The separator, which is placed in the line from the crankcase, tappet chamber or rocker cover, is cleaned by washing in solvent and blowing dry with compressed air. The job should be done about once a year for proper maintenance.

If you keep your engine in good tune, however, the engine will burn the fuel more completely the first time, leaving less for the PCV system and therefore requiring less frequent maintenance.

Don't Blow Your Gasket—Fix It

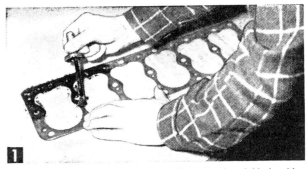

Coating gasket that goes between cylinder head and block with Permatex *Form-A-Gasket* cement. Some gaskets (such as those of the steel and asbestos head type) usually have a sealing coat put on by the manufacturer, thus do not require another coat.

LOTS of gaskets, particularly engine cylinder head gaskets, "blow." Maybe it's happened to you, and maybe you thought the fault lay in the quality or construction of the gasket. Actually, gaskets usually blow because of incorrect application. It's the way you do or do not prepare the surfaces to be gasketed together that counts. And counts heavily. The gasoline mileage you get, the engine's cooling efficiency, compression, lubrication, silencing of the exhaust, tightness of the rear axle housing and a lot of performance factors depend on the ability of gaskets to seal well; to maintain pressure, and to keep out dirt and water. The oil, water or even fuel that drips on your garage floor overnight may indicate leaky gaskets. And the leakage may be worse when the car is running because parts get hot, metal expands and the gasket-packed joints widen, creating greater leakage. If you want to track down guilty gaskets, first inspect the car's engine carefully (Fig. 2). If you see rusty and gooey looking seepage around the cylinder block and head joint, your engine needs a new head gasket. The same evidence around the crankcase and oil pan joints, the water inlet elbow flange and head, the fuel pump connection to crankcase, the front end chain housing cover, and the water pump flange and manifolds —is a sign that gasket trouble has arrived.

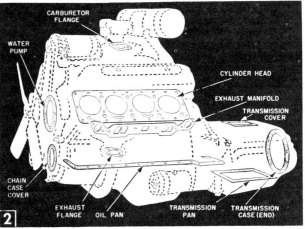

Here's your guide to checking the engine for guilty gaskets.

It's always a good rule to install a new gasket every time a joint is broken. The old gasket might "look good" but it has done its job even if it hasn't "blown," so toss it out and use a new one. There's always the temptation to use the old cylinder head gasket, for example, especially if it comes off clean, stays flat and has that nice shiny copper color. But you can't re-seal the joint adequately with the old gasket, as E in Fig. 3 shows. In the first place, the joining surfaces between the cylinder block and head, while "milled" to substantially smooth surfaces, are never completely smooth. Under a microscope, you see a lot of hills and valleys (B) in Fig. 3. When the head is bolted down tightly, the copper of the gasket (usually made of asbestos between two thin layers of copper or steel) squeezes into the tiny imperfections of the metal and with the asbestos filler makes a tight seal

against compression and coolant losses. Obviously, this compression of the gasket flattens and conforms it to irregularities of the block and head, so that if the head is later removed, it's practically impossible to replace the gasket (which has lost much of its compressibility) and get a perfect seal against all the little irregularities again.

Figure 4 also shows how the old gasket may be bent in removing it so that the asbestos filler breaks when the gasket is straightened for re-use—and the gasket is liable to burn through at this weak spot and lose its effective seal.

You can find out whether you have a broken and leaky head gasket by checking these points. If the coolant boils at normal atmospheric temperatures and your radiator takes a lot of water, it could indicate a broken gasket. When you make a cylinder compression test and find two adjacent cylinders reading much lower than the others, the gasket may have blown at the spot between the two cylinders (Fig. 5). Sometimes

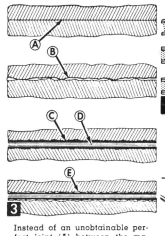

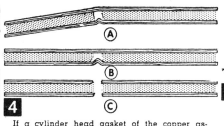

4

If a cylinder head gasket of the copper asbestos type is bent, the asbestos filler may break as at A. If the gasket is then straightened (B) it may look okay but later burn through and "blow" at the break in the asbestos (C).

3

Instead of an unobtainable perfect joint (A) between the machined surfaces of a cylinder head and engine block, there are a series of microscopic hills and valleys (B). Note how the metal of the gasket (C) fills the irregularities of the block and head, making a tight joint. (D) is the asbestos filler. After a gasket has been compressed it is almost impossible to again seal the irregular surfaces (E).

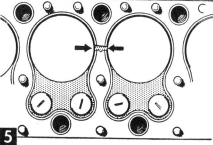

5

Occasionally a cylinder head gasket breaks at a point between two adjacent cylinders, shown by the heavy arrows.

6

A handy tester to check for a blown gasket can be made by brazing or soldering a tire valve into a spark plug shell. You can buy a set of 4 such testers for $8 from Easy-Living Products, 7361 N. Hoyne, Chicago.

you can see bubbles in the top of the radiator, which can be from a blown gasket. Figure 6 shows you a homemade tester you can use to find out whether the head gasket is faulty and allowing leakage into the coolant. To use it, fill the radiator to the top with coolant, run the car until it reaches normal operating temperature, then remove the spark plugs and test each cylinder as follows: Take off the distributor cap so you can watch the rotor. Turn the engine slowly (with fan belt or by jacking up one rear wheel with the transmission in gear), until the rotor is lined up with one of the cap electrodes if the cap were in place. The valves of that cylinder will then be closed. Screw the tester into the spark plug hole of that cylinder and from a hand pump or air supply, apply air to the tester valve. If there is gasket leakage you can see or hear the bubbles at the radiator neck with the filler cap off to allow you to look in.

To replace this gasket, you'll have to strip the engine of such parts as the air cleaner, carburetor, spark plugs and wiring harness, perhaps the oil filter bracket, the hose connection at the water inlet elbow and other parts depending on the make and type of engine. Then you take out the head bolts or loosen the nuts on the block studs so you can lift off the head. But before you loosen the nuts and bolts, let the engine cool to the surrounding temperature of the atmosphere or room.

Next, clean the block and cylinder head of all carbon deposits by scraping, wire brushing, and with a metal parts cleaner. You can use an ordi-

nary hand tire pump to blow out any foreign matter on the piston heads, bolt holes and water passages. Also, blow out the passages inside the cylinder head to prevent any carbon particles from dropping on the new gasket (such particles can form pockets in the gasket and cause leakage). With the block and head surfaces clean, check the surfaces with a straight edge for indications of distortion or warping (Fig. 7).

Since the cylinder head gets hotter than the block, warpage is more likely to occur in the head. If you run into such a condition, better have your car repair shop true the surface of the head on a surface grinder. This removal of metal, however, should be held to a minimum as it increases compression ratio—perhaps more than is good for the engine. On old engines, especially, if the cylinder has been remachined more than once, it's wise to replace the head with a new one.

Make a careful inspection of the cylinder head studs in the block (or the bolt holes, if the head is held down with bolts). If you find there is a buildup of metal around the studs or bolt holes (A in Fig. 8), you can use a chamfering tool (B in Fig. 8) to trim enough off so the studs or bolts can be firmly tightened with clearance for the gasket (C and D in Fig. 8). But make sure you don't remove too much metal with the chamfering tool, particularly where a stud is located very

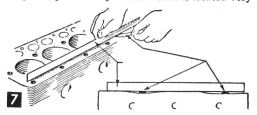

7

Checking the machined surface of a cylinder block with a straight edge and feeler. The same procedure can be used for checking the cylinder head.

59

close to two cylinders (removing too much metal in such places may cause gasket to blow). Some mechanics prefer to dress the block with a large file, which also removes the rough spots.

Now check the new gasket for correct fit on the cylinder block. Some gaskets are marked "Top," "Front" or "Up." Check for these markings before installing and follow the directions

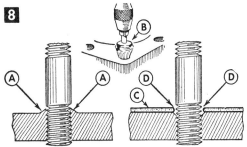

8

Good gasket fitting demands that the block metal not be raised or "drawn up" around the studs or bolts (A). You can use a file or a chamfering tool (B) to cut down the metal as at D, so gasket (C) lies smoothly.

they indicate. All of the water holes and bolt holes should tally with those in the block. On some engines like the 6-cylinder Ford, be sure that the gasket is positioned with the cut-off corner at the left front corner of the cylinder block (Fig. 9); otherwise water will leak externally at the left rear corner of the engine between the cylinder head and block. Never enlarge any of the water passage holes in the gasket, as the rear cylinders might overheat. Watch out for a bent gasket as in Fig. 4. The method of applying the gasket depends on the type of gasket material. The steel and the asbestos head gaskets usually have a sealing coat put on them by the gasket manufacturer. This clear coating ordinarily does not require any additional gasket cements. But if this type of gasket does not have a coating you can use a non-hardening gasket compound such as Permatex *Form-A-Gasket*. This material is a liquid applied with a brush and changes in a few seconds to a paste. It produces a non-drying, elastic, adhesive, heat-resisting seal. You can also use it with copper asbestos gaskets. If you wonder why both steel and copper asbestos gaskets are used, each has certain advantages. For example, where high octane fuel is used and detonation is likely, steel resists break-down better than copper. But this advantage is offset to some extent by the superior heat conductivity of copper. Copper also makes a better seal with less likelihood of compression leakage that might cause burning of the gasket back of the edge of the cylinder opening. Steel has a natural tendency to corrode where exposed to the coolant at water holes or where the gasket itself is exposed to the coolant. Some steel gaskets are made with copper grommets at the water holes. Remember, however, that gaskets with copper ferrules must never be used with aluminum heads. Some recent cars, Buick, Cadillac, Chrysler, Ford and

Lincoln, use an embossed type of steel cylinder head gasket. This is said to provide an even and uninterrupted flow of heat between the cylinder head and engine block. The design and formation of the embossing makes the flow of metal under compression even, producing a good seal.

If you don't want to blow your new gasket, better check for clearance of the new gasket around the cylinder bores. The engine may have been rebored and fitted with oversize pistons. In this case the edge of the metal around the gasket might be very close to or even slightly overlap the cylinder bore openings. Thus, on the upstroke, the pistons might strike the head of the gasket, causing early gasket failure or blowout. The minimum clearance from the edge of the gasket to the edge of the cylinder bore opening should be $\frac{1}{32}$ in. This permits correct gasket compression and prevents direct flame contact burn-out. If you find you can not get this clearance check the tops of the pistons for a number such as +.010 which indicates an oversize piston, and buy a gasket to match it. As a last resort, you may have to have the cylinder bores sleeved.

If the new gasket meets requirements, place it on a sheet of paper bottom side up and brush coat it with gasket cement. Then place the gasket with the coated side down on the cylinder block, and coat the upper side. With a rag wipe the cylinder bores of any compound that may have gotten into them. Make a final check to make sure that the gasket is correctly centered. If the head is held by studs, this is easy. But if long cap screws or bolts are used, buy a couple of longer bolts, cut off the heads and screw these into a couple of holes at the end of the block. These will serve as pilots and after the head has been dropped and a half dozen or so of the head bolts inserted finger-tight, remove the pilot bolts with pliers.

You are now ready to tighten the head, which

9

On the Ford 6-cylinder engine the gasket must be applied so the cut-off end (A) is at the left front end of the block; if reversed, leakage occurs because of the water hole shown at the right.

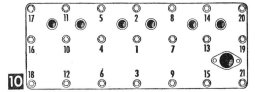

10

17	11	5	2	8	14	20
16	10	4	1	7	13	19
18	12	6	3	9	15	21

Tightening sequence of cylinder heads varies with each engine but in the absence of the manufacturer's specifications, this method should work.

unless carefully done can cause gasket failure. You can obtain a shop manual from your dealer or by writing the factory, for anywhere from $3.50 to $5. This will show the approved sequence in which you should tighten the head bolts, or nuts as the case might be, as well as special instructions regarding the procedure to use, and this should be done with a torque indicating wrench. These torque wrench readings vary with different engines. For example, an engine with an aluminum head may require a recommended tightening torque of 34 to 42 ft lbs; the same engine with a cast-iron head would have approximately 55 to 60 ft lbs torque. If you don't have a torque wrench use an ordinary socket wrench with about a 12-in. handle and follow the tightening sequence shown in Fig. 10. Don't tighten any one bolt or nut all the way "home." Tighten each one a little at a time to draw the head down uniformly, compressing the gasket evenly.

After you have replaced the accessories you previously removed, run the engine for 15 or 20 minutes at a fast idle and then go over the head bolts on the cast-iron head again, once more tightening them about a quarter turn. On aluminum heads the engine must first be cooled to room temperature before tightening the bolts down. You should tighten again after about 300 or 400 miles of operation, using the same recommended sequence.

When you install intake and exhaust manifold gaskets, alignment is important. If the gasket does not line up with the port holes (Fig. 11) the reduced port opening area cuts down on engine power and, in the case of the exhaust, might cause engine overheating. On manifold gaskets, the gaskets are positioned by the bolts holding the manifold on the head. On overhead-valve V8 engines, tighten the bolts holding the intake manifold. If they are loose, air is pulled into the manifold, making a lean mixture, and also ruining the gasket.

Also, check the gasket between the lower edge of the crankcase and oil pan for leakage. If you have removed the engine oil pan for sludge cleaning, check the pan for dents in the flange. If

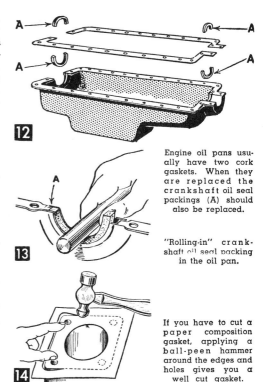

Engine oil pans usually have two cork gaskets. When they are replaced the crankshaft oil seal packings (A) should also be replaced.

"Rolling-in" crankshaft oil seal packing in the oil pan.

If you have to cut a paper composition gasket, applying a ball-peen hammer around the edges and holes gives you a well cut gasket.

there are dents, place the flange upside down on a bench, and hammer out the dents. Usually two cork gaskets are used on the oil pan flange (Fig. 12); in applying them, first coat the flange surface with cup grease. When the oil pan is replaced, install new oil seal packings (A in Fig. 12). You can do this by cleaning the grooves at the ends of the oil pan and rolling-in the seals with a short piece of shafting (Fig. 13). The oil seals come in a pan-gasket set. On some engines, the oil seal ends should come flush with the pan gaskets. On others, such as Chrysler-made engines, the oil seals have strips of cork that project above the gasket and are to be crushed up against the block when the pan is bolted in place. Before bolting the pan, check the crankshaft against which the packings seal for nicks or burrs and smooth them with an oil stone.

For carburetor and fuel pump, you can buy gasket kits which contain all of the necessary ones you need for the job. Also you can buy composition, rubber or paper gasket material in sheet form. In an emergency, you can make a gasket out of composition paper as in Fig. 14. Place the material over the surface to be gasketed, hold it in place with one hand and then with a ball-peen hammer, hammer lightly around holes and edges.

Do not use shellac to apply gaskets. Use good gasket cement because it sets slowly and you can move the gasket about until it is positioned right. Remember to draw the bolts or cap screws up evenly whenever you tighten a gasketed joint.

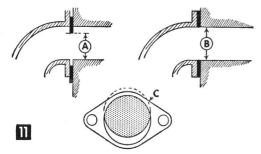

Intake and exhaust manifolds must have their gaskets in alignment; otherwise the port openings are reduced. Note the small opening (A) compared to what it should be (B). The effect of misalignment on port opening is shown at C.

Taking the TAP out of TAPPETS

Strange noises under the hood of your car? A tap-tap-tapping? If you want a little peace and quiet, fix those tappets

Listening to the valve action with a 2-ft. length of garden hose can tell you a great deal.

Feeling the valve action with finger on valve spring retainer.

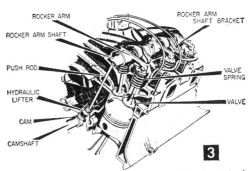

ROCKER ARM
ROCKER ARM SHAFT
PUSH ROD
HYDRAULIC LIFTER
CAM
CAMSHAFT
ROCKER ARM SHAFT BRACKET
VALVE SPRING
VALVE

Artist's drawing of the valve drive train typical of some Chrysler products. Construction is similar on all V-8's using hydraulic lifters.

MANY motorists with some of the finest and latest cars are plagued by a tapping sound under the hood. This noise may be light or heavy; it may continue for only a few seconds when the car is first started, or it may not clear up for many miles. And, in some cases, the noise may not stop at all.

The sound is probably caused by the hydraulic tappets. These tappets were designed to assure quiet engine operation with maximum power but, when they fail, the result is noisy operation and loss of power.

To picture the vital job of the valve lifter—we won't call it a *tappet* any longer, because we are going to quiet this part—look at Figs. 3 and 4. Here we see the lifter riding on the camshaft and carrying a push rod which operates the rocker arm, which in turn opens and closes the valve. Strictly speaking, the rocker arm does not *close* the valve. This job quite obviously is done by the valve spring as the cam allows the valve lifter to descend and the push rod and rocker arms are allowed to "retreat."

There is always the possibility in any engine that carbon is causing valve sticking, with resultant noise and loss of engine performance. And, while we are concerned at the moment with the quiet and efficient performance of valve lifters, we cannot ignore valve conditions. It is a good idea on any engine checkup operation to use one of the commercial valve oils in order to be sure of smooth valve performance. One-pint containers, holding enough for an average engine, may be purchased at automotive supply stores. The instructions on the container usually recommend on overhead valve jobs that the oil be squirted directly onto the valve stems while the engine is running, and frequently also suggest that some

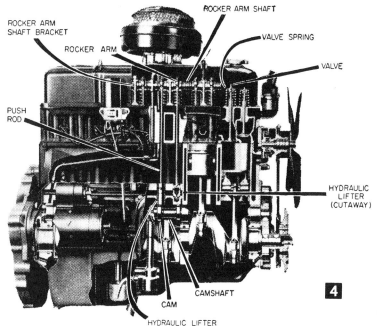

ROCKER ARM SHAFT BRACKET
ROCKER ARM
ROCKER ARM SHAFT
VALVE SPRING
VALVE
PUSH ROD
HYDRAULIC LIFTER (CUTAWAY)
CAMSHAFT
CAM
HYDRAULIC LIFTER

4

Modern in-line engine using overhead valves and hydraulic lifters.

operation. This begins with the intake stroke in which the intake valve is opened and the piston is going down into the cylinder bore. This fills the cylinder with a combustible mixture. Somewhere near the bottom the intake valve closes. The exhaust valve is already closed. So the piston goes up to top dead center, compressing the charge. Near top dead center the spark occurs and, with both valves still closed, the piston goes down on the power stroke. Near the bottom of the stroke the exhaust valve opens and remains open while the piston goes up on the exhaust stroke.

So we see that there is a complete cycle of valve movements at every other revolution of the engine. This fact can help in identifying tapping sounds. For example, if a tapping sound is present in the engine at what appears to be about engine speed, then the piston pins, rings, or connecting rods are more likely to be to blame than the valves. But, if the sound occurs at what appears to be about *half* engine speed, there is good reason to believe that the fault lies in the valve action somewhere. Now, let's see where.

To check for valve lifter noise you can either listen or feel, or use both methods as a double check. The first step in either case is to remove the rocker box cover. Be careful of the gasket: it can often be used again. With the rocker box cover (of a straight six or eight) or the covers of a V-8 removed, start the engine and let it idle (about 400-450 *rpm*). To listen to the sound of individual valves and their lifters, hold one end of a length of garden hose firmly to your ear and hold the other end close to one valve at a time (Fig. 1). Some noise will be picked up from each valve. But if you come to one that sounds like a lonesome woodpecker on a drainpipe, you've located your trouble.

To *feel* the valve action, place one or two fingers on the top of one valve spring retainer at a time, while the engine runs slowly (Fig. 2). If the valve lifter is not performing as it should, there will be a distinct stinging or snapping effect on your finger. In other words the hammering that you hear will be the hammering that you feel. Now let's see what causes this annoying and power-destroying action.

If you experience a hard rapping noise contrasted with a moderate rapping noise, it is likely

oil be introduced through the air intake of the carburetor (air-cleaner removed) while the engine is running.

Note in Fig. 4 that there is basically no difference in the job of the hydraulic valve lifter in a straight engine (whether six or eight cylinder) and the job performed in a V-8. The thing to get clearly in mind is that an engine warms up at varying rates and consequently is subject to varying degrees of expansion when going into service. This varying expansion upsets valve clearances in any engine utilizing solid valve lifters. Picture in Fig. 4, for example, what happens when the engine first starts up. Combustion at extremely high temperature is present in each cylinder and on each piston so the engine begins to warm up through the cylinder block. The first heating up takes place near the top of the block. As the heat progresses down the cylinder walls and up into the cylinder head, expansion actually lifts the whole valve rocker assembly, since this is mounted on the head. To the extent of a few thousandths of an inch this increases clearances in the valve train. With hydraulic valve lifters the clearance is taken up and valve action remains unchanged. With solid lifters the lifter has to travel a little farther to take up the clearance that has developed before it can open the valve. This influences valve timing slightly and has an adverse effect on engine power. True, the difference is small. No driver would notice this. But engineers who are trying to corral the very last horse in their favorite engine consider these fine points. Naturally, this valve action goes on at one-half engine speed.

To clear up that point, let's review the engine

63

Using ratchet wrench with extension for quick and easy removal of intake manifold with carburetor on V-8 engine. Reinstalling the manifold is just the reverse of removing it.

Running out rocker arm hold-down bolts in order to remove the push rods.

that the plunger is sticking in the bore of the lifter body. This means that the return spring within the valve lifter is unable to push the plunger into the working position to take up play or looseness (see sketch at right). This trouble is generally due to gum or varnish deposits from the oil used or to carbon formation.

There is also the possibility that the metal itself has galled. This galling, or picking up of metal, is commonly the result of the presence in the engine oil of abrasive dirt that was not filtered out. The best preventive is the use of heavy-duty or high-detergent oil and the frequent replacement of the oil filter — at least every 5,000 miles on a car using hydraulic valve lifters.

A moderate rapping noise heard during the garden hose check indicates considerable wear within the valve lifter. This allows an excessively high leakdown rate of the oil in the space between plunger and lifter body. There is also the possibility of a leaky check valve due to a bad valve or seat.

If you find it hard to determine which valve is the noisiest and yet the whole system is an-

noyingly loud, check up on the quantity and quality of the oil in the engine. Frequent short runs in cold weather, excessive use of the choke, or cold running will contribute to crankcase di-

Before you attempt to quiet your valves, be sure you understand

How Hydraulic Valve Lifters Work

WITH engine valve closed there is no pressure on the push rod (1 in Fig. A), so the plunger spring (2) pushes up the plunger (3). Oil from the engine's lubrication system enters at (4), passes through the lifter valve (5) into space (6) below the plunger into the lifter body (7).

When the cam has turned to open a valve as in Fig. B, lifter valve (5) closes making the body (7) and plunger (3) a solid hydraulic ram. Thus the hydraulic lifter acts like a solid unit forcing up the push rod and opening the engine valve.

So we see that automatic *takeup* of *clearance* in the valve train is handled by the relatively light plunger spring (2 in Fig. A) moving up the plunger as any play develops. The oil then holds the plunger up.

Continuous pressure on the plunger, however, will force the plunger down due to *slight intentional leakage* between the plunger and the body. This continuous pressure is present on one or two valves when a car is left standing, for example overnight. This is why hydraulic lifters may be noisy for just a second or two when the engine is first started after having been idle for a period. Understanding that a *tight* plunger spring takes up noise-producing clearance explains why even a little gum within the lifter body or foreign matter between the plunger and the body will cause noise. The plunger spring simply isn't strong enough to take up the clearance that develops in the system as the engine expands and contracts with changes in temperature.

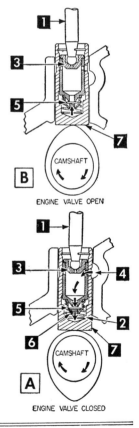

CAMSHAFT

B

ENGINE VALVE OPEN

CAMSHAFT

A

ENGINE VALVE CLOSED

lution. And this dilution of the crankcase oil will allow a rate of leakdown that will let the lifters become noisy. The first step in this case is to drain the oil while the oil is thoroughly hot and put in oil of the correct grade as specified by the engine manufacturer for the particular time of year.

If the valve lifter noise is the type that comes and goes, it may be caused by a very small piece of dirt which prevents the check-valve in the lifter from sealing tight. There is, of course, the possibility that the valve itself may have a small defect on it. And as the valve shifts around this defect may occasionally interfere with action and cause the valve lifter to be noisy. At other times the defect does not interfere and the valve lifter is quiet.

Before undertaking expensive mechanical work, try a commercial gum-dissolving solvent or special oil that will clean up any varnish or gum deposit in the hydraulic valve lifters. The methods of using the hydraulic valve lifter oil vary all the way from a normal oil change to a highly specialized lubrication system servicing.

For example, one additive maker specifies that the engine should be drained, the oil filter cartridge removed and the engine then refilled with a quart of SAE 10 oil plus 4 qts. of kerosene in which his additive has been installed. Then, due to the cleansing effect of this mixture, the engine must be run at what would give 15 to 20 *mph* for two hours, *outside* of the shop or garage. Then it is drained, the oil filter chamber cleaned, a new filter element added, and the regular oil for the particular engine put in. Usually this clears up the entire valve lifter problem. Where the valve lifter noise has continued so long that mechanical damage has occurred or where the noise was due originally to wear or damage to the parts, then of course the use of a special solvent will accomplish nothing. So this brings us up to the job of removing, cleaning, inspecting, reassembling and installing the lifters.

First, you will have to remove the one rocker

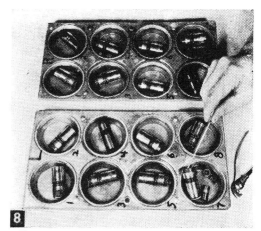

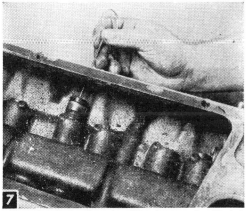

Removing hydraulic valve lifter from engine block with a piece of stiff wire with ⅛ in. "L"-shaped hooks bent at each end.

Using muffin tins as an easy way of keeping hydraulic lifters from a V-8 engine identified as to location, while also soaking them in a solvent to remove gum, varnish and carbon. Lifters must always be returned to their original engine position.

Removing the lock ring or plunger retainer wire that holds the plunger in the lifter body.

box cover on a straight engine or two covers on a V-8. On an engine such as shown in Fig. 4 the side plate over the push rods will also have to be removed. In a V-type engine the intake manifold will have to be taken off (Fig. 5). Then, whatever the engine design, the valve rocker arm assembly must either be loosened sufficiently to release the push rods or removed entirely if that becomes necessary in order to get the push rods out (Fig. 6).

Now use the starter to turn the engine over at least two revolutions. This will push all of the hydraulic valve lifters up as high as they go in normal operation. If they fall down again, it merely indicates that they are fairly free in their guides. Sometimes carbon or gum in the valve lifter guide *above* the normal travel of the lifter will interfere with lifter removal, requiring a strong hook in order to get the lifter up (Fig. 7). The lifters have one or two holes near the top to facilitate removal. To make a hook for one with two holes, straighten out a 20-in. length of heavy wire coat hanger and bend over exactly in the middle. Then bend the two free ends out with a ⅛-in. base for each "L" shape. Spread the wire sufficiently so that it will tend to spring out in the top of the valve lifter and grip the holes.

Place each valve lifter in the cup of a muffin tin (Fig. 8). Use one muffin tin to represent the

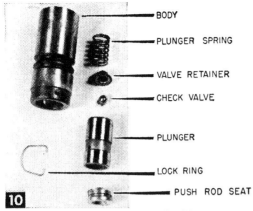

BODY

PLUNGER SPRING

VALVE RETAINER

CHECK VALVE

PLUNGER

LOCK RING

PUSH ROD SEAT

10

Disassembled hydraulic valve lifter.

left block, another for the right block, and number the individual compartments from front to back so that each lifter can be returned to its original engine position. Soak each lifter in a commercial gum and varnish solvent or in lacquer thinner, *Gum-Out,* or acetone; then, for complete cleaning, disassemble each lifter and return parts to the solvent (Fig. 8). Keep the parts of each lifter together in the properly numbered compartment of the muffin tin. Plungers and lifter bodies are a selective fit when manufactured, and as they wear together it becomes increasingly important that the same parts continue to work together.

Disassemble lifter by pressing the plunger down with one of the push rods from the engine and lift out the lock-ring (Fig. 9). If, with the wire out, hydraulic lifter assembly cannot be shaken apart due to gum on the plunger or inner core of the body, let it soak for a half-hour. Then strike the assembly softly against a piece of soft wood, holding it in the right hand with the opening facing down. The inertia of the plunger will carry it out of the bore. Occasionally brush the parts soaking in the solvent with a 1 in. varnish brush to speed up the cleaning action. Then lift out the assemblies one by one and shake them dry. Compressed air may be used, but do not wipe parts with a cloth as the lint can cause trouble. Inspect each part for damage such as scratching or galling. Then try the plunger in the lifter body. It should move in and out freely of its own weight but should not have any noticeable looseness or side play.

Now replace all parts in the order in which they were removed. Be sure that the locking spring has not been collapsed. Spring it outward about ⅛ in. before installing so that it will snap firmly into the groove in the lifter body. When the lifter is assembled, you should be able to hear the check valve (Fig. 10) rattle when the assembly is shaken. Reassembly is easiest when done with all parts upside down. That is, place the push rod seat on the bench and put the plunger in position on top of the seat. Then put the check valve with its retainer on top of the plunger and

the plunger spring on top of the valve-retainer. Pour about a spoonful of SAE 10 engine oil over this plunger assembly, then slide the valve lifter body down over it. Holding the assembly in place in the body with the tip of one finger, turn the lifter right side up. Then, using a push rod to force the plunger down into the body, put the spring lock ring into position in the body groove.

Now submerge the lifter in a clean container of SAE 10 engine oil. Pump the plunger up and down so that the lifter becomes filled with oil, then press down firmly on the plunger. If the plunger can be pushed down into the lifter body, it indicates excessive leakage between the lifter and the body or through the valve. Discard such lifters and substitute new ones purchased from your car dealer or automotive supply house. Test these as previously described before installing.

Now you can reassemble the engine. Remember, there is a limit to the takeup of a hydraulic lifter. For this reason on engines that provide no mechanical adjustment in the rocker arms each lifter should be collapsed after it is installed by applying continuous pressure on the push rod. When the lifter is collapsed by having forced out all the oil there should be .030 to .070 in. of clearance between the rocker arm and the valve stem (Fig. 11). In checking this, crank the engine until the piston of the cylinder in which the valves are being checked is at top dead center of the compression stroke. On many engines it is possible to see the camshaft. On these it is only necessary to have the valve lifter on the "heel" of the cam—the lifter's lowest position

CLEARANCE OF .030 TO .070 REQUIRED HERE WITH LIFTER COLLAPSED

ROCKER ARM SHAFT BRACKET

VALVE CAN BE REMOVED AND STEM GROUND FOR CLEARANCE — OR — SHIM HERE TO INCREASE CLEARANCE

11

Where clearance is measured and how to increase it if less than .030 in. with lifter forced all the way down.

—when checking the clearance. Obviously there can be no clearance when the cam is turned so as to open the valve. And it is very important that the cam is not in some mid-position which eliminates *some* of the clearance though the valve has not yet opened.

Another easy way to check for dead center position of the piston is to use the distributor rotor. The rotor points to the distributor cap terminal of the piston that is at top dead center of the compression stroke. Should the clearance when checked prove to be less than .030 in.—which is most unlikely—it will be necessary to grind the end of the valve stem to give the required clearance. If the clearance is greater than .070 in., replacement of the worn parts will be necessary. This could involve rebushing the rocker arm, renewing the rocker arm shaft or installing a new valve. No one can tell which will be required until the job is inspected. Occasionally where no adjustment is provided, mechanics have improvised by shimming up or filing off the

brackets that support the rocker arm shaft. A .004 in. shim between the base of the rocker arm support bracket and the cylinder head will increase valve clearance about .008 in.

Since checking the hydraulic lifters in the block required compressing them and thus discharging all oil, they will be a little noisy until the engine oil has worked into them again. With the lifters in place, the pushrods replaced and the rocker arm assemblies tightened down, start up the engine and let it idle. With the rocker arm covers still off, take a recheck of operations by listening at each valve for unusual noise, then feeling each valve spring as the engine idles. There should be no stinging shock on your fingertip. If you have followed the foregoing procedure step-by-step you have saved at least $50, and you have the plus-satisfaction that comes from realizing that hydraulic tappets don't have to be noisy—that they can, in fact, give you a bonus of silence and power when properly used and serviced.

Be Sure Your Horn Won't Blow at Midnight

BY installing a simple push-pull switch on your dash, and cutting into one wire, you can be certain that *your* car horns will never blow at midnight.

First, drill a hole large enough to accommodate the switch at a convenient spot on the dash. Lift the hood and locate the horn relay. If you're unsure about which metal box is the horn relay, trace the wires from the horn. Take two lengths of #14 insulated wire and thread through the firewall; if possible, using a hole in the firewall through which other wires pass. If you drill a new hole, install a rubber grommet so that the insulation on the wires won't scrape against metal.

Loosen the screw on the horn relay terminal marked "S" (switch or horn button) and remove the wire from the horn relay. If there is no "S," the smallest wire leading to the relay is the horn-ring, or button, wire.

Attach one of the new wires to the "S" terminal on the relay; lead the other end of the wire through the firewall and attach to either switch terminal. Solder and tape one end of the second piece of new wire to the end of the wire removed from the "S" terminal on the horn relay.

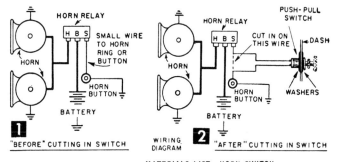

MATERIALS LIST—HORN SWITCH

Amt.	Description
1	push-pull switch
2 pcs.	#14 insulated wire twice as long as the distance from dashboard to horn relay

Lead the free end of this wire through the hole in the firewall and attach to the other switch terminal. Install the switch, using washers.

Now to test your job With the switch pushed *in*, a tap on the horn-ring or button should make the horns blow. With the switch pulled to *off* position, the horns should not blow. If it's the other way around, reverse the two switch wires.

When you leave your car, get in the habit of pulling the switch to the *off* position. This cuts the horns out completely.

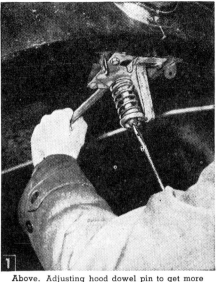

Above. Adjusting hood dowel pin to get more tension on hood lock when closed.

Right. "Listening" rod made from 4-ft length of broom handle tracks down knocks, clicks and rattles, much like the doctor's stethoscope.

How to Spot That Noise—and Cure It

You can silence that shake, rattle and roll

WOULDN'T you like to choke that little "Canary" somewhere in the front end of your car that's been pestering you? Or, maybe you've got one of those thumpy clunks that only shows up now and then at certain speeds. Suppose your car runs like the proverbial jackrabbit but when you hit around 45 or so, some sort of a howl or wheeze comes in that makes your passenger ask "What makes it do that?"

Noises often come from a source least expected as knocks, growls, groans, squeaks, whistles and so on have a way of seeming to be where they ain't. Even the best shops are often stumped by odd sounds, especially when everything seems to be tip top. There is always that "mysterious" knocking or rattle, hard to pin down. But even the most evasive squeak can be located by following these methods.

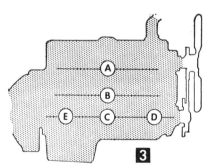

Divide engine into zones to help localize foreign noise when you use a listening rod. (A) Cylinder block casting zone. (B) Camshaft zone (L-head engine). (C) Crankshaft center main bearing zone. (D) Front main bearing zone. (E) Rear main bearing zone.

Unwanted noises plague new and old cars, big and little cars. Those little tingling noises that are often heard only when the car is in motion can keep you guessing. And for the life of you, you can't reproduce them by bouncing or shaking your car. Weather has a lot to do with car noise too. Some squeaks and rattles ride with you on hot, dry days but fade away during rainy weather. Sometimes all you can do is localize foreign noise, and you'd have to tear down the unit to find the cause. Like a transmission, for example. You may have traced a low speed "howl" to a conventional gear transmission. Tearing down the transmission might show a defective clutch pilot bearing, binding clutch hub or misalignment of the clutch in the flywheel as the direct cause of the growl.

While a complete chassis lubrication, includ-

68

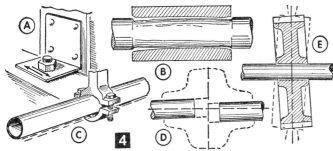

A few causes of knocks, squeaks, and rattles. (A) Friction of loose, dry parts rubbing together. (B) Excessive wear in a shaft and its bearing or bushing. (C) Loose part, like muffler tail pipe. (D) Misaligned shafts, causing excessive wear and "pound." (E) gears, pulleys, etc., which run out-of-true.

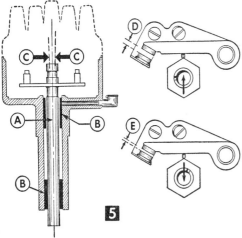

Engine's "wump, wump, wump" at idle may be caused by a worn or bent ignition distributor shaft. Note how shaft (A) in top bushing (B) wobbles so its center line oscillates from C to C. As the distributor cam is pushed towards or away from the contact point breaker arm the point opening is either too great (D) or too little (E).

ing under hood engine units—distributor oil or grease cup, oiler on generator, fan bearing, water pump, lubricant or wax on glazed fan belt stops many noises, don't depend too much on a chassis lube job to take care of the squeaks and groans permanently. There may be a worn spring shackle that quiets down with a lube job, but grease won't take the place of worn metal. Once you've traced such a noise, better get some new bushings in the shackle. Higher car speeds and more powerful engines tend to amplify small noises you never have heard before at lower speeds.

When trying to locate noises under the hood and coming

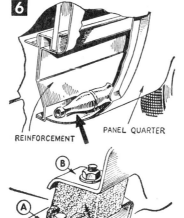

REINFORCEMENT PANEL QUARTER

principally from the engine, a sounding rod helps to localize the source. The rod can be $\frac{5}{16}$ or $\frac{3}{8}$-in. dia steel, and about 3 ft long. Or, use a broom stick of about the same length. To "sound" a noise, place one end of it on the spot to be tested and bring the other end close so your ear rests on your closed hand (Fig. 2). To organize your attack, split up the engine section into zones (Fig. 3).

While using the sounding rod, "short out" the spark plug of the cylinder being tested. If the engine knock becomes less audible, louder or changes in any way with a spark plug dead, you are pretty sure to have located the troublesome cylinder. Of course, if all connecting rod bearings are worn and loose, you'll hear a clatter no matter where you put the end of the sounding rod on the crankcase. Speeding up the engine makes such clatter louder.

Actually the foreign noises we are interested in are those "funny sounds," klunks, whistles and squeaks that might come from any part of your car.

Since many car owners recognize run-of-mine knocks, spark rap, valve tappet clatter, hydraulic valve lifter click, carbon knock and such, we'll skip those and talk about the ones that are harder to track down.

Table A lists the more common noises, parts affected, probable trouble, how to check for it and how to fix it. You can't always apply the same information to every make of car. Take #9, if the car has an automatic transmission, you can't check for end play as prescribed because there's no pedal to push. In this case check for excessive end play with the oil pan off using a heavy screw driver or pinch bar between the main bearing cap and crank cheek. Or, in #13, piston slap may occur in even a new or rebuilt engine with some types of aluminum pistons when the engine is cold, but the pistons will quiet down as the engine reaches correct operating temperature.

Whether you call it a knock, squeak, hiss, rattle, or pound (see Table B for definitions)

Fig. 6. A "mysterious" rattle like the cola bottle which some factory employee unthinkingly welded in the panel quarter is usually found only by sheer accident.
Fig. 7. Typical forward engine mounting. (A) Frame bracket. (B) Engine leg. (C) Rubber shock dampening insulator. If rubber deteriorates, a knock or thump may result as the engine rocks during accelerating.

ENGINE AND UNDERHOOD NOISE

	CHARACTERISTIC SOUND OR BEHAVIOR	PART OR PARTS AFFECTED	PROBABLE NATURE OF TROUBLE	CHECKING	REMEDY
1.	Hissing	Spark plug	Broken or loose	Squirt oil around plug base; bubbles indicate leak	Tighten or replace plug
2.	Click or rattle	Fan	Bent blade, broken ball, loose bracket	Look for shiny spot on blade. Inspect bearings and bracket mountings	Straighten blade. Replace bearing. Tighten bracket
3.	Loud report in muffler	Muffler	Exhause valve not seating. Ignition out of time. Rich or too lean mixture	Accelerate engine for smoke from exhaust pipe	Reface & regrind valve. Retime ignition to engine. Clean carburetor jets or adjust fuel level
4.	Sharp snap Engine pulling	High-tension Ignition System	Cracked distributor head. Cracked plug insulator. Damaged wire insulation. Loose distributor wire.	Wipe distributor head and plugs. Examine wire insulation. Test wires in distributor sockets	Wipe parts clean or replace with new. Tape wires or replace. Push wires firmly into sockets
5.	Dull thump or Pound upon acceleration	Engine mount or mounts	Loose or deteriorated rubber in mount	Visual inspection	Tighten bolts of mount or replace rubber blocks
6.	Metallic rattle upon acceleration	Muffler or tail pipe	Muffler baffles loose. Tail pipe strikes frame	Use sounding rod on muffler (rear end on jacks) shake tail pipe	Install new muffler. Bend tail pipe and tighten clamps
7.	Squeal (generally at idling speed)	Generator Fan bearing Water pump	Generator brushes too hard. Fan bearing dry. Dry water pump seal	Use sounding rod on suspected units	Install new generator brushes—or sand commutator Lubricate fan bearing. Use soluble oil in cooling system
8.	Knock (upon accelerating or pulling)	Ignition Distributor	Automatic advance stuck. Spark timed too early. Vacuum control not functioning	Remove breaker plate from distributor and test governor weights for free action. Check timing with a timing light. Check vacuum control	Clean and lubricate governor advance. Retime ignition to engine with timing light. Install new diaphragm
9.	Intermittent rap (engine idling)	Crankshaft	Excessive end play in crankshaft	Noise affected by applying or releasing clutch	Install new end-thrust bearing or bronze washer
10.	Loud knock or "bump" (engine pulling hard at low speed)	Crankshaft main bearing	Loose or worn main bearing	Short out spark plugs with screwdriver on block or head	Replace worn bearing or bearings with new or adjust with shims
11.	Well defined knock or "tap" on accelerating more pronounced when releasing pedal	Connecting rod	Worn bearing	Allow engine to "pull" at approximately 35 mph. then release accelerator pedal pressure	Install rod or rods with new bearings
12.	Light metallic knock or tap (engine idling)	Piston pin	Worn pin	Hold sounding rod on block from cylinder to cylinder. Short out plugs one by one	Install new pin or pins
13.	Decided "slap" or knock with cold engine	Pistons	Pistons loose in cylinder. Connecting rod misaligned. Excessively worn cylinders	See whether noise disappears as engine warms up	Recondition cylinders. Install new pistons, rings, pins and align connecting rods
14.	"Spark" knocks (wide open throttle)	Ignition Distributor	Sticking distributor breaker plate. Governor advance springs weak	Visual inspection of plate. Test distributor, after removal in test machine	Clean and "free-up" breaker plate. Install new governor springs.
15.	"Whistle" (partly open throttle)	Heat riser tube	Loose tube	Idle engine. Remove air cleaner. Hold bundle of rags over exhaust tail pipe. Stop engine. Check for smoke from carburetor air intake	Install new riser tube to replace burned out tube
16.	Hissing sound (in crankcase)	Pistons and Rings	Loose pistons or stuck rings causing "blow-by"	Look for smoke coming from breather pipe or crankcase. Insert rubber hose in breather. Crank engine and place ear on other end of hose	Recondition cylinders, new pistons and rings, or free up rings with solvent

DRIVE LINE NOISE—CLUTCH, TRANSMISSION AND PROPELLER SHAFT

17.	Chatter	Clutch	Facings worn or glazed	Accelerate car slowly. (also check for excessive end play in rear spring front shackles)	Install new clutch facings. New pressure plate may also be required
18.	Grinding noise	Clutch	Worn release bearing. Bearing requires lubrication	Press clutch pedal intermittently	Install new release bearing or lubricate bearing
19.	Squeaks	Clutch	Insufficient pedal-to-floor board clearance	Test for pedal striking floor board	Adjust screw or pedal shaft clearance, to correct specification
20.	Whining noise	Fluid flywheel	Fluid level low	Constantly audible	Add fluid to correct level
21.	Whistle—long, low	Driver or passenger	Curvaceous blonde on street	Glance quickly around area	Turn sharply at next corner
22.	Gears noisy when shifting	Transmission and Clutch	Wrong clutch pedal adjustment	Noise evident when shifting into any speed while pressing clutch pedal	Adjust for correct "lash" and floor board clearance
23.	Grinding noise from transmission at high speed	Transmission and Propeller shaft assembly	Worn transmission rear bearings. Worn universal joints	"Whip" of propeller shaft usually can be felt at high speed	New transmission bearings (other parts may be needed too). Renew worn universal
24.	Howl (shift lever in "low")	Transmission	Worn clutch pilot bearing in flywheel recess	Noise usually disappears in 2nd and high	Remove clutch & transmission assembly & install new pilot bearing
25.	Growl or hum (in "neutral")	Transmission	Pinion shaft bearing and gear probably excessively worn	Depressing clutch pedal usually stops noise	Overhaul transmission (other gears and bearings usually are worn, too)
26.	Whirring noise (under car, with considerable vibrating)	Propeller shaft	Worn universal joints and unbalanced propeller shaft	Drive at fairly high speed. Shift to neutral. Let engine idle. If vibration persists, suspect propeller shaft	New universal joint parts (also perhaps, transmission rear bearing)

CHASSIS, SPRINGS, SHACKLES, AND SHOCK ABSORBER NOISE

	CHARACTERISTIC SOUND OR BEHAVIOR	PART OR PARTS AFFECTED	PROBABLE NATURE OF TROUBLE	CHECKING	REMEDY
27.	Rattle	Under hood chassis parts (front)	Loose radiator shell. Independent coil spring pads missing. Car heater bracket loose	Visual inspection of parts; test for looseness with heavy screwdriver	Replace missing parts, screws or bolts and tighten securely
28.	Rattle	Muffler or Tail pipe	Muffler and tail-pipe bracket loose	Grasp and shake end of tailpipe. Visual inspection underneath car	Replace missing parts screws or bolts and tighten securely
29.	Drumming noise	Under hood parts	Loose engine mountings	With carburetor throttle rod accelerate engine in short "jerks" and observe engine mountings for movement	Tighten engine hold-down bolts (or replace rubber mounts on newer engines)
30.	Heavy bumping noise	Under hood	Battery loose in its cradle	Visual inspection	Tighten battery hold-bolts (also see if cable has been chafing)
31.	Dull thud	Spring shackle or bolt	Worn or loose rubber or metal bushings	Place pry bar between frame and leaf spring and apply pressure to test looseness	Install new rubber bushings (some equipped with metal bushings)
32.	Squeaky noise (slowing down or stopping)	Shock absorber	Linkage joints	Examine for lack of lubrication	Lubricate linkage
33.	Rattle (from vicinity of wheels)	Shock absorbers	Loose on frame—Arm striking frame or other parts. Bushings or attaching eyes (telescoping type) worn or loose	Visual examination of parts. (Also check spring shackles, sway bar mounting and spring U-bolts for looseness)	Tighten bolts, align parts or rebush attaching parts. (Noise seldom within shock absorber itself)
	REAR AXLE NOISE				
34.	Humming noise (continuous)	Rear axle pinion and drive gear	Pinion bearing incorrectly adjusted giving high tooth contact	Best done by driving on asphalt road. (Have correct seasonal lubricant in axle). Often can be tire noise	Move pinion towards drive gear (drive gear may require shifting also). Axle must be "taken down" for work
35.	Gear noise (decelerating)	Rear axle Differential	End play in differential bearings excessive	Audible when releasing accelerator and car slows down	Rear axle must be opened. Loosen bearing saddle clamps and adjust bearings. Lock assembly
36.	Hum while coasting	Axle wheel bearings	Excessive end play in axle shafts (or both shafts)	Audible when coasting. Jack up rear wheels and pull and push on wheels in line with axle shaft	Remove wheel, brake drum and adjust end play with shims inside backing plate
37.	Noise or Growl on turns	Rear axle side gear thrust washers or inner axle oil seal	Thrust washers worn, seal burned out	Most audible when making left turn	Remove, disassemble differential and install new thrust washers (perhaps gears also). Install new axle oil seal
	BRAKE, TIRES AND WHEEL NOISE				
38.	Chatter (applying Brakes)	Brakes (one or more wheels)	Loose wheel bearing. Loose spring U-bolts. Loose spring shackle	Jack up wheel, grasp it top and bottom and test for "play". Inspect U-bolts for tightness. Test shackles	Adjust wheel bearing. Tighten U-bolts. Re-bush spring shackles
39.	Loud squeal—when applying brakes	Brakes	Non-concentric shoes produce local high pressure areas. Drums distort under braking pressure	Remove wheels and brake drum. Check lining for uneven wear spots. Have mechanic check drums with gages	Have shop true-up brake shoe linings with lining grinder. Install new brake drums
40.	Squeal or whistle (on curves)	Tires	Lateral slippage caused by front wheel misalignment	Check tires for uneven tread wear, scuffing and cupped condition; check for bent frame	Front end alignment for toe-in camber, caster and king pin inclination. Straighten frame
41.	Thumping noise	Tires	One or more tires "egg-shaped"	Jack up wheel; place carton or box on ground close to center of tread. Rotate tire slowly; note variation in distance between tire and box	Tire should be retrued (new tires should be driven 1500 miles or so for breakin before truing)
42.	Rattle (front wheel)	Bearings	Broken ball or roller	Remove bearings and make visual inspection	Install new bearing assembly and adjust bearing
	BODY NOISE				
43.	Rumble or Rattle (front end)	Hood	Hood fastener has insufficient spring tension. Anti rattlers missing	Testing for trouble is also the cure. Loosen lock nut and turn dowel inward with screwdriver for correct fit and tighten nut. Check for missing rubber or fabric anti-rattlers	Correct tension removes "play". Install new anti-rattlers
44.	Squeak	Door panel	Panel scrapes against hinge pillar	Look for "rusty" or shiny edge on door panel and hinge pillar	Open door, insert screwdriver in crack and press on door so as to close against it. Metal will spring back at flange
45.	Front fender "squeak"	Fender and door	Too little clearance between fender and door	Visual inspection	Loosen bolts (engine compartment) holding fender rear edge to cowl. Shift fender forward or rearward with pinch bar for clearance, tighten bolts
46.	Rattle (cowl)	Ventilator	Gasket rotted out or deteriorated	Visual inspection of gasket	Remove old pieces of gasket, clean channel, fit new gasket
47.	Squeal or whistle (40-50 mph)	Body louvers on side of car	Air stream passing through louvers	Fasten a cloth over louvers and see if noise ceases	Break up air stream with wire fastened lengthwise in louvers
48.	Rumbling sound	Doors and body panel	Vibration due to insufficient sound deadening	Difficult to check	Undercoating possibly best answer
49.	Bumping noise (rear end of car)	Spare wheel and tire	Loose in its mounting. Loose body bolts	Visual inspection	Tighten clamp screw or nut. Tighten body bolts
50.	"Buzzing" sound	Speedometer	Cable tip not correctly seated in speedometer head drive gear. Cable too long	Unscrew sleeve on rear of speedometer and examine parts	Seat tip into drive gear and tighten sleeve. Install cable of correct length

71

Loosening deck lid hinge bolts before aligning lid. After alignment carefully raise lid and tighten nuts.

a noise can be caused by one or more of the conditions shown in Fig. 4. Friction will set up a squeak, for example, when a bolt becomes loose enough to allow adjacent parts to rub together. Squirting a little oil around the parts usually quiets it, but for a permanent remedy, tighten the bolt. It's friction, too, that produces the squeak from a glazed fan belt. A little wax on the belt quiets it for a time, but you really need a new belt.

Out-of-round parts that wobble or hop can produce a wump-wump-wump noise like an out-of-balance wheel or engine flywheel. One grumble, accompanied by noticeable car vibration, often traced to an unbalanced propeller shaft with undercoating on one side. Undercoating is fine for fenders or gas tank, but if a blob gets smeared on the propeller shaft (actually a tube) it can set up a mighty unpleasant vibration at high speeds. Since the undercoating is not evenly spread around shaft, it runs lop-sided—the higher the speed the worse it gets. It takes only a few ounces on the shaft to cause a noise.

An out-of-round or worn ignition distributor shaft can cause your car's engine to run "rough," particularly at low speed, along with a sort of "loping" exhaust. Fig. 5 shows why. Note that wear has turned the bushing oval allowing the distributor shaft to be pushed back and forth in

Loosening hood hinge bolts before aligning hood to center it between front fenders.

the oval opening by pressure from the bent shaft. In a six-cylinder engine distributor, for example, only two of the cylinders have the correct "dwell" or closure time for the contact points. Other cylinders are firing "early" or "late," causing an unbalanced or "rough" running engine.

Misaligned parts, such as two shaft ends which do not slide concentrically into a coupling (Fig. 4D), cause severe strains on the supporting bearings and wear the bearings excessively to produce noise. Clutches, transmissions, propeller shafts and rear axles are subject to these misalignments, particularly on older cars or those recently repaired. Transmission noises are difficult to track down because some noises, which seem to be coming from the transmission, actually are being "telegraphed" from their origin in the rear axle.

Adjustments for correcting misaligned parts are provided, for example, at the hood hinges, hood lock dowel and guide (Figs. 1 and 8). Usually elongated holes at hood hinges permit fore and aft movement of the hood hinge brackets. To align hood, loosen hinge adjusting screws, grasp front of hood and shift it around until it is centered. Then carefully raise the hood and tighten the hinge screws.

Minor adjustments can be made on the trunk lid at the hinges. To find out if an adjustment is necessary, chalk the edge of the body flange with white chalk and close the lid. If chalk marks on the weatherstrip are not visible all around (spotty), adjustment is necessary. Loosen hinge support bolts (Fig. 9) and shift the deck lid in elongated holes at the body hinge support brackets. After alignment, tighten the bolts.

Shock absorbers are often blamed for noise when actually the fault may be elsewhere. There may be loose parts in the car's trunk, or spring shackles and clips may be loose. Fenders or bumpers may require tightening. Most shock absorber noise results from units that are empty or low in fluid, have worn links and bushings or loose mountings. Simplest way to correct shock absorber noise unless fluid is low is to replace units.

Hoses: Your Car's Lifeline

Check them often and you can save yourself time, trouble, and money

Fig. 1: Hoses should be inspected about every six months to check for wall separation, cracks, and leaks. If hoses are in good condition and the engine still runs a fever, remove hoses to see if they may be clogged with rust.

IF YOUR car runs too hot, or if your windshield wiper runs too slow, the solution may be as simple as installing a new hose. A leaking hose may mean that you'll end up at a dead stop. So, it's good practice to check them periodically to make sure they're in good condition.

The engine draws cool water from the bottom of the radiator and a pump forces it through the water jackets of the cylinder block and head where it absorbs much of the engine heat. The hot water then flows into the upper tank on the radiator and as it works its way through the radiator to the bottom, it is cooled.

Most late model cars use a sealed cooling system, using water under pressures of 2 to 15 lbs. psi above normal. The increased water pressure raises the boiling point of the water allowing the engine to be operated at more efficient higher temperatures without boiling the water out of the system. Raising the pressure 1 pound at sea level will raise the boiling point of water about 3°.

Water boils at 212° F at normal sea level pressure (15 lbs. psi). If the cooling system

on your car is pressurized 5 lbs, the total pressure in the system at sea level would be 20 lbs. and the water inside would boil at 228° F.

A special radiator cap is needed to hold this higher than normal pressure inside the cooling system. The pressure cap used on most cars has two valves: one for pressure, the other for vacuum.

The pressure valve stays closed while pressure in the cooling system is within safe limits. If the engine heats up, raising water pressure, the valve opens to permit the excess pressure to escape. The vacuum valve opens automatically to admit outside air when the engine cools and the pressure in the cooling system drops.

When you remove the pressure cap: be careful. If the cooling system in your car is highly pressurized or if the water temperature is above normal, the sudden release of the cap may send boiling water shooting out. To protect you, the cap has two "on" positions. In the first position, the cap is fully sealed. A slight twist relieves the pressure but keeps the cap firmly on the radiator stem.

Pressure and hot water can escape from the second position, but the cap cannot blow. A further twist on the cap will release it from the stem.

Danger Signs. If your engine is running hot or using water, check the hoses in both the cooling system and the heater system. Since the system is pressurized, a poor hose in either system could mean trouble. A soft-walled hose may collapse inwardly, restricting the flow of water from radiator to engine. A worn hose, cracked or split, may leak water. A hardened hose may leak water around the connections. A leaky hose may also allow air to seep into the cooling system, and as the air bubbles form in the cooling system, they may promote rust. The rust, in time, can clog the radiator and the hoses.

In a recent survey, automotive engineers found that 15% of all cooling system complaints were caused by rotted or age-hardened hoses or by hoses with loose, leaking joints. The trouble may be in the age of the hose, but it can be in the quality of the hose itself.

Hoses are generally made with reinforcement, either an inner layer of fabric or an inner spiral of wire, or, in cases of extreme pressure, both. A hose without some kind of reinforcement can break without warning. In a recent test, Prestone engineers checked reinforced hoses against unreinforced types. Of all non-reinforced hoses, 54% failed during the test. Only 15% of the reinforced types gave any sign of trouble.

To be safe, check the condition of hoses about every six months (Fig. 1). Inspect them for cracks, splits and signs of leaks. Squeeze radiator hoses. Be sure they are springy and resilient, not spongy and lifeless (Fig. 2). If any hose collapses under finger pressure and does not instantly spring back, it should be replaced. Hoses which are too hard may leak at the connections. Replace these. If the hoses seem in good condition and your engine still runs a fever, remove the hoses to see if they may be clogged with rust.

Replacing Hoses. When you replace a hose, use one with the recommended internal diameter. If there is any doubt about the hose clamps, replace them.

There are two types of clamps used on cars built in the U. S. The spring clamp, (Fig. 3) such as is now standard on Chrysler products, and a screw-type clamp (Fig. 4) used as both a stock item and replacement part on many cars. The spring clamp consists of a double circle of wire which can be expanded by compressing two "L" shaped tabs with pliers and which contact tightly against the hose when the tabs are released. The screw-type clamps use either a screw and nut which tighten the circular clamp or a ratchet arrangement which screws one end of the clamp against the screw.

You can glue the new hoses to their con-

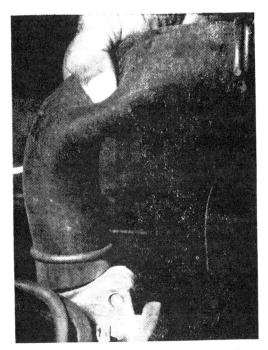

Fig. 2: If hose springs back quickly, feels strong to finger pressure, it is in good condition. If it feels spongy or lifeless, it should be replaced.

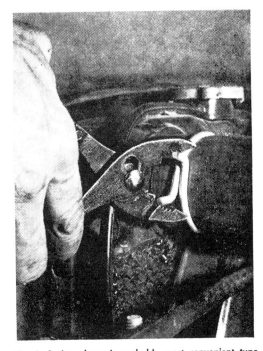

Fig. 3: Spring clamp is probably most convenient type to use. When the tabs are compressed, the clamp releases. When the tabs are released, the clamp holds the hose tightly against the connection.

Fig. 4: Screw type hose clamp is also popular; has a screw-ratchet adjustment which, as the screw moves, tightens the clamp against the hose. A sealing compound can be used under the hose to ensure snugness.

Fig. 5: Easy way to replace hose: place lower end on engine connection. Bend center section in by squeezing to spring hose inward to the connection. Be sure to place clamps on hose before installation.

nections with a coating of sealing compound if you wish, but this is not necessary when you use the right clamp. But whether you glue the new hoses to the connections or rely on clamp pressure, be sure to clean the connections before you fit the new hoses.

To replace the upper radiator hose, drain the radiator by opening the petcock at the bottom. Drain only enough liquid from the radiator to lower the coolant below the level of the upper radiator pipe.

To replace the lower radiator hose, drain the entire cooling system. Open both the petcock on the radiator and the petcock on the engine.

To replace the heater hose, check the intake and exhaust levels of the hoses. If they take off and empty above the upper radiator pipe, you'll have to drain only part of the coolant from the radiator. If they fit to connections below the upper radiator pipe, it may be necessary to drain the entire cooling system to replace them.

After you've drained the system to the safe level (or empty, depending upon the car and the hose to be replaced), loosen the hose clamps and remove the worn hose. If the hose to be replaced is a straight section, you can cut a new length to match. If the hose is premolded, buy one to match. Use the old hose as a pattern. If the hose is a flexible type, be sure you have the right replacement.

Place two clamps over the new hose. Clean the two connections and slip the hose onto the engine connection first. Attach the other end to the radiator connection, bending the hose near the center to fit over the radiator pipe (Fig. 5). Tighten the clamp at the engine connection, then slide the hose upward on the radiator connection as far as it will go. Tighten the radiator clamp.

Refill the cooling system with water (or anti-freeze) and start the engine. Check the hose for leaks, then retighten the clamps after the engine has warmed.

Your windshield wiper, if it is vacuum operated, should operate at a speed of about 100 strokes a minute on dry glass. If it runs slower, the trouble may be in either the vacuum lines or in the motor. Be sure to check the lines. They should be straight and strong. If they are collapsed, kinked or split, be sure to replace them.

Many late model cars are equipped with automatic windshield washers. These too can become fouled or inoperative because of worn or clogged hoses. Most washers will use two hoses, similar in size to the wiper lines. One line will lead to the vacuum source. Check these for splits at the connections and for kinks and rot. Replace them if you find anything that's not right.

If you find signs of leaks or aging on cars equipped with power steering and power brakes drain the system and replace the hose.

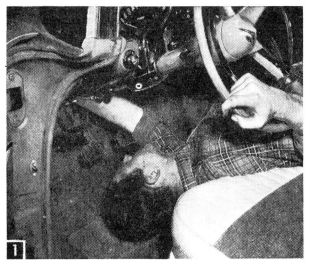

Although some cars have fuses on the firewall in the engine compartment, many have them under the instrument panel, making an awkward position necessary for repair work.

NEW STANDARD FUSES   **OLD TYPE "AG" FUSES**

SFE 4

SFE 6

Actual Size

SFE 7½ & SFE 9

SFE 14

SFE 20

SFE 30

AGA formerly called 1AG

AGW formerly called 7AG

AGX formerly called 8AG

AGC formerly called 3AG

AGY formerly called 9AG

AGU formerly called 5AG

Servicing Electrical Controls

Knowing how your car's electrical circuitry operates will help you make minor repairs yourself in either a 6- or a 12-volt system

MOST car owners have experienced blown fuses in their homes and know how and where to remove the damaged fuse and replace it with a good one. Your car's light and electrical-accessory wiring system isn't very different from your home's, and if you carry several new fuses—and know where the fuses are located—the job of handling a blown fuse is simple.

Correcting the trouble that was responsible for the fuse blowing isn't always so easy, however. Besides, your lighting system most likely is protected with a "circuit breaker," which, unlike a fuse, does not "blow," but intermittently opens the circuit to reduce the current and serve as a warning that a "short" exists and something must be done about it.

The small fuses used on cars are of the cartridge type (Fig. 2), and easily slip into fuse clips or in-line retainers. Do not attempt to remove fuses with a screwdriver; you may touch one clip with the screwdriver's blade and at the same time ground the blade on nearby metal. The resulting sparks may not only startle you badly, but on a 12-v system could instantly burn out every wire under the instrument panel, since the overload factor inherent in the older 6-v systems is missing. Use a small wooden stick to remove fuses. Better still, purchase a small, inexpensive plastic or hard-rubber fuse puller that not only permits you to get a good grip on a cartridge fuse, but also is completely insulated. Such pullers are available at auto-supply stores.

Now let's suppose, for example, that the electric clock in your new car doesn't work. You go about troubleshooting it as you would if the lights in your home go out—you look for a blown fuse. (A chart that tells you the specified size, type, and location of car fuses for all makes and models of cars for the last 15 model years is available free from the Bussman Mfg. Division of McGraw Edison Co., University at Jefferson, St. Louis 7, Mo.) Once the fuse is located, you can tell by looking at it that the link inside the glass casing has melted to interrupt the circuit. Usually, clock fuses are in the line and you have to undo the bayonet lock on the fuse housing to drop out the fuse. If the fuse is blown, replace it with one of correct type and size. Correct fuse amperage is important. Installing a fuse of greater capacity than specified may damage the unit it is intended to protect.

The single-wire system, wherein the metal parts of the car serve as a return wire or ground, is universally used on cars. With the switch on a car lamp closed, the circuit to and from it is complete and, consequently, the lamp lights. If a connection to the lamp loosens, or becomes corroded, or begins to chafe, resistance is set up in the circuit, heating occurs, the lamp burns dimly and—if the wiring grounds—the battery will discharge. Heavy discharge reading on an ammeter would warn of this, but if a light is used instead of an ammeter (as is common with later model cars) a very heavy short would be required to cause the lamp to glow.

If such a simple circuit is protected with a fuse, however, any of the conditions mentioned above will melt the fuse link, breaking the circuit, thus protecting the units and wiring and preventing danger from fire.

To locate the cause of a blown fuse, always check wiring terminals for tightness first. Look for spots where a wire is rubbing against a sharp metallic surface. And if you do put in a new wire, don't let it hang loosely. Tape it wherever possible to a bracket, or insert it in the regular clips made to hold it.

If any of the car lamps fail to light and the bulb is known to be okay, then it can be due to a blown fuse and replacement often restores the circuit. If a second fuse blows, the trouble lies elsewhere in the circuit. Vibration of a headlight circuit breaker always means a short which you must find and correct. To do this, disconnect the switch wires one at a time until the relay stops vibrating; that is the line or wire in which the trouble will be found. If you get no light and the lamps are okay, the circuit breaker contacts could be disengaged. Clean the contacts with a fine file and regap according to the manufacturer's specifications. You will find, too, that electrical circuits will work better if you occasionally take out the fuses and clean the fuse clips and the ends of the fuses to remove corrosion.

The lighting system is the largest and most involved as to wiring and the likelihood of shorts or grounds. The circuit basically includes head lamps, parking lamps, taillights, stoplights, directional lights and interior lamps. It often is supplemented by spotlights, back-up lights and fog light, all of these circuits usually being fused. Fuses also are used in the accessory circuits such as heaters, radio, underhood lights, hand brake lights, cigarette lighters, overdrives, trunk lights, air conditioners and many other units.

Fuses seldom are used for headlamps except in older cars, and on late-model trucks. Protection for headlamps, tail lamp, parking lamps and instrument lamp circuits on most cars before 1955 is through a thermostatically-controlled limit relay (Fig. 3) or a bi-metal type circuit breaker (Fig. 4), usually attached to the main light switch. On most cars built in the last few years all circuits but the headlamps have been removed from the circuit-breaker line and are fitted with separate fuses. The reason for this is that the headlamps and tail lamps are used the most and are the most important in operation of the car.

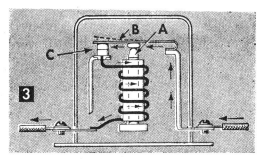

Current-limiting relay. Arrows show flow of current from battery. Heavy current, a short or loose connection, causes plunger A, to be pulled into the core and push against spring B, breaking contact points C and thus opening the circuit. Upon cooling, contacts again close and cycle repeats until trouble is remedied.

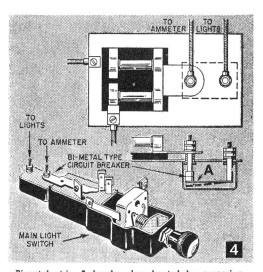

Bi-metal strip A bends when heated by excessive current and separates the contact points to open the circuit. Bottom view shows circuit breaker attached to main light switch.

You can drive with the lights flickering off and on, although it is a tremendous irritation, until you reach a service station where repairs can be made. Excess current, due to a short, causes the relay points (C in Fig. 3) to open and close rapidly to reduce the current enough to protect the wiring from damage. The action continues until the short is eliminated.

On the 1951-52 Henry J cars, the headlights had a 30-amp fuse located on the headlight switch, rather than a circuit breaker. The 1953 models had the fuse in the wire, near the ignition switch.

The circuit breaker used for headlight protection on some cars (like the 1949-52 Lincoln) has a 14-amp fuse mounted on it to protect the interior lighting circuit. The breaker circuit protects the headlamp, the stop light, and the taillight circuits only, and is mounted on the rear of the instrument panel in earlier models.

On some cars the tail lamp circuit includes tail lamps and license plate lamp which are protected

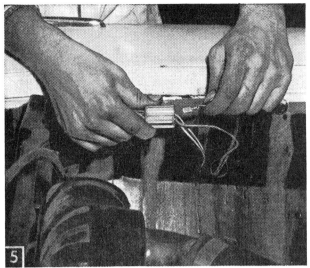

On older model cars, clips at wire ends were held with screws. On later model cars, wire ends are fitted with small metal "shoes" that fit into connector blocks, such as is shown here.

with a 7½-amp fuse. The instrument lights have a separate circuit, protected with a 4-amp fuse. On some of the older models a 14-amp fuse protected the tail lamps circuit, which included the license plate lamp and the instrument lights.

On cars using the Autronic-eye headlamp control a 14-amp SFE fuse is used in the amplifier unit, usually placed on the cowl under the hood. To inspect the fuse, the amplifier cover must be removed. The Anti-Creep on 1950-53 Studebakers used a SFE 14-amp fuse located in the wire under the hood. The 1954 models used the same size fuse located on the firewall under the hood. The 1955-57 also used a 14-amp fuse in the hood wire.

The bi-metal type circuit breaker is thermostatic in nature. If the current is too heavy due to a short, the bi-metal arm (A in Fig. 4) heats, pulls away from the contact points and breaks the circuit. As soon as the breaker cools, however, the contacts close again to restore the circuit. Thus the lights going on and off alternately by this action is your cue that too heavy a load exists and a short must be repaired.

The circuit-limit relay (Fig. 3) takes the place of fuses or thermostatic circuit breakers. Current-limiting relays are vibrating or lockout type. With the vibrating type, when excessive current flows in the circuit, the relay begins vibrating and cuts down the amount of current flowing to avoid damage. The lockout type works the same except that the contact points (C in Fig. 3) are held open by a separate winding connected between the points. A small current keeps flowing through this winding but not enough to operate the electrical equipment. The contact points automatically close when the trouble is fixed and normal action is restored. In this type there is a plunger (A in Fig. 3) inside the winding core and above the core is a flat spring (B) with one con-

tact point and a brass button. Normally the circuit through the relay is completed through the contact points. But with excessive current, the magnetism of the winding is enough to draw in the plunger which strikes the brass button on the spring and the contact points open. The current stops and the plunger falls back to permit the points to close again. The resulting vibration of the points prevents the current flow from being excessive.

Remember that the wiring circuits in your car are like those in your home. If you have too many lights and appliances on one circuit, a blown fuse will result. The same thing is true in a car. Using a larger capacity fuse will prevent a blown fuse, but trouble is built in. The best method is to run a new circuit, with its own proper capacity fuse to protect the new spotlight or other accessory. In some cases there is a junction block wired to the ignition switch that has spare connections that can be used. This heavy-duty circuit will handle the added electrical load, and has the added advantage of shutting off the current when the ignition key is turned off.

Penny-match-box in size, the Electronic Light-Minder can save you recharge costs or even the cost of a new battery.

For those of you who are inclined to park your car with lights on—and then leave it that way—or who have wives or teen-age children who make this bad practice a practice, a novel auto accessory called the Electronic Light-Minder (see Fig. 6) should prove a boon.

Automatically, when the engine is stopped, the Light-Minder illuminates the word LIGHTS on its dial if either the bright lights, the dimmers or the parking lights have been left on. This accessory contains no moving parts and installs fairly easily on cars or trucks, without changes in original wiring. It's designed to mount on the steering column or the instrument panel, and is produced by Unitron Corp. of Dade City, Fla., for either 6-volt or 12-volt electrical systems. Don't say we didn't tell you about it.

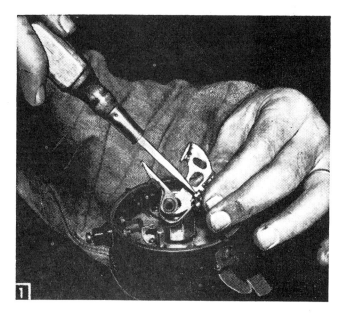

Lift the rotor straight up to remove it from the distributor shaft.

Connecting the leads to a new set of ignition points prior to installing them in the distributor.

Servicing the Ignition System

How to service the distributor and replace points

THERE are many little things you can do to the ignition system of your car that will make it start quickly, improve its mileage and give

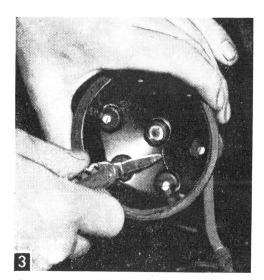

Scraping away carbon deposits from a crack in the inside of a distributor cap.

it the pick-up zip you would like it to have.

Checking the Distributor. First disconnect one spark-plug wire at a time from the plugs and, with the engine idling, hold the terminal of the disconnected wire about ¼ in. away from a good ground such as the shell of the plug or a cylinder-head bolt. A good "fat" spark should jump regularly from wire to ground. If the wires have rubber protectors over the ends which cannot be slid back, place a key in the end of the terminal to make contact with the end of the wire and let the spark jump from the key to the ground as in Fig. 4.

To avoid getting a shock when testing each spark-plug wire, have someone start and turn off the engine each time you disconnect a wire, or use pliers with insulated handles to place the key into the rubber socket.

If you get a very weak spark or none at all from one of the wires, it could be due to a wet or dirty distributor cap, a worn or burned rotor or the wire itself may have worn spots in the insulation or make poor contact in the cap.

Unclip the distributor cap and, without removing the wires, wipe the cap clean both inside and out with a dry cloth. Carefully inspect the inside of the cap for cracks or carbon deposits along a crack extending from one contact point

Using a key as an extension for the spark-plug wire terminal. A spark during this test proves that coil, condenser and points are in good working order.

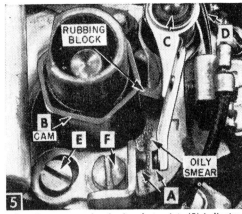

An oily smear under the breaker points (A) indicates that the oil is getting on the points.

to another. Carbon deposits, particularly on caps having a smooth inner surface, can conduct electricity and cause engine "miss."

Either replace the cracked cap with a new one or, for an emergency repair, scrape off the carbon along the crack with the point of a knife blade as in Fig. 3. Seal the scraped-out crack with lacquer or a dab of nail polish to prevent future carbon deposits.

While you have the distributor cap off, remove the rotor (Fig. 2), and carefully inspect the tip. If it is burned and pitted so that the edge is irregular, replace it with a new one. Any attempt to file the edge clean would increase the gap between rotor and cap terminals and interfere with delivery of a good hot spark to the plugs.

Distributor point failure is sometimes due to oil being thrown on the point contact surfaces (A in Fig. 5) by the rotating cam. If you notice a black oily smear on the point support plate as in Fig. 5, it is evidence that oil is getting on the points and interfering with engine performance.

One motorist made an emergency repair that solved the problem with an ordinary pipe cleaner. First he bent the pipe cleaner around a pencil and twisted the ends so as to form an "eye" in the middle of the cleaner. Then he slipped the "eye" over and around the points as in Fig. 6 and bent the ends of the cleaner so it could be fastened under a convenient screw. With the pipe cleaner in place, any oil thrown by the cam is caught by the cleaner instead of landing on the points.

Clean the oil from the contact points by pulling a strip of paper between the closed points. If the points need dressing or surfacing, use a contact-point file (available at automotive accessory stores for 20 to 25¢). Then reset the gap between the points as recommended by the car manufacturer.

Keeping oil off the points is only the first step in creating a good spark. Let's suppose, for example, that your car's acceleration and top speed is not what it used to be. Since the dis-

tributor points must open and close about 10,000 times a minute at 60 *mph*, any binding of the movable contact-point arm on its shaft (C in Fig. 5) or weakness of the arm spring (D in Fig. 5) will interfere with spark generation at any speed and particularly at high engine speeds.

Lacking spring-tension specifications for the distributor of your car, you can still get satisfactory engine operation by having a spring tension that will bring the points together under a pressure of 16-18 ounces. Ignition servicemen check this spring tension with an accurate scale. A surprisingly close approximation, however, can be made by first feeling how much finger pressure it takes to support a one-lb. package of butter. Then take hold of the movable point arm as in Fig. 7 with the same finger used to lift the butter and feel if the spring exerts about the same pressure on your finger. This crude but handy method is quite accurate and used by many mechanics to "spot" check a distributor.

If the spring tension is too high, the movable arm will bounce, causing the engine to "miss" because of an interruption in the current flow in the coil. If the spring tension is too weak, the points will not close quickly enough.

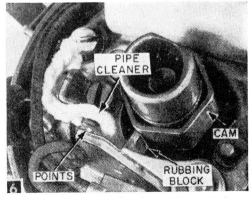

A pipe cleaner surrounding the points protects them from oil thrown by the cam.

80

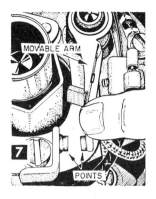

If, after making the finger test for spring tension, you suspect that spring D in Fig. 5 is too weak, place a rubber band over the movable contact arm and stretch it around some convenient support like the condenser in Fig. 8. The rubber band isn't going to last very long, but it will give you a quick check to see what increased spring tension will do for the performance of your car.

Stretch the rubber band so that you will have about a 50% increase in tension on the movable arm. Test by pulling the movable arm with your finger as in Fig. 7, first without the rubber band, then with the rubber band in place. Then start your car and drive it a mile or so.

This simple test, which will only take a few minutes of your time, may give you some interesting information. For example, if pick-up and top speed improve, it indicates that tension spring should be replaced. When doing this, it's a good idea to replace the points with a new set too. To remove the points, take out the screws labeled E and F in Fig. 5, lift out the point set and disconnect the wires with a screwdriver as in Fig. 1. Reverse this procedure when installing the new set.

The new points should be adjusted to open about .016 in. on most cars. You can get the exact point-setting gap for your car from a local distributor. To measure and set the point gap, turn the engine over slowly with the fan belt until the rubbing block reaches a high point on the cam as in Fig. 5. Then measure the gap between the points with a feeler gage. If the gap is not .016 in., or as recommended in the

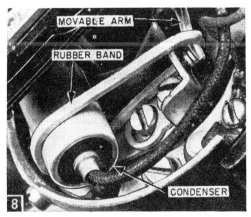

Placement of rubber band in distributor to increase spring pressure on movable point arm.

specifications, just barely loosen clamp screw **F** in Fig. 5 and very slowly turn the eccentric screw E until the stationary point has moved enough to give you the .016-in. gap. Then tighten both screws.

To do a thorough job of cutting down resistance in the delivery of current to the sparkplug, take a 1-in. wide strip of #00 emery cloth and roll just enough of it on the end of a pencil so that you can get it down into each distribution cap tower terminal as in Fig. 9. Use a rubber band to keep the emery cloth in place. Then twirl the pencil to clean and polish the inside of the cap terminals. Although Fig. 9 shows all the wires removed from the cap, it would be wise to remove and replace the wires one at a

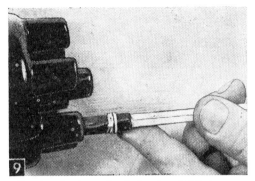

Cleaning the tower terminals of a distributor cap with emery cloth wrapped around the end of a pencil.

time to make certain each wire is returned to its proper terminal.

If the terminals on the ends of the wires are burned or corroded, remove them, strip off ¼ in. of the insulation and solder a new terminal to the end of the wires. These metal terminals can be purchased at auto accessory stores for a few cents each.

Servicing the Spark Plugs. If one cylinder is missing due to a fouled plug, here's an emergency tip that will put it back in service quickly and without having to remove the plug from the engine. First start the engine and let it idle. Then, if you know which plug is fouled, pull off the wire, slide the protector back to expose the wire terminal and hold it ¼ to ⅜ in. from the plug terminal as in Fig. 10. (*Caution: Grasp the wire well back from the terminal to avoid getting a shock.*) Allow the spark to jump from the terminal to plug for about one minute, then reconnect the wire to the plug. This simple treatment increases spark intensity at the plug electrodes and will often put a fouled plug back in service.

If you do not know which plug is fouled, slide back the protectors on each plug one at a time and ground the plug terminals to the engine with a plastic-handled screwdriver. When you ground a good plug you will notice a drop in engine idling speed. When you ground the fouled plug the idling speed will remain unchanged.

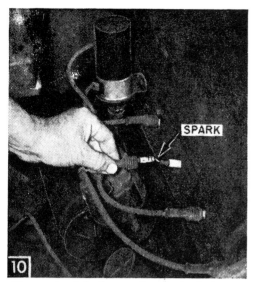

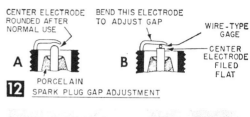

12 SPARK PLUG GAP ADJUSTMENT

13 A contact-point file cleans spark-plug electrodes.

10 Disconnect and slowly move the wire terminal away from the spark plug terminal until the spark is about ⅜ in. long.

Although the above-mentioned hint may help you out in an emergency, there will come a time when all of the plugs must be removed for cleaning. Since you cannot do a good job cleaning spark plugs yourself, many motorists have a spare set of plugs all cleaned and adjusted that can be installed when the old set is taken out. The old set can then be left at a gas station for sandblast cleaning. Inspect the cleaned plugs carefully to see that all deposits are removed from the inner part of the plug. Deposits up in the plug could short out the inner insulator.

Next, check the condition of the spark plug electrodes C and G in Fig. 11. If the center electrode C is rounded over as in Fig. 12A, file it flat on the end as in Fig. 12B with the same file you used for cleaning the distributor points (Fig. 13). Touch up the other electrode with the file too, but do not remove too much metal—just enough to show a bright surface.

When resetting the gap between the two electrodes, make all adjustments by bending the outer, or electrode G in Fig. 11. Never bend the center electrode because the surrounding porcelain will crack. Use a round, wire-type spark-plug gage to determine the electrode gap setting. If you know the exact setting for the plugs in your car use that size "feeler" on the gage. If you do not have this information, set all of the plugs to .030 in. Do this by lightly tapping the outer electrode on the bench top and then trying the wire of the gage between the electrodes

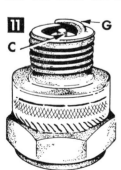

as in Fig. 12B.

Before installing cleaned and adjusted spark plugs replace the old copper gaskets with new ones and turn the plugs down finger tight. Then, with a socket wrench on the plugs tighten them an additional one-half turn. Over-tightening the plugs may break the porcelain or upset the distance between electrode gaps.

If the engine does not idle smoothly, try increasing the plug gap two thousandths of an inch using an .032-in. gage. On the other hand if the engine idles well but "stumbles" on acceleration or fails to hit the top speed you had expected, try closing the plug gap two thousandths using a .028-in. gage. This variation from the basic setting may be tried up to .005 in. oversize for better idling and .005 in. undersize for higher engine speeds.

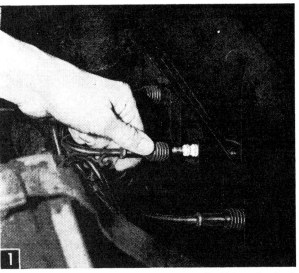

To get at your spark plugs, first remove the high tension leads by pulling gently and rotating lightly until the snap terminal releases.

2 Wet, oily deposits indicate a severe oil pumping condition in the engine.

3 Hard, black, baked-on deposits are an oil-fouling condition caused by using too cold a plug in an old engine.

Spark Plug
Troubleshooting

Ailing plugs cause engine miss, hard starts and poor fuel mileage. Here's how to both locate and prevent such troubles

YOU can learn a lot about a car by inspecting its spark plugs.

For example, the type of deposit on the firing end of the plug can reveal how the car has been operating.

If the deposit is wet, black and oily as in Fig. 2, the car probably pumps oil, due to worn rings, pistons or cylinder walls, or worn or sticky valves. Or the ignition system may not be supplying enough power to the plug.

If, however, the electrodes and inner insulator are covered with black carbon deposits which are hard and baked on (Fig. 3), you can suspect that too cold a plug is being used in an oil-burning engine, and you need either a hotter plug or, if fouling continues, an engine overhaul.

The plug itself may be faulty—with a badly worn electrode or even a cracked insulator. These, too, are clues to the condition of the car, and to the type

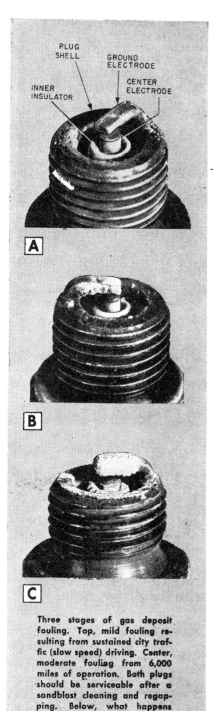

A

B

C

Three stages of gas deposit fouling. Top, mild fouling resulting from sustained city traffic (slow speed) driving. Center, moderate fouling from 6,000 miles of operation. Both plugs should be serviceable after a sandblast cleaning and regapping. Below, what happens after 8,000 miles without cleaning. Deposits are so compacted they would be extremely difficult to remove, and plug should be replaced.

4

Use new washer if previous one was insufficiently tightened and has appearance of the one above.

Properly tightened washer

Excessively tightened washer flattens out.

5

Checking condition of gasket washer.

of service attention it has been receiving. Once you learn how to read such clues, you can usually correct the trouble, and avoid some burdensome repair bills.

Before removing a spark plug for inspection, carefully blow any dirt out of the spark plug well. This will keep dirt from falling into the combustion chamber when the plug is taken out. Pull the wires from the spark plug terminals *gently* until the snap fitting comes free (Fig. 1). If you jerk them, you may separate the wire from the terminal connection, and although a broken lead wire isn't visible, it will form a secondary spark gap and eventually burn through the ignition cable, causing electrical failure.

As you remove the plugs, first check each gasket washer (Fig. 5). The surfaces of the washer which contact the plug and cylinder head should be bright, clean, uniform and unbroken. And the washer itself should not be completely flattened.

If the gasket washer is discolored, corroded, or irregularly marked, the plug was not tightened enough during installation. This produces an incomplete seal which allows gases to leak by, and the plug to overheat. And such overheating will cause rapid wear of the electrodes and pre-ignition.

On the other hand, an entirely flattened washer (Fig. 5) means that the plug was tightened too much, and this will often cause a fracture in the plug shell, stretched threads, or a cracked insulator.

Flash Over Versus Corona. When an insulator has been cracked during installation (Fig. 9 right) and this crack fills up with a film of dirt and oil you'll have a condition known as "flash over." Electricity flows directly from the top terminal to the grounded plug shell, completely by-passing the electrodes and spark gap. The plug is thus short circuited, and the only remedy is to replace the plug.

You can also have a "flash over" condition when an accumulation of dirt and oil coats the top insulator enough to allow current to pass through it. The cure here is to wipe the insulator with a cloth moistened with a gasoline or alcohol solvent which will cut the oil film.

When "flash over" occurs at the upper insulator, it may be visible in the form of a dim blue *spark discharge* around the plugs. This is sometimes confused with corona—the *steady blue light* that will appear around the base of the upper insulator, indicating a high tension field. Remember that the corona blue light is steady, and it will not affect ignition performance. In fact, corona often repels dust particles and will sometimes leave a tell-tale clean white ring around the base of the upper insulator, just above the plug shell. Such a ring does not indicate a gas leak between the plug and cylinder head.

Inspecting the Electrodes is your next step. Here you may encounter the examples of fouling or deposit accumulation we mentioned earlier. If the electrodes are covered with a wet oily deposit (Fig. 2), the plugs will probably give you good service after they have been cleaned and regapped. Such deposits are tell-tale signs of oil pumping in the engine, however, and you should check for worn rings, piston and cylinder walls. New rings might cut down the pumping. Or the battery or generator might be ailing to the point where not enough power is being delivered to the plug for proper ignition.

When the electrodes are coated with a hard, baked-on deposit (Fig. 3), it's a sign that too cold a plug is being used in an oil-burning engine. You should change to a hotter plug. If such oil fouling then continues, you'll need an engine overhaul to correct the trouble at its source.

What do we mean by *cold* or *hot* plugs? Well, to function properly, a spark plug must operate within a specific temperature or heat range. So all plugs are classified by heat ranges as well as by size, thread and reach (Fig. 7).

The heat range of a plug is primarily controlled by the length of the center insulator, and is, basically, the speed with which the electrodes will cool after the cylinder fires. The electrodes must remain hot enough to prevent fouling, but must not get so hot that they will ignite the fuel mixture without an electrical spark (pre-ignition).

The problem is that combustion chamber temperatures vary greatly with the type and condition of the engine, how fast it is run and the load it is pulling. For example, when an engine fitted with spark plugs of intermediate heat range is run at slow (city traffic) speeds for a long time, the electrodes will stay cool enough to allow deposits to form rapidly.

This electrode fouling causes the plugs to misfire, and you get hard starting, poor gas mileage and a loss of power. But when the same plugs are given a high speed workout on the open road, many of the deposits may be burned away, in effect cleaning the plug. So, if you are getting spark plug miss from

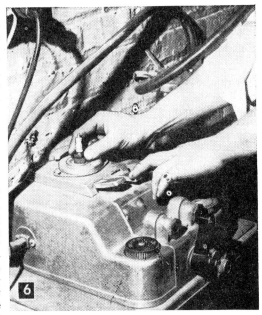

Sandblast cleaning a plug—the only good way to remove deposit fouling from inner insulator and inner wall. Most gas stations have such a cleaner and most attendants will let you use it, frequently without charge.

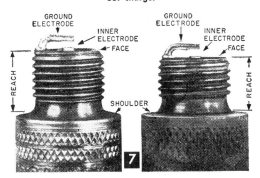

Plug at left is a "long-reach" plug. One at right is of "standard reach."

city driving, take your car out on the open highway and run it hard for an hour or so. Really run it up to peak engine speed and hold it there for a few seconds before you change gears. Such a "hard run" treatment may be the cheapest tune-up you can get.

It helps to clean away the type of fluffy dry carbon deposits in the electrode and inner insulator which are caused by gas-fouling. To prevent a re-occurrence of such rapid fouling, you might—in addition to regular high-speed workouts—lean down the fuel mixture by adjusting the carburetor. Then, if you still get rapid fouling, even after a carburetor adjustment, it might be wise to change to a hotter range of spark plug.

White, Yellow, Brown Deposits. The most common form of deposit fouling results in white, yellow, brown or red coatings on the electrodes (Fig. 4). These are normal by-products of combustion which result from the many additives in today's fuels and lubricants. In their original powdery form, they usually have little effect on spark plug operation. But when high speeds or heavy loads raise the engine temperature enough, such deposits melt and form a glaze coating on the inner insulator. When hot, this glaze is an excellent conductor, and allows the current to follow the glaze instead of jumping the spark gap.

Cleaning underside of ground electrode with distributor-point file, after sandblasting.

Periodic sandblast cleaning (Fig. 6) usually removes these coatings and restores the plugs to proper operation. If the deposits are compacted between the plug shell and the inner insulator, however, replace the plug. It's almost impossible to remove such compacted deposits without damaging the insulator.

The sandblast treatment, available at most good service stations, is the most effective way to clean the face of the plug and the inner insulator. It won't always remove all the scale and oxide deposits from the center electrode and from the underside of the ground

At left, a broken inner insulator, a rare condition resulting from center electrode being bent during regapping. Right, cracked upper insulator causes "flash over," and such a plug should be replaced.

electrode. So, to ensure clean firing surfaces, try bending the ground electrode up slightly and cleaning both surfaces thoroughly with a flat distributor-point file (Fig. 8).

After a cleaning, you frequently discover other faults, such as a broken inner insulator (Fig. 9). This may be caused by carelessness in regapping, or sustained operation with heavy detonation and pre-ignition.

If the lower insulator is cracked and the center electrode worn to a fine point, while the ground electrode shows no sign of wear, the plug is operating too hot. The solution is to discard the damaged plug and replace it with one of a lower heat range.

Damaged plug shells are unusual. They are always the result of such mishandling as overtightening during installation. The damage generally shows up as a crack in the threads near the gasket seat, and such a plug should be promptly replaced.

Electrode Wear. Once the fouling deposits have been cleaned off the electrodes, you can check them for wear. As a rough guide, remember that a set of spark plugs, properly cared for and regularly cleaned and regapped, should give you good service for about 10,000 miles. Considering that the spark

Note the wear on the underside of the ground electrode at the tip. This would be normal wear for 4,000-6,000 miles but the plug has only been run 1,000 miles. Suspect faulty installation, too lean a carb mix, an over-advanced spark, a damaged gasket or too hot a range.

plug must give off from 1,000 to 3,000 sparks per minute while operating in gas temperatures as high as 4,000° F.—and also withstand explosive pressures of up to 800-lbs/psi—this is a remarkable life expectancy.

These intense pressures and temperatures, when combined with the corrosive gases in the combustion chamber, gradually wear the electrodes down to the point where the gap can't be effectively reset. Replace such plugs.

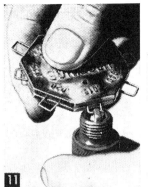

When setting the gap on spark plugs, a flat feeler gage CANNOT give a correct gap reading because of the concave hollow produced by normal electrode wear

ONLY a round wire gage will give an accurate gap reading

Checking spark plug gap to specs given by engine manufacturer. Use round gage, since flat feeler gage cannot give correct gap reading (see inset).

Using a torque wrench and deep socket to insure proper plug seating. Hand-thread the plug until it seats finger-tight, then torque in according to Table A. If plugs won't turn by hand, remove and clean threads with wire brush and solvent on a nubbly fabric. Then reinstall and torque in place. When I started torquing plugs on my Porsche, I increased mileage ten times.

TABLE A—PLUG SEATING TORQUES

PLUG THREAD	CAST IRON HEAD	ALUMINUM HEAD
10 mm.	12 ft/lbs.	10 ft/lbs.
14 mm.	25 ft/lbs.	22 ft/lbs.
18 mm.	30 ft/lbs.	25 ft/lbs.
7/8 in.	35 ft/lbs.	30 ft/lbs.
18 mm. taper seat	15 ft/lbs.	12 ft/lbs.

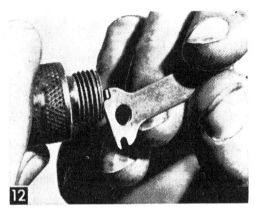

Make any gap adjustments by bending the ground electrode, preferably with a spark plug gapping tool. Don't pry against center electrode—you may break the inner insulator.

When the plug is fairly new, and shows substantial wear, as is the case in Fig. 10, you know that the rate of wear is too rapid. In such cases, the trouble may be faulty installation, too lean a carburetor mixture, an over-advanced spark, dirty or damaged gasket seats, or a plug which has too hot a heat range.

Cleaning and Regapping. A good rule of thumb for spark plug servicing is to remove, clean and regap plugs at least once every 5,000 miles on a new car with less than 30,000 miles on the odometer and about every 2,000 to 3,000 miles on an older car.

Always regap an old plug to the exact specifications set by the engine manufacturer (Fig. 11). If you use a new plug, check it before installing to make sure it also meets the engine specs. Make the gap adjustment by bending the *ground* electrode (Fig. 12). If you bend the center electrode, you'll fracture the inner insulator tip.

Always use a round wire gage (from an auto supply store) when setting the plug gap. Because the wearing away of the electrode tends to form a concave hollow on the underside, a flat feeler gage cannot give an accurate gap measurement (Fig. 11 inset).

When your plugs have been cleaned and regapped, *be sure to fit them with new gasket washers before installing.* The old washer can't give a good seal and the plug can't function properly without it.

Seating the Plug. The ideal way to ensure a correct seating of the plug is to use a torque wrench for tightening down the plugs (Fig. 13). If you own one, and put in your own plugs (or can talk your garage-man into using his) follow what the manufacturers recommend, as shown in Table A.

If you can't torque in your plugs, hand turn the plug in until it seats finger tight on the gasket. Then, using a *proper fitting* spark plug socket wrench, give it an additional ½ turn. This will produce the proper seal between the plug and the cylinder head.

Is Your Driving Average? When you go to buy a new set of plugs, remember that the manufacturer's chart gives the recommendations for *average* driving (about 40% city and 60% highway). If you are on the highway a lot, covering most of your distance at fairly high speed, you may need a plug that's a little cooler than average. If you're a "stop and go" driver, putting most of your miles in the city at slow speeds with lots of waits at traffic lights, maybe a hotter plug will keep you going longer between tuneups.

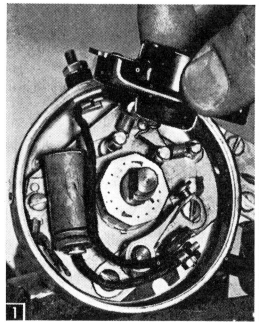
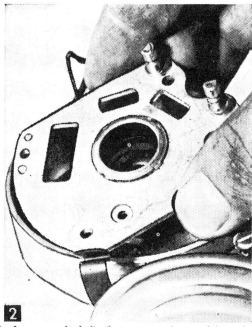

Top views of breaker plate as seen fully assembled after removal of distributor cap and rotor (left) and stripped of its working parts (right). Generally mounted on ball bearings, this plate should be replaced if loose or wobbly.

𝓘𝓼 𝓨𝓸𝓾𝓻 **Breaker Plate OK?**

Here's how to get peak performance from the nerve center of your ignition system

THAT nerve center of your car's ignition system, the breaker plate in the distributor, will give you more power and better performance if you keep it and its parts in perfect shape.

Unless you have checked your distributor within the last 10,000 miles, now's the time to do it before ignition trouble catches up with you.

In the principal makes of distributors, the breaker plate surrounds the shaft and is usually mounted on ball bearings (Figs. 1 and 2). The shaft slides through the distributor housing and has a gear on the lower end which mates with the drive gear on the camshaft. Portions of the housing which surround the shaft may be fitted with bronze bushings or ball bearings on which the shaft rides.

On the breaker plate you'll usually find the condenser, which is a story in itself when it comes to troubleshooting (see "Double-Check that Condenser," p. 129), as well as the contact breaker points and tension springs. One point is stationary, the other hinged for opening and closing by cam action. Some distrib-

Setting new points with a flat feeler gauge.

FEELER GAUGE ⟶   ⟵BREAKER ARM

Incorrect Point Opening Obtained with Feeler Gauge

CONTACT SUPPORT

4   CONTACT POINTS

Buick Div., General Motors Corp.

Incorrect opening obtained when gapping old points with a flat feeler gauge.

88

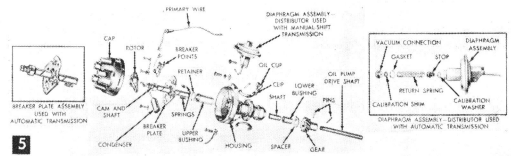

PRIMARY WIRE

DIAPHRAGM ASSEMBLY— DISTRIBUTOR USED WITH MANUAL-SHIFT TRANSMISSION

CAP

ROTOR

BREAKER POINTS

RETAINER

OIL CUP

OIL PUMP DRIVE SHAFT

CLIP

SHAFT

LOWER BUSHING

PINS

CAM AND SHAFT

SPRINGS

BREAKER PLATE ASSEMBLY USED WITH AUTOMATIC TRANSMISSION

BREAKER PLATE

CONDENSER

UPPER BUSHING

HOUSING

SPACER

GEAR

VACUUM CONNECTION

DIAPHRAGM ASSEMBLY

GASKET

STOP

RETURN SPRING

CALIBRATION SHIM

CALIBRATION WASHER

DIAPHRAGM ASSEMBLY—DISTRIBUTOR USED WITH AUTOMATIC TRANSMISSION

5

Ford Motor Co.

utors will have one set of breaker points; others two. Most will use one cam lobe per cylinder; a few will have one for each pair of cylinders.

Preliminary Steps. The first check is to inspect the distributor cap. Then remove it and look over the side. Wipe the interior clean, then look for cracks, chips, and carbon paths which would allow the high voltage current to leak to the ground. Clean all cap and rotor terminals with a sharp knife blade, never emery cloth or sandpaper. If you find carbon paths, deep pits, or grooves in any terminal, replace cap with a new one.

Wires should fit tightly in the cap. If there's any sign of moisture, try a little paraffin at points where wires join the cap. It's an effective way to stop hard starting caused by moisture.

Point Wear, Gap, and Tension. Next, examine the surfaces of the points on the breaker plate. Be sure they make good con-

tact. It is normal for used points to appear dull and gray. If they are blackened, slightly burned, or pitted, however, clean them with a contact file, never sandpaper or emery cloth which may embed particles in the points to cause burning. It's best to replace worn or burnt points. They cost little and assure a good job.

Check points for the proper gap listed in your instruction manual. You can set new points with a flat feeler gauge; old ones with a round feeler (Figs. 3 and 4). On most distributors, the gap is set by loosening a lock screw on the movable arm, moving it to the proper gap, then relocking. Be sure the points are aligned when you regap. Misalignment causes a host of troubles. Since the point opening decreases as the rubbing block wears, set new points as close to the high limit setting as possible to allow for wear.

Contact Arm Tension, if incorrect, can cause misfiring, especially at higher speeds

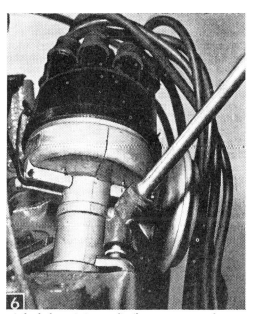

6 **7**

Left, before timing a distributor, you must loosen a clamp. This quarter-circle type clamp on a Mercury. Right, when clamp is removed, distributor can be pulled upward from engine after marking position of housing and rotor.

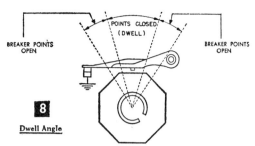

Dwell Angle

Lincoln-Mercury Div., Ford Motor Co.
Explaining the meaning of the mysterious word, "dwell," which is the period of time, in degrees, that points are closed. Proper attachment of timing light on distributor. One terminal goes to primary circuit, the other to a good ground.

with low pressures. Weak contact point pressure allows the points to chatter or bounce, which prevents a firm electrical contact and causes intermittent missing. Too much pressure causes exaggerated cam lobe wear. A worn lobe and rubbing block may reach the stage where there is no break between the points.

To set the arm tension, you'll need a spring-tension gauge. A postal or fish scale which reads in ounces of pull will do. Tension on most arms is between 17 and 23 oz.; some go to 25 oz. or more. An elongated slot in the breaker plate is provided to adjust tension of most springs. Loosen the anchoring screw and push it in the direction of the contact point for more tension; push away for less.

Check and adjust the point gap and tension before you attempt to change distributor timing. Too wide a gap will cause advanced timing; a narrow gap will retard it.

Reasons for Burnt Points. You'll be wise to do more than merely replace badly burned contact points. Check for the cause among these six common troubles:

1. Coil resistance unit not properly connected into the circuit between ignition switch and the coil positive.

2. Defective condenser.

3. Points do not open widely enough.

4. Oil vapor may seep into the distributor and get on contact points to cause arcing and rapid burning. A smudge line on breaker plate under the points is a clue to this.

5. High voltage condition may cause excessive flow through points and produce a blue scale on the points.

6. Radio capacitor connected to distributor terminal may cause excessive pitting.

Distributor Removal. No matter how well you adjust the points, a distributor may not give good performance if considerably worn or inadequately lubricated. A worn shaft or bushing may cause the points to open unevenly. An over-greased distributor may pick up enough dirt to interfere with operation of advance governors.

With such troubles, the distributor must be removed. This is not difficult, if you take a few simple precautions. Disconnect the wire from distributor to coil and either remove the cap or disconnect wires from cap to the spark plugs.

Now crank the engine until the No. 1 piston is at top dead center on its compression stroke, as indicated by pointer mark on the front of the engine. If distributor is properly timed, make a mark on its housing to show the rotor position and another on the block to indicate position of the housing. Then take off the distributor as in Figs. 6 and 7.

Dwell Measurements can be used to set points and tune the distributor. To understand what a mechanic means by "dwell angle" or "cam dwell," see Fig. 8.

First adjustment of a distributor on a car is best done with a timing light. If not in a position to do this, you can have it done by a mechanic or perform a fairly accurate job this way:

Remove the No. 1 plug. Rotate engine until piston starts up on its compression stroke. To feel this, hold your thumb over the plug hole. Continue the upstroke until the timing mark is lined up with the pointer. Then connect a test lamp parallel with the distributor primary circuit. Connect one lead to this circuit and the other to a good ground.

Loosen the distributor clamp and turn the distributor slightly in either direction until the light goes on. At this instant, the points will have opened and the engine is timed so that the spark will occur in the No. 1 cylinder with piston in the position indicated by the timing marks. This should be the proper firing for idle speed.

If you have no timing light, you can approximate timing as follows: Remove the high tension center lead from the distributor cap and hold terminal about ⅛ in. from the closest ground. Loosen the distributor clamp and slightly rotate the distributor until a spark jumps from terminal to ground. The engine is then timed as it would be with a light.

Many car fans like to make final timing adjustments on the highway, turning the distributor a degree or two until the engine sounds just right. If you try this, be sure the engine is well warmed up.

As you make final adjustments, set the distributor so that you hear a little ping when accelerating from 15 to 20 *mph* on level ground. If you have an automatic transmission, you may have to increase the load slightly to do this.

The ping may occur regardless of timing accuracy. It could be caused by overheating, low octane gas, wrong gears, or carbonization in the combustion chamber. But if the rest of the car is right, you'll notice a big difference in performance. A perfect distributor could help to make a hot rod out of an old clunker.

Check That Condenser

Burned or pitted contact points, hard starting, and other ignition troubles point to the condenser as the culprit

A condenser seldom goes bad, but when it does, watch out. As a first step toward its removal from distributor, the pigtail leading from it is being loosened from the distributor terminal.

A CERTAIN amount of distributor contact point pitting is to be expected: on most cars, one point or the other will develop limited pitting within six months. When pitting becomes serious, however, it could be a sign that something is wrong with the condenser (Fig. 1).

A hole on the negative point may be caused by an under-capacity condenser, a hole on the positive side by an over-capacity condenser. A faulty condenser can also cause burned points.

There is no industry standard for the polarity of contact points: it varies with the make of car. On a few, the polarity changes every time a driver steps on the starter—a gimmick designed to prevent point wear.

The Condenser Is an Integral Part of the ignition system. Without it the points would be pitted, burned, and worn in a couple of days. There's an easy explanation.

In order to force the electrical current to jump the air gap between the spark plug case and the electrode, the relatively insignificant current from the battery must be built up to 20,000 volts or more. The build-up takes place in the primary and secondary windings of the coil. The low voltage battery current flows into the primary winding of the coil, setting up a magnetic field in the coil. When the voltage is abruptly stopped, the magnetic field collapses and induces a higher voltage in secondary coil windings.

The low voltage is stopped by the opening of the distributor contact points. The moment the points separate, the current stops flowing from battery to coil. Collapse of the magnetic field not only keys the needed high-voltage induction in the secondary windings of the coil, but also induces, as a by-product, a higher voltage in the primary circuit, a voltage high enough to jump the point gap. If this were allowed to happen, the contact points would soon become useless, and the arcing would drain needed power from the higher secondary voltage.

The condenser saves voltage and points by acting much like a refrigerator. It offsets the unwanted build-up by storing the surge of electrons. The electrons are crowded into the condenser where they continue to build up. As they work they set up a reverse direction to their flow pattern. Because the points are still open, the flow is toward the grounded side of the condenser. At a point, the build-up collapses and reverses, building up toward

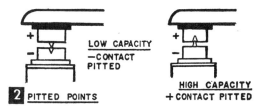

LOW CAPACITY
−CONTACT PITTED

HIGH CAPACITY
+ CONTACT PITTED

2 PITTED POINTS

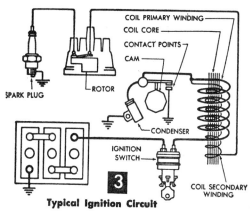

Typical Ignition Circuit

How the condenser fits into the ignition setup and
how it works to ground.

the insulated side of the condenser, then the flow and build-up reverses again and again.

Each time the flow is reversed, the magnetic field it creates collapses, then builds up in the opposite direction continuing from side to side until the electrons are dissipated or stopped by closing of the points. The condenser thus helps retard the flow by impeding or blocking the electrons and keeping them where they can do no damage.

Inside Your Condenser are four strips, two of metal foil and two of insulating paper. Almost 15 feet long, they are rolled tightly (metal foil sheets are slightly narrower than

the insulation to prevent leakage of electrons around the edges) and the roll is placed in a metal case. The case is hermetically sealed to shut out moisture—the enemy of a condenser.

One foil strip is connected to the cap of the condenser and an exterior terminal. The second is connected internally to the condenser case. A pigtail soldered to the outside terminal connects to the primary distributor terminal, placing the condenser in parallel. The case acts as ground so the condenser is wired across the circuit (Fig. 3).

Automotive condensers are rated in microfarads. It is important to replace a worn condenser with one of the proper rating for your car. For average driving conditions, a condenser rated between .18 and .25 microfarads is right, but if you drive at high speeds over open roads, try a slightly lower-capacity condenser. If you drive most often at low city street speeds, try one of higher capacity.

Although the condenser in your car is a reliable, long-lasting item, trouble could strike when least expected. A weak or leaking condenser usually has absorbed enough moisture to weaken the insulating papers and can no longer hold the build-up charge it was designed to handle. A condenser with poor insulation can drain enough energy from an ignition system to lower the secondary voltage substantially. A weak or intermittent spark at the plugs can be a disastrous result.

Before lifting out the condenser, check its pigtail lead for loose connection, corrosion, and worn insulation.
They cause as much trouble as a faulty condenser.

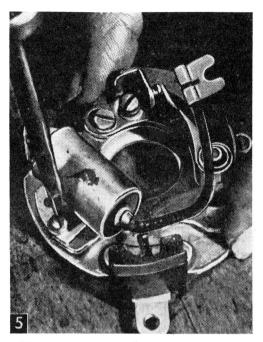

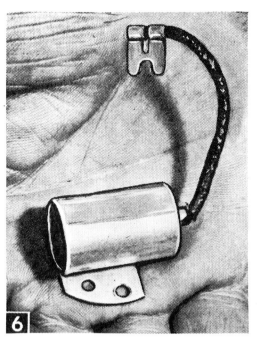

After freeing pigtail lead, you can remove condenser by loosening the hold-down screw which mounts it to breaker plate. Since screw serves as a ground, it should also be checked. Distributor need not be removed to take out condenser.

An indication of size of the typical condenser which polices the high voltage path in a distributor. It will do its job well unless terminals are corroded or moisture seeps into the insulation. Replacement is a jiffy job and costs little.

Signs of Trouble may go unnoticed except when the engine is hot. It is unlikely a leaking condenser would cause misfiring at low or medium speeds, except under conditions which cause it to heat.

Frayed pigtail, broken terminal, or loose insulation can all increase point wear. Under severe conditions, they can render the points useless. If you're experiencing ignition trouble, burned points, hard starting, check the condenser. Remove it from the distributor as in Figs. 4 and 5. Check for broken leads, frayed or loose insulation, corroded terminals, signs of moisture, or poor ground at the mounting.

Some Simple Tests. Condensers are generally tested on equipment giving three readings: microfarads, leakage, and series resistance. But test equipment costs money and condensers cost but a few pennies. You'll be money ahead if you make these few simple tests; then if the condenser seems faulty or if you're in doubt, replace it and test again.

A condenser can be tested for excessive leakage (short) by charging it from a spark plug as the engine is turned over. Be sure the spark used for the test has a gap no greater than .030. The small gap will limit the voltage involved.

Ground the condenser case to the cylinder head or block, then touch it to the plug terminals. Remove the plug, turn off the engine, and wait one minute. With a *well-insulated* screw driver, short the condenser terminal to the outer case. One heavy spark should result. If the condenser will not hold such a charge for one minute, it should be replaced.

Caution: Charged in this manner, a condenser can give you a severe shock. A plug gapped to .030 in. and operating in low compression with the engine at idle, will develop about 300 volts. This is not enough to injure the condenser insulation, but plenty "hot" if you touch it. Be sure the screw driver is well insulated before you short the condenser.

A safer test is to check the condenser with the coil. Remove the high tension lead from the coil terminal and fit a 12-in. jumper wire to the terminal. Now make certain you are properly insulated from the jumper wire, then turn on the ignition switch and hold the open end about ¼ in. from the cylinder head as the engine is cranked. If a spark leaps across the gap regularly, coil and condenser are OK. If there is no spark, or if it is weak or irregular, either the coil or condenser are at fault.

Replace the condenser and repeat the test. If there is still no spark, the trouble lies in the coil. If the spark now jumps the gap, the condenser was at fault and the trouble has been fixed.

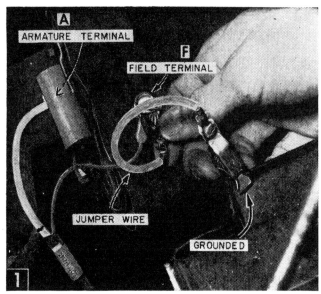

To test an externally grounded system, ground field terminal on generator with a jumper wire to any part of body and run engine at fast idle. Charge indicator bulb or ammeter should indicate generator is charging if it is in good operating condition.

GENERATOR TROUBLESHOOTING

Sure cures for some devilish problems that are known to start small and end up as oversized repair bills

YOU may save yourself a long walk to the "nearest service station" some day with an on-the-spot repair if you know what to look for when your generator gives out.

But if you inspect the generator-voltage regulator system every 10,000 miles or so, you may forestall more serious trouble by making bench repairs before they become emergencies. At any rate, you can do most of the work yourself.

These electrical powerhouses for your car are of three types. The generator field in some Delco-Remy and Auto-Lite systems is externally grounded through the mounting bolts (Fig. 1). In types used in cars made by Ford, and some others (Ford, Bosch systems), the generator field is internally grounded (Fig. 2). Beginning with 1958, many General Motors cars have a third type controlled by Delco-Remy dual contact regulators.

All systems with an internal ground can be identified by the presence of a ground terminal (marked "G" or "GND") on both the generator and regulator. All dual contact regulators are plainly marked with a red tag and also bear the warning *"do not ground"* plainly stenciled in white pencil. This cannot be overemphasized. A momentary grounding of this new system will burn the second set of points in the dual contact regulator and may easily burn out the whole generator system.

What Can Go Wrong? Basically, only three things: no charge (complete failure of the output), insufficient charge or too much charge.

When there is no charge—the usual fault—the generator is not taking over for the battery the job of supplying elec-

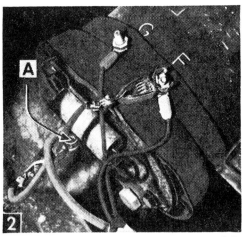

Jumper charge test is similar for internally grounded generator, except that wire connects field terminal to armature terminal (A).

trical power to run your car. In a late model car, you can tell this by your charge indicator bulb (irreverently dubbed "idiot light," as any idiot supposedly can tell when his generator isn't charging). It will light when you switch on the ignition and refuse to dim no matter how fast you run the engine. If you have an ammeter, the needle will stay on the negative side through these operations.

Left, to clean a dirty commutator, wrap a strip of 00 sandpaper around end of a block of wood, insert it through generator inspection hole and let it ride gently against commutator surface as engine idles. Right, properly seated new brush indicated by pencil should be about even with top of brush holder. Brush worn to about half this length should be replaced.

Before running any tests, open the hood and check that the generator drive belt has not broken or slipped off its pulley. If in place, but loose, tighten the drive belt adjustment.

Basic No-Charge Tests. You need only a length of insulated wire, preferably with an alligator clip at each end, to check all generators except those using dual contact regulators. Connect one end of this jumper wire to the generator field terminal (marked with a big fat "F"). If generator field is externally grounded, connect the other end to a good ground as in Fig. 1; if internally grounded, connect it to generator armature (marked "A" or "ARM") as in Fig. 2.

Now start the engine and run it at a fast idle. If the idiot light goes out or ammeter needle swings to the plus side, the generator is OK and the trouble is in the wiring or regulator.

If you have a Delco-Remy system with a double contact regulator—once again—*don't ground anything.* This must be checked at the regulator, requires some equipment and is somewhat involved. If you want to try it, here's what to do.

Secure a voltmeter-ammeter and connect it in series between the battery terminal ("B" or "BAT") on the regulator and the *non-*

grounded terminal of the battery as in Fig. 3. Disconnect field wire from "F" terminal on regulator and connect it to one lead of a 25-ohm, 25-watt variable resistance rheostat (an old "clamp-under-the-dash" heater control will work). Ground the other rheostat lead to the regulator body and set rheostat to wide open position.

Turn on all car accessories (lights, radio, heater, etc.). Start engine, run about one-third throttle and slowly turn off the rheostat until voltmeter reads slightly under 15 volts. A charge on the ammeter indicates regulator trouble. If no charge shows, make one more check.

Drop engine speed to a fast idle, remove the previous set-up and turn off the accessories. Connect jumper between the battery terminal on the regulator and the regulator armature terminal ("A" or "ARM"). If you get a charge now, the trouble is in the circuit breaker or current regulator. If not, the regulator is OK and the generator is at fault, or possibly the wiring.

Dirty Commutators, probably responsible for most generator failures, are one of the easiest ailments to cure. Sand commutator surface gently as in Fig. 4. *Never use emery cloth* since particles will imbed in the commutator surface to cause hot spots and burning. Do not use your fingers to hold the sandpaper. If you are stuck on the road somewhere, you can do an emergency cleaning job with an ordinary lead pencil eraser.

Where commutator appears worn or rough, you will be wise to have it turned down and the mica undercut at a garage. The cost is slight ($5 at most) when compared to that of a new or rebuilt unit.

Midnight Burr. While burring may not be so common, it happened to me. Apparently

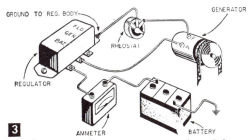

No-charge set-up for generator system using a Delco-Remy dual contact regulator.

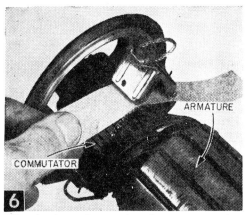

New brush can be seated against commutator by pulling a strip of 00 sandpaper between them, with sanding side against the brush holder. Repeat until end of brush is shaped for full contact.

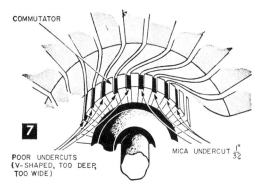

COMMUTATOR

POOR UNDERCUTS (V-SHAPED, TOO DEEP, TOO WIDE)

MICA UNDERCUT $\frac{1}{32}$"

something got caught under a brush and dug a small groove in the commutator—just deep enough to form little burrs that shorted all commutator segments into each other. This was one of those "middle of the night and 90 miles from nowhere" emergencies, but by scraping along the mica separators with a pocket knife, I managed to cut away enough burr to restore charging capacity. In fact, it worked so well, I never did have it turned down. In any event, it saved me a long walk on a cold night.

Assuming we have pinned down the problem to the generator, but have not yet located it, remove the unit from the engine for the following tests and repairs.

Take off the cover band and clean the commutator thoroughly. Remove all grease, using a rag dampened with carbon tetrachloride and follow with the wood block-sandpaper technique for a good polish job.

Sticking or Worn Brushes. If brushes do not move freely in their holders, slip the holder retaining springs and lift out the brushes. Clean both brushes and holders thoroughly with a toothbrush and some carbon tet. If brushes are worn to half original

length (Fig. 5), install new ones. Seat new brushes against the commutator with sandpaper as in Fig. 6.

The common practice of wrapping sandpaper around the commutator and rotating it back and forth is not recommended. Since brushes usually face different directions, such procedure will not seat one of the brushes properly, which will lead to arcing in the generator.

If brush connecting wires or tension springs are broken, replace them. The same goes for any spring with tension so weak it will not hold a partly worn brush firmly against the commutator.

Commutator Out of Round; High Mica. This usually accompanies severe commutator wear caused by a lot of generator mileage. In a case of severe wear, the remedy is turning the commutator on a lathe and undercutting the mica (Fig. 7) $\frac{1}{32}$ in. below the surface of the segments. You can do the latter job alone (and often get many more miles of generator service before having the commutator turned) with a section of hacksaw blade stoned down to proper thickness.

Thrown Solder on Cover Band. If little dabs of solder are splattered on inner surface of the cover band, something caused your generator to overheat, melting solder that holds the armature windings to commutator segments. In this case, some winding ends are probably loose and not contacting the commutator. If the separation is not too severe, you may be able to save the armature by a resoldering and reinsulating job as in Fig. 8.

Bench Tests. Where trouble is still not located, lift the grounded brush and insulate

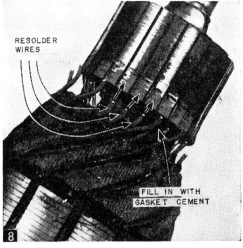

RESOLDER WIRES

FILL IN WITH GASKET CEMENT

Ends of field windings work loose when soldered connections melt due to overheating. Resolder connections to commutator segments and pack hard-setting gasket cement behind wires with a small stick.

it from the commutator with cardboard. Hook one clip of the test set-up in Fig. 9A to the "A" terminal and ground the other to the generator frame. If the generator is inoperative, has passed all other tests and shows negative (no short) on this one, you had better replace it. Further tests would

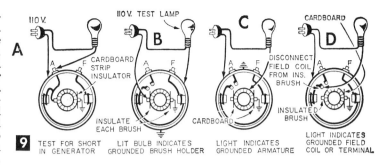

9 TEST FOR SHORT IN GENERATOR — LIT BULB INDICATES GROUNDED BRUSH HOLDER — LIGHT INDICATES GROUNDED ARMATURE — LIGHT INDICATES GROUNDED FIELD COIL OR TERMINAL

require an investment in specialized knowledge and equipment to detect the trouble and repair it.

If the test bulb lights up, however, the short is in the brush holder, armature or field coils. Determine which, by close visual inspection, if possible; otherwise make the tests in Figs. 9B, C and D. Once the short has been pinpointed, the chances are you can correct it by taping the bared wire or replacing the faulty terminal insulator.

For low or irregular generator output, any of the conditions previously discussed may be the answer, except the loose drive belt. The cure is also the same.

For the cause of an overly high output in an externally grounded generator, make the test as in Fig. 9D. Trouble in the internally grounded type is probably a short between the field and insulated main circuits. Correct this by taping up the exposed leads and eliminating the short.

What Kind of Replacement? If you decide to install another unit, let your pocketbook be your guide. Prices for new current model generators exchanged for your old unit are approximately $20 to $25; rebuilt units com-

pletely overhauled, turned, undercut and with new brushes installed average $15 to $20. You can get a junkyard unit taken from a wreck (no guarantee, but they usually work) for $5, or sometimes less if you bring your own tools and take it off yourself.

Regulator Checks. A typical voltage regulator as in Fig. 10 consists of three distinct magnetic switch units which automatically control the rate of charge within the battery-generator circuit. One switch, a cut-out or circuit breaker (Fig. 11), automatically connects the generator circuit to the battery wherever engine speed is above an idle; disconnects when engine is idling or stopped.

The other switches regulate voltage and current, cutting resistances into or out of the generator field circuit. When battery charge is low, resistances cut out, allowing the generator to deliver maximum power to the battery and bring it up to a full charge. At this point, resistances automatically cut back into the circuit to reduce generator power so it will just maintain the battery charge and keep its voltage within safe limits.

If trouble is indicated in your regulator, make the ground test first. Connect the jumper from regulator base to a good ground on the car body. If your regulator has a separate ground terminal, see that connections here and at generator ground terminal are

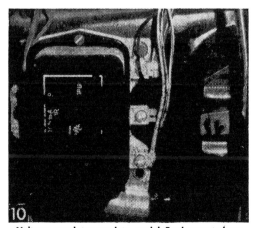

Voltage regulator on late model Ford mounted on front of body alongside radiator. When removing "hot" battery lead, tape exposed end to prevent a direct short by accidental contact with body.

Typical generator regulator with cover removed to show the three basic units, each an electromagnetic switch. On this Delco-Remy unit, from left, are cut-out relay, current regulator and voltage regulator.

97

clean and tight. After starting up and running engine at a fast idle, your idiot light should go out or ammeter show positive. If not, your regulator grounding is defective.

For further tests of a dual contact regulator in a Delco-Remy system, refer back to the generator test procedure.

If you have an externally grounded generator, connect jumper between field terminal on regulator and a good ground. If the regulator has a ground terminal, connect jumper between it and the regulator body. If you get a charge signal during a fast idle, the regulator is at fault.

On internal ground systems, make this test by connecting jumper between armature and field terminals of the regulator. This hookup can be used in an emergency to drive the car short distances at low speeds until you can get the regulator fixed or replaced.

Too Much Charge. If your battery is fully charged and a high charge rate is still indicated, run engine at a fast idle and remove wire from the regulator field terminal. If charge rate continues, you probably have a grounded or shorted wire somewhere in the wiring harness of the car. If the rate drops to zero, the trouble is in the regulator. Continued high charging may seriously damage generator armature, contact points and coil as well as burn out your car lights prematurely.

Too Little Charge. If battery and charge rate are both low, check for the most common causes—loose battery cable connections and corroded battery terminals. If they are cleaned and tight, run engine at a fast idle and cut the regulator out of the charging circuit. To do this on externally grounded systems, place a jumper between field and ground terminals of the regulator; on internally grounded systems, make the hookup between field and armature terminals of the regulator. If trouble is in the regulator, the charge rate should increase noticeably.

Since few faulty regulators are repairable without special tools and equipment and many require complete rebuilding, it's a good idea to buy a new one (around $5-$6) when you find yours at fault.

Repolarization. After testing or repairing a generator, make sure its polarity is the same as that of its regulator and the battery it will charge. Before starting, if you have a dual-contact regulator, slip cardboard strips between brushes and commutator for insulation.

On externally grounded generators, make a "flash" jumper wire connection between "B" (battery) and "A" (generator armature) leads at the regulator. Polarizing action occurs instantly. On internally grounded units, remove field lead from regulator and contact it momentarily with the "B" regulator terminal.

MAINTAINING ALTERNATOR OUTPUT

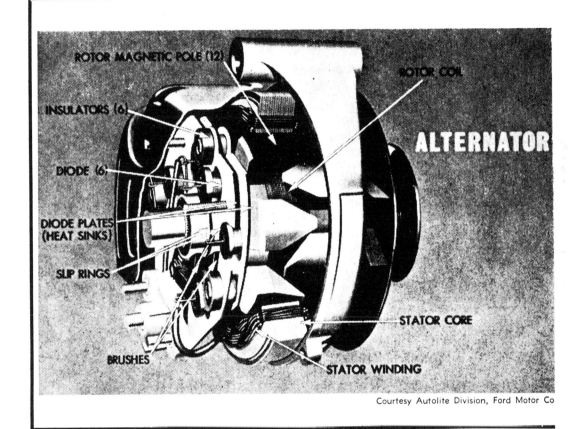

ROTOR MAGNETIC POLE (12)

ROTOR COIL

INSULATORS (6)

DIODE (6)

ALTERNATOR

DIODE PLATES (HEAT SINKS)

SLIP RINGS

STATOR CORE

BRUSHES

STATOR WINDING

Courtesy Autolite Division, Ford Motor Co

The increased capability and improved output characteristics of the

Most of the automobiles being built today are equipped with an AC generator—more commonly called an alternator. It does the same job as the DC generator—or simply, the generator—we've already discussed.

Just as the modern engine represents a high state-of-the-art in the power available from a given displacement, so the alternator electrical system represents a high achievement in obtaining the most electrical power from a minimum draw on engine output. It has been termed the ultimate electrical power source for automotive use.

The alternator offers the potential for longer battery life in addition to its primary advantage—higher output. The higher output is obtained due to the comparatively low weight of the rotor and coil assembly allowing greater pulley ratios for higher r.p.m. The

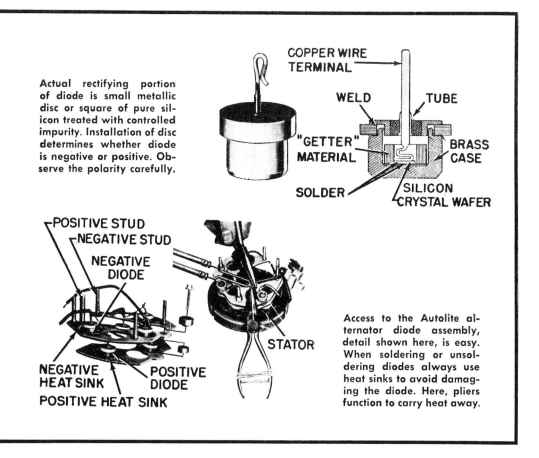

Actual rectifying portion of diode is small metallic disc or square of pure silicon treated with controlled impurity. Installation of disc determines whether diode is negative or positive. Observe the polarity carefully.

COPPER WIRE TERMINAL

WELD   TUBE

"GETTER" MATERIAL   BRASS CASE

SOLDER   SILICON CRYSTAL WAFER

POSITIVE STUD
NEGATIVE STUD
NEGATIVE DIODE

STATOR

NEGATIVE HEAT SINK   POSITIVE DIODE
POSITIVE HEAT SINK

Access to the Autolite alternator diode assembly, detail shown here, is easy. When soldering or unsoldering diodes always use heat sinks to avoid damaging the diode. Here, pliers function to carry heat away.

alternator over the generator are only kept with the proper care

result, of course, is higher output—even at engine idle. Maintaining the advantage an alternator gives your electrical system is just a matter of knowing the alternator and keeping it in top tune.

Construction. All alternators consist of a stator, which corresponds to the generator's field circuit, and a rotor, which corresponds to the generator's armature. The only essential difference between the two is the method

used to convert alternating current to direct current. Alternator construction can be seen in the accompanying illustrations.

In generators, as you've seen, brushes are used to pick the alternating current off a commutator, converting that current to direct. Alternators, however, employ silicon rectifiers or, for short, diodes. Don't be confused by the fact that alternators also contain brushes because they are used for a different

Alternator Output

purpose than in a generator. Alternator brushes supply field current to the rotor by connecting two slip rings mounted concentrically on the rotor shaft.

The rectifier in the alternator is a chemical disc that changes alternating current to direct current since it permits current to flow in one direction only. In other words, the rectifiers used in alternators have a low resistance to the flow of electrical current in one direction and a high resistance to the flow of electrical current in the other direction.

This low resistance allows current to flow from the alternator to the battery, but the rectifier's high resistance prevents a return flow from the battery to the alternator when battery current exceeds alternator ouput, as it does when the engine idles.

Both alternator and generator have regulator units, but the makeup of each is different in one important respect—the absence of a circuit breaker (the cut-out relay) in the alternator regulator.

In the generator's regulator, as you've seen, the circuit breaker connects and disconnects the battery and generator at the proper time. Since the alternator is self-rectifying, though, allowing current to flow only in one direction—toward the battery—there is no need for a circuit breaker. The constant, steady flow of current from the alternator to the battery allows the battery to maintain a full state of charge.

Maintenance. The alternator is no harder to tune than the generator. What makes it even easier is that if trouble's apparent, you don't usually have to replace the entire unit. The unit breaks into two parts—the stator and rotor—allowing you to replace the one that's giving the trouble.

Fan belt tension is critical with the alternator. Always make sure the belt is in good condition and adjusted to specification.

The one precaution you must keep in mind when working with the alternator is guarding against reverse polarity. Reverse the polarity of the alternator or the battery for even an instant and you stand a chance of burning out the rectifiers. To prevent accidental grounding, furthermore, you should always use insulated tools when working in the area of the alternator.

Following adjustment of the fan belt, turn your attention to the regulator. Make sure all connections at this unit are tight. Follow this by checking the condition of the regulator points. If you find they're burned or pitted, you'll have to replace the regulator. Now, check and tighten all connections in-

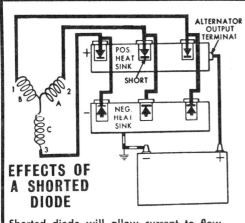

EFFECTS OF A SHORTED DIODE

Shorted diode will allow current to flow in both directions. It will flow back to the A winding instead of to the battery.

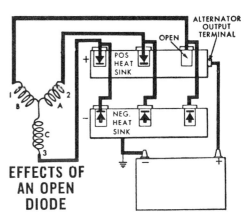

EFFECTS OF AN OPEN DIODE

Open diode will not let current flow in either direction. The circuit is not complete through the B winding to battery.

cluding those to the ignition switch, the ballast resistor, the regulator and the conducting surfaces of the fuse and holder.

Unscrew the brushes from the alternator and inspect them for wear. If worn, replace them.

In some cars, the brushes can be removed from the alternator with the unit in the car. This is done by unscrewing the external cap screws to which the brushes are attached. In other cars, the unit must be removed from the car to reach the brushes, which can then be unscrewed.

If it becomes necessary to take the unit apart, remove it from the car and split it open, separating the stator from the rotor. Test the rectifiers first. This can be done with a commercial diode tester, although you could use an ammeter calibrated in 1-amp units. Simply touch each rectifier with the meter probe. The meter should read at least 1¾ amps. If not, the rectifier is not giving good service and should be replaced.

Next inspect the stator winding carefully for breaks. To be absolutely sure there are none, you should test from the stator leads to the stator core with a 110-volt test lamp or other suitable tester. If the lamp lights, the stator is grounded and should be replaced.

Finally, test the field windings in the rotor part of the alternator. This is done with an ammeter hooked to the alternator battery output terminal while turning the rotor shaft by hand. The correct field current draw should be recorded on the meter. This reading differs from car to car, so check your service manual.

The above description tells you what to do if you are not getting output from the alternator. However, there are things a faulty adjusted or malfunctioning alternator can cause—most can be checked on the car.

Low Charging Rate. A low charging rate is indicated when the ammeter or troublelight in your car begins to show discharge at low engine speed and idle. It is also indicated if a battery gets rundown.

Look at the fan belt first and make sure it's properly adjusted. Then check the battery terminals where high resistance could be causing the trouble. Remove the cables and clean the terminals and posts. Make sure the ground cable is clean and tight.

Finally check at the alternator for loose connections. If the trouble still persists, replace the brushes in the alternator since poor contact between brushes and slip rings is a major factor for a low charging rate. As a final tuneup procedure, remove the alternator from the car and check the stator. Open windings cause an unsteady low charging rate.

If the ammeter troublelight flicks on and

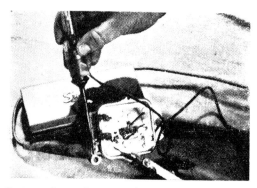

Test regulator air gap with a gauge and troublelight. Lamp should dim when armature is pressed.

Check for a grounded condition in the alternator by touching stator winding assembly and case.

Alternator Output

off at all speeds and you get a rundown battery, which indicates low voltage output, check the regulator first. To do this, hook the negative lead of a voltmeter to the battery's negative post and the positive to the positive post. Connect a jumper wire from the ignition terminal to the field terminal on the regulator and then start the engine. The voltmeter should read about 14.3 to 15.0 volts for a 12-volt charging system and 7.0 to 7.5 volts for a 6-volt charging system. If not, the regulator is faulty. Try adjusting the regulator points; if that does not increase the voltage output, get a new regulator.

But if the regulator does check out, go to the alternator and tighten all connections. The trouble could also be a shorted rectifier or grounded stator, so check them as well.

High Charging Rate. It is possible for the alternator to throw out too much charge. An over-charge condition will show up by acid salts on the battery and the battery beginning to use too much water. Check the regulator first; if it's set too high, adjust the points. If this doesn't help, don't scrap the regulator yet.

First remove the unit and clean its mounting surface. A poorly grounded regulator could be causing the problem. If not, the problem's either that the regulator points are stuck or there are open windings in the unit. If so, replace the regulator.

If the battery's using too much water or a lot of acid salts begin to form, it could also mean that the regulator points are oxidizing. The cause could be a loose or dirty ground connection, so clean the mounting surface and tighten all attaching bolts. Now, test the regulator. If the meter shows a high voltage, set the points.

Finally, check and adjust the regulator air gap to specification as given in your car's manual. To do this, connect a test lamp between the regulator ignition and field terminals. Insert the proper wire gauge (usually one of 0.48 in.). Press the armature plate down. The contacts should open and the test lamp should dim.

Now, insert a larger wire gauge in the same position (usually one of .052 in.). Depress the armature plate. The upper contact should be closed and the test lamp should remain lighted. If the air gap doesn't check out, adjust it by bending the upper contact support

until you get the right openings and test readings.

Another reason for oxidized points could be shorted field windings in the rotor pole. In this case, the rotor has to be replaced.

Again, excessive use of water by the battery and acid salts on the battery are indications of another condition—burned regulator points. The trouble is probably a regulator set too high or shorted field windings in the rotor pole. In the former case, adjust the points—in the latter, replace the rotor.

Mechanical Problems. An alternator that's noisy is one that's either loose on its mountings or one that has internal problems. First check the mounting bolts and make sure the alternator is tightly connected. The drive pulley could also be causing the noise, so ensure that it is tight.

If this fails to stop the noise, remove the alternator from the car and break it open. Inspect the rotor fan blades. If bent, replace the rotor. Now test each rectifier for a short. If this doesn't stop the trouble, the problem's a sprung rotor shaft, worn shaft bearings or open or shorted windings in the stator and a rubbing rotor pole.

In the event of a sprung rotor shaft, replace the rotor. If the problem boils down to worn shaft bearings, you can have them replaced too. If, though, the stator windings are shorted and the rotor poles are rubbing, you'll have to replace the entire alternator.

If the battery keeps running down for no rhyme or reason, it indicates that the regulator points are stuck closed. This was probably caused by a poor ground connection between the alternator and regulator. The only course is to replace the regulator and make sure the new unit is properly grounded so the trouble doesn't recur.

SETTINGS FOR SOME ALTERNATOR VOLTAGE REGULATORS		
MAKE	AIR GAP	POINT GAP
Buick	.057	.014
Cadillac	.057	.014
Oldsmobile	.060	.014
Chevy	.057	.014
Chrysler	.048-.052	.015
Dodge	.048-.052	.015
Plymouth	.048-.052	.015
Valiant	.057	.015
Ford	.045-.052	.010-.015
Lincoln	.045-.052	.010-.015
Mercury	.045-.052	.010-.015

Be Sure Your Brakes Work Well

Your best life insurance is a brake system that works well. Here's what you should know to check and repair it

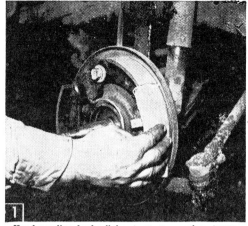

Hand sanding brake lining to remove surface traces of grease or dirt.

SOME wise wit once summed up the basic problem of car ownership. "When your engine quits," said he, "*there* you are. When your brakes quit, *where* are you?"

Which naturally leads to the next question: How can you tell when your brakes are likely to fail you? Actually, most of us know some familiar symptoms that signal brake trouble—noisy brake operation, swerving and pulling to one side, fading, dragging, wet weather grabbing, and spongy pedal action.

The trick is to learn first how to spot the conditions that cause such troubles, and then correct impending ailments before they can become dangerous. So let's start first with a correctly operating brake system—and then see where and how parts of this system can fail—if improperly adjusted or not serviced regularly.

Figure 2 shows the basic operating parts of a complete brake system. Each brake drum revolves as a unit with a wheel. Anchored inside each drum are the brake shoes. Each shoe carries brake lining on its outer surface. The shoes are so pivoted (at the bottom in this particular design) that they can swing outward and contact the inner surface of the revolving drum.

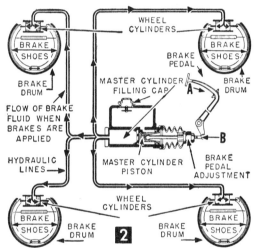

Schematic layout of modern brake system showing how mechanical parts at the wheels are operated by hydraulic pressure developed in the master cylinder, and delivered to the wheel cylinders.

Fig. 3. Weakening, due to removing too much metal, caused this thin drum to break, resulting in a tragic accident.

Fig. 4. Using simple gage composed of rod and feeler blades to check taper or out-of-round conditions, as well as diameter of brake drums.

5

Shop-type universal wheel and hub puller.

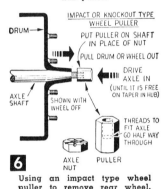

6

Using an impact type wheel puller to remove rear wheel.

The outward movement of each shoe is the result of hydraulic pressure within the wheel cylinders acting on pistons in the ends of the cylinders. Some cars use two single piston cylinders at each wheel, but the fundamental action is the same. To keep the brake shoes from dragging against the drums, coil springs hold the shoes out of contact.

So much for the mechanical operation of the system, with its anchored shoes creating mechanical friction within the brake drum.

Brake *application* is the result of the build-up of hydraulic pressure in the brake lines. This hydraulic pressure is built up when the brake pedal moves as indicated by arrow A in Fig. 2. The lower end of the pedal moves as indicated by the arrow B. When brakes are applied, the master cylinder piston moves against the brake fluid in the master cylinder, building up pressure in the master cylinder.

As this pressure transfers into the brake lines, the brake fluid moves into the four wheel cylinders. This causes the wheel cylinder pistons to move outward, forcing the brake shoes against the brake drums.

A false theory regarding modern brakes is that they are self equalizing. They are not. The hydraulic pressure is equalized. But mechanical

TABLE A—BRAKE TROUBLE-SHOOTING

Brake trouble can be due to a combination of ailments—both inside and outside of the braking system. This chart will discuss troubles within the braking system—but you should also check for such outside conditions as sagged springs, weak shock absorbers, worn tires, bad wheel bearings—any one of which can give you balky or faulty braking action.

Where the cure of brake trouble specifies the use of brake shoe gages, pressure gages, or would necessitate other specialized equipment, the car owner lacking such facilities should take the job to a brake mechanic.

Likely CAUSE	Probable CURE
Trouble: NOISY OPERATION	
1. Lining worn, glazed or greasy.	1. Have relined. Surface glaze can be removed by sanding.
2. Warped shoes causing poor lining contact.	2. Have shoes trued, lining ground to fit or replaced.
3. Brake backing plate sprung or loose.	3. Tighten backing plate or have straightened or replaced, and shoes fitted to drums.
4. Wheel bearings in bad order or improperly adjusted.	4. Adjust or have replaced.
5. Brake drum out of round, surface flared, tapered, scored or glazed.	5. Have drum braking surface refinished.
6. Low hydraulic pressure.	6. Isolate location of trouble with pressure gage. (100 pounds on pedal should give more than 500 pounds at each wheel.)
7. Stuck wheel pistons.	7. Free up, overhaul or replace as necessary.
8. Cups in master cylinder sticking.	8. Flush system, renew cups, refill with new fluid.
Trouble: BRAKES ERRATIC—	
Car pulls to one side, brakes grab	
1. Master cylinder check valve not holding hydraulic system at 7-12 pounds above atmospheric pressure.	1. Service master cylinder.
2. Hydraulic fluid gassing, or air in lines.	2. Flush, refill with heavy duty fluid, bleed system.
3. Clogged or dented lines causing unequal pressure at wheel cylinders.	3. Inspect and unclog or replace.
4. Stuck or rusted linkage at shoes.	4. Free up and lubricate.
5. Rear wheel parking brake controls adjusted too tight.	5. Readjust parking brake.
6. Power vacuum booster check valve faulty, or hoses collapsing.	6. Have valve serviced, and hoses replaced.
7. Lining greasy, wrong type, loose.	7. Reline.
8. Drum and shoe radii unequal.	8. Fit shoes to drum.
9. Looseness in backing plates, spring U bolts, front system bushings, or shock absorbers ineffective.	9. Check and repair as necessary.

trouble at the individual wheels, or difference in lining, can cause annoying if not dangerous action.

You'll find the more frequent and hazardous brake faults summed up in Table A. Note that this includes symptoms from both the mechanical and hydraulic parts of the braking system. Actually, the brakes used on today's cars are *mechanical*—but they are *hydraulically* applied. So maintenance and service divide naturally into *mechanical* and *hydraulic* units. First, we will investigate in detail the care and repair of the *mechanical parts* of the braking system. When they have been covered, we'll proceed to an investigation of the *hydraulic* parts.

One word of caution before we dig into servicing problems. Brakes are often blamed when the trouble is due to conditions in the car springs, shock absorbers, shackles, tires, and other related parts. Also, a serious brake problem can be the result of a combination of conditions. So, if you

Likely CAUSE	Probable CURE

Trouble: BRAKES FADE UNDER HARD, REPEATED USE

Likely CAUSE	Probable CURE
1. Hydraulic fluid gassing.	1. Refill with heavy-duty fluid.
2. Rubber cups sticking.	2. Replace.
3. Master cylinder primary cup leak.	3. Overhaul master cylinder.
4. Power reserve tank of vacuum booster too small.	4. Add additional tank.
5. Clearance excessive between shoes and drum.	5. Have brakes given major adjustment.
6. Excessive expansion of drums.	6. Install new drums if they have been turned over .060 in. oversize.
7. Oil, grease or brake fluid in lining.	7. Reline and correct cause.

Trouble: DRAGGING BRAKES

Likely CAUSE	Probable CURE
1. Clogged ports in master cylinder.	1. Remove dirt from port, or adjust so primary cup uncovers the port.
2. No play between master cylinder and pedal rod.	2. Adjust rod.
3. Sticking pistons in wheel cylinders.	3. Overhaul cylinders and replace fluid.
4. Shoe linkage at wheels stuck or rusty.	4. Free up and lubricate.
5. Brake shoes too close to drums.	5. Have proper adjustment made.
6. Hydraulic line dented or clogged.	6. Inspect and correct as necessary.
7. Weak, sagged or bent brake shoe return springs.	7. Replace with new springs.
8. Backing plates or shoe supports out of line, anchor pins or bushings frozen.	8. Have plates aligned and tightened.
9. Faulty adjustment of shoes.	9. Have major adjustment made.
10. Shoes not fitted to drums.	10. Have shoes fitted and adjusted.

Trouble: WET WEATHER GRABBING, OR FAILURE TO HOLD

Likely CAUSE	Probable CURE
1. Rusted wheel cylinders.	1. Replace rubber boots after cleaning cylinders.
2. Dust in drum forms "goo" that causes slipping or grabbing.	2. Clean all parts thoroughly.
3. Water held in brakes by scored drums.	3. Have drums refinished or replaced if refinishing would make too thin.
4. Backing plate gasket damaged, permitting water to enter brakes.	4. Inspect and renew gasket. Have backing plate repaired.

Trouble: PEDAL SPONGY—BRAKE FADE

Likely CAUSE	Probable CURE
1. Incorrect hydraulic fluid.	1. Flush and refill.
2. Dirt in master cylinder ports.	2. Clean ports and bleed system.
3. Old flexible hose expanding.	3. Install new flexible hose lines.
4. Air leak in system.	4. Renew rubber cups, tighten all connections.
5. Master cylinder primary cup leaking.	5. Service master cylinder.
6. Shoe and drum radii differ.	6. Have shoes ground or replaced.
7. Anchors improperly set.	7. Have brake specialist with precision gages reset the anchors.
8. Drums too thin from wear or refinishing.	8. Have drums replaced if more than .060 in. oversize.
9. Axle housing shifting upon brake application.	9. Have U clips tightened and springs and saddles checked.
10. System not maintaining pressure of 7-12 pounds above atmospheric, so air enters at wheel cylinders.	10. Overhaul master cylinder, paying special attention to check valve.

have brake trouble in your car, be sure to consider all of the possibilities before buying or performing services intended to correct the fault giving you the trouble.

Noisy Operation. Noise in the brake system develops in somewhat the same manner as the noise a youngster makes when sliding his hand down a banister. The hand squeaks when sliding along, the squeak varying with the pressure. Dry and moist spots on the palm of the hand add to the noise.

In brakes, noise may result from improper fit of the shoes resulting in varying pressure between the shoes and the drum, and varying the degree of friction between the brake parts and lining. Thus, anything that keeps the brake drum from furnishing a *firm foundation* for the shoes can cause noise trouble. The brake drums themselves must be perfectly round and free of taper for satisfactory brake operation. And each drum must be strong enough to withstand the high shoe pressure required in emergency stops (Fig. 3).

Brake mechanics use a caliper to check for oversize drums. Drums when new are generally 10, 11 or 12 inches in diameter and engineers agree that they should not be enlarged more than .060 in. In other words, .030 in. is the maximum cut that should ever be made in a drum. When

7 To prevent damage to the springs or injury, use spring pliers when removing brake retracting springs.

8 Note the order in which small parts are removed to assure speed and accuracy when reassembling.

turned any thinner, you may get the kind of breakage shown in Fig. 3, an example salvaged after a tragic wreck caused by the broken drum.

An inexpensive means of checking drums is a ¼-in. dia. rod with rounded ends that is cut exactly 10, 11 or 12 in. long depending on the original diameter of the drum you want to check. This rod is used with a thickness gage, as in Fig. 4. By using the rod in two positions at right angles to each other, the drum can be checked for out-of-round. By using the rod at the outer edge and also as far in as possible, a flared or bell-mouthed drum can be detected.

Inspection of your brake shoes and drums is not too difficult. General wear conditions can be determined by what you find at the front wheels, which not only are easy to remove, but also reveal the greatest wear. This is because the center of gravity of the car shifts toward the front when brakes are applied. So the front brakes do more work and get more wear than the rear brakes.

To be sure that the brake noise you hear is not due to grease or brake fluid on the linings at the rear wheels, go under the car and look for any sign of grease or fluid at the bottom of the brake backing plate. If you see any, the rear wheels should be pulled.

Figure 5 shows a professional type of puller used by brake mechanics for removing rear wheels. This is heavy and too expensive for the motorist who does his own repair work. But you can use the impact type puller (Fig. 6) which merely protects the axle threads. It is like a nut in which the hole does not go all the way through. In use it should be screwed tightly on a shaft so that the nut-like puller is tight against the end of the shaft.

The actual wheel removal from the rear axle results from driving against the protected shaft with a heavy hammer. But remember that *failure to take up play* in the differential, by *pulling*

out hard enough on the wheel, may allow **the** axle shaft to strike and damage differential parts. So when you use the impact puller, *pull outward hard on the wheel as you pound.*

Brake specialists put the car on a hoist or steel horses while doing an extensive brake job. Chances are you don't have a hoist handy but, before starting any brake work, be sure the car is safely supported at all corners on its axles (not bumpers), with the wheels clearing the ground.

When handling brake shoe removal or replacement, remember that brake retracting springs (Fig. 7) are powerful. These springs pull the shoes away from the drums when the brakes are released, so don't stretch them out of shape when removing or installing them. For personal safety, and to prevent damage to the springs, always use spring pliers as in Fig. 7.

Note the order in which small parts are removed. For example, the horse-shoe-like washer, and oil felt, with retainer pictured in Fig. 8

Chalk mark brake shoes before removal. LFF identifies left front wheel, front shoe; LFR is left front wheel, rear shoe.

To keep piston from coming out while working on brakes, either use cylinder clamp as at A or tie cord around piston and cylinder as at B.

should be carefully preserved for use when reassembling. And the idea of marking each brake shoe as it comes off (Fig. 9) is a good one.

Of course, if the linings are not worn down to the rivets, are tight on the shoes and free of grease, oil, or brake fluid, you don't need to disassemble the shoes from the backing plate. Instead, you can remove any glaze on the lining with No. 0 sandpaper (Fig. 1). This will do much to quiet your brakes and improve their action.

While the shoes are removed, to keep the pistons from coming out and protect the hydraulic system, use a cylinder clamp (A in Fig. 10), or tie each cylinder and piston together (B in Fig. 10). Also, make sure that no one presses on the brake pedal while the shoes are removed.

Braking Erratic. If your car pulls to one side, or the brakes grab, attention to the items just discussed may clear up the entire problem. Unpredictable action, however, can also be due to rusted and sticking parts at or near the wheels.

As we noted earlier, the brake-applying energy delivered to the wheels by the hydraulic system may be uniform at each wheel. But the brake action will vary seriously if shoe movement is hampered by rust or dirt. So, when working on brakes, apply a few drops of No. 20 SAE oil to a small piece of No. 1 emery cloth, and use this to remove rust (Fig. 11).

When reassembling the brakes, many brake experts apply a thin film of Lubriplate (from car dealers or auto supply stores) to each moving mechanical part. But be doubly sure no Lubriplate gets on the brake drum or brake lining.

While checking free fit of brake shoes on their anchor bolts, test for sprung shoes by placing each shoe on the corner of a surface plate (Fig. 12) (plate glass will take the place of a surface plate in an emergency).

Never attempt to use lining that has been soaked with grease or brake fluid. Sanding the lining surface does not remove dirt or fluids that have penetrated, and washing linings with gasoline removes only surface grease or fluid. Then under the heat and pressure of use, the oil, grease or brake fluid that has penetrated the lining will come to the surface and cause dangerously unpredictable brake action.

Brake Fade. When traffic or grades make it

Emery cloth with oil will polish rust off of anchor bolts.

Checking for sprung brake shoe by testing for uniform clearance on a level surface.

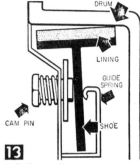

Lack of alignment between the shoe and the drum reduces the frictional contact area and thereby brings on brake fade.

necessary to apply the brakes repeatedly from high speeds, they may fail to hold. Some causes for this dangerous condition are thin brake drums, worn linings, or the presence of oil, grease or hydraulic fluid on the lining. We have discussed the cures for these. Figure 13 shows still another cause of brake fading, where only a fraction of the braking surface is in use. Under easy application this might get by. When used hard, however, it would fail. The cause of this misalignment may be a bell-mouthed or flared brake drum, a sprung shoe, a bent backing plate or an improperly installed shoe. The point is to see that the shoes when installed stand square and operate against a brake drum surface that is parallel with the surface of the shoe.

Dragging Brakes. Perhaps you have had the annoying experience of applying the brakes which later refused to "let go." First check for free pedal play. You should be able to move the brake pedal by hand about $\frac{5}{16}$-$\frac{7}{16}$ inch before resistance is felt. If you can't, the instructions for adjusting given in Fig. 20 will explain what to do. Lack of free play interferes with the return of the hydraulic fluid to the master cylinder. And if the fluid cannot return, then the brakes cannot release.

Adjusting the brake shoes too close to the drum, or operating with shoes that have oil, grease or brake fluid on them may also cause dragging. Also, recheck those brake shoe retractor springs to be sure they are in good condition. If they have been overstretched, or are rusty, replacing them with new springs will probably clear up brake drag.

Wet Weather Grabbing. Experienced motorists realize that after passing under a flooded viaduct or through a shallow stream or a series of deep puddles, they should drag their brakes slightly while accelerating. Doing this produces friction which causes heat, and the pressure and heat tend to squeeze and dry out water on linings.

If the grabbing seems particularly severe, however, check the brake drums for slight scores or grooves. These grooves hold water—not much water, it's true, but enough to furnish lubrication where none is desired.

Excess water may be getting in through loose backing plates or damaged backing plate paper gaskets. Occasionally, rubber boots are left off from the wheels' cylinders, letting rust get in the cylinders to interfere with proper piston action.

Finally, your brakes may be just simply very dusty. This dust forms a slimy "goo" that makes the brakes slip until the heat generated by friction has dried up the mess, and the brakes.

The cure for this, of course, is to remove wheels to expose brake parts and clean out all dirt with a wire brush and compressed air.

Spongy Pedal. If your brake pedal feels as though you had a rubber sponge on top of it, you probably have air in the hydraulic system, and we will explain the cure for this later on. But

Star wheel type of brake adjuster. Star wheel is reached through opening in brake backing plate.

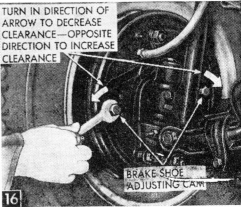

Cam or eccentric type brake adjuster.

there are also mechanical causes for a spongy pedal. One of the most dangerous is the rotting and expanding of the flexible lines in the hydraulic system (Fig. 2). Age combined with careless lubrication can hurt these flexible lines. To check their condition, have someone apply the brakes firmly while you hold these flexible lines in your hand. They will become very stiff when the brake is applied. But if they also increase measurably in diameter, replace them.

A cracked or broken brake drum (Fig. 3) can also signal its condition with a spongy pedal, as can brake shoes poorly fitted to the drum. Brake specialists when assembling a job lay each shoe in its drum. If a .005 in. feeler blade can be slipped between the *center* of the shoe and the drum, the shoe is too large for the drum (probably due to using too thick a lining). But, if the center of the shoe contacts the drum and the ends show clearance, the shoe is too small for the drum (the lining may be too thin).

The radius of the shoe and the drum must be identical. Specialists accomplish this by using

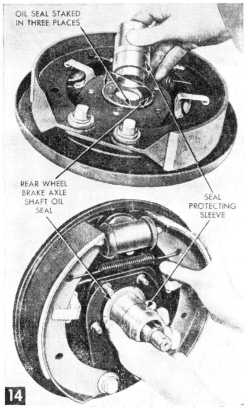

New oil seal installed in brake backing plate. Note how seal-protecting sleeve is used to avoid damage to seal when the axle shaft passes through the seal.

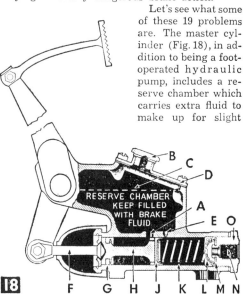

the brake shoe toward the drum, thus compensating for lining wear.

But remember that these critical clearance adjustments determine your safety on the highway, and most motorists prefer to leave this part of brake servicing to brake mechanics.

Now, let's take the major hydraulic parts step by step (see Fig. 2). The master cylinder, operated by depressing the brake pedal, causes brake fluid to flow through the solid hydraulic lines from the master cylinder and the flexible lines at the wheels to the wheel cylinders. Specialized brake service stations have gages for checking the delivery of the hydraulic pressure, though such gages are not commonly required, since the system is relatively fool-proof. But where hydraulic line corrosion has become severe, or other types of foreign matter or mechanical damage have interfered with the transfer of energy, a scientific check must be made.

Right now it is sufficient for you as a car owner to realize that all the hydraulic lines in the brake system are designed to handle *extreme pressure*, and care should be exercised to prevent chafing of the flexible lines or mechanical injury to the solid lines. Careless lubrication that allows grease to accumulate on the flexible lines may soften them and cause eventual failure.

Experienced brake men would not be surprised if they counted up and found 27 mechanical causes for brake troubles. But many might be astonished to realize that 19 different conditions within the hydraulic system contribute to annoying or deadly dangerous brake action.

Master cylinder located under floor boards on driver's side of car.

grinders which fit the shoe to the drum. These grinders are of various types: some are used after the shoes are installed on the car, others grind the shoes before installation. This machining of drums and shoes is a highly-developed specialty requiring expensive equipment and extensive know-how. Automotive wholesalers with machine shop facilities do this specialized work for many garages and service stations. And many of these automotive jobbers or wholesalers will do this work for the car owner directly.

Finally, to protect any brake job, make sure wheel bearings and their lubrication seals are in good order. Most experienced brake men renew all oil or grease seals on any major brake job, (as in Fig. 14). Bearings should have no noticeable play, because brakes run with a clearance of anywhere between .007 and .015 in. between the shoes and drums. And the wheel bearing is thus just as critical an element in maintaining this clearance as the brake drum itself. One word of warning. Never upset the anchor bolts when changing brake shoes. If these are upset, only a major brake adjustment done by a skilled brake man with proper gages is safe.

For those mechanically inclined (and for the tricky work of brake servicing, you should either be quite skillful—or leave the job to a professional) let's look at the *essentials* of a minor adjustment. Note the star wheel between the bottom ends of the brake shoes (A in Fig. 15). You reach this star wheel through an opening in the brake backing plate when the wheel is replaced. Turning it is like turning a turnbuckle.

By means of this star wheel the shoes can be pushed out toward drum to offset lining wear.

Another basic design is pictured in Fig. 16. Here each bolt is integral with a cam or eccentric. Pulling downward on the wrench moves

Let's see what some of these 19 problems are. The master cylinder (Fig. 18), in addition to being a foot-operated hydraulic pump, includes a reserve chamber which carries extra fluid to make up for slight

Section through master cylinder with principal parts identified: (A) breather hole, (B) filler plug, (C) reserve chamber, (D) chamber cover, (E) compensating port, (F) piston rod, (G) secondary cup, (H) piston, (J) primary cup, (K) main spring, (L) check valve, (M) check valve washer, (N) outlet to hydraulic lines (O) end nut.

Master cylinder located on engine side of dash panel.

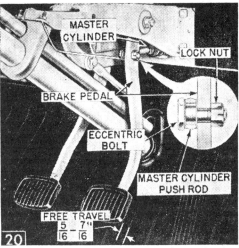

Freeplay adjustment. After loosening the lock nut, the eccentric bolt that passes through the brake pedal is turned to establish 5/16—7/16 inch of freeplay.

fluid losses. In addition to developing pressure to apply the brakes, the master cylinder also maintains pressure on the hydraulic system. This keeps the system in readiness for immediate application. It also prevents the entrance of air at the wheel cylinders when the brakes are suddenly released. From the safety standpoint, the most important thing that a motorist can do is to *see that the reserve chamber in the master cylinder never runs dry.* In fact it is dangerous to operate with the level down more than halfway. Careful motorists have the brake fluid level checked *at least* twice a year.

To do this, brush all grit and dust away from the filler plug. Remove the plug, and add new, clean, high-grade brake fluid until the level is within ½ in. of the top of the chamber. Use only an approved fluid. Never use mineral oil because it will expand and rot the rubber parts of the hydraulic system, and cause early and total failure. A good brake fluid is one that will not gas at the highest operating temperatures, and which will flow freely at the lowest temperatures. Fluids of different kinds should not be mixed. If there is any doubt, the system should be drained, flushed with denatured alcohol, and refilled. Details on performing these services will be covered later.

The master cylinder, until recently, was mounted underneath the floor boards on the driver's side of the car, as in Fig. 17. Now many of them are found on the engine side of the dash panel (Fig. 19). Wherever located, the fundamentals of operation are the same. Master cylinders vary slightly in design. All, however, of the compensating type have similar major parts.

The ⁵⁄₁₆ to ⁷⁄₁₆ in. of freeplay in the pedal (Fig. 18) allows the piston to move back so that its rubber primary cup clears the compensating port. Dragging brakes will result if the primary cup covers the port or if any foreign matter clogs the port. When the brakes are released, the brake shoe retractor springs put pressure on the hydraulic system from the wheels toward the master cylinder. Pushing the pistons in at each wheel also forces fluid back into the master cylinder. The surplus fluid must return to the

reserve chamber by way of the compensator port. It is the strength of the main spring (Fig. 18) operating against the check valve that maintains 7 to 12 pounds of pressure above atmospheric pressure in the hydraulic system.

So far as the car owner is concerned, servicing of the master cylinder is limited to exchanging it. Car dealers and automotive wholesalers carry new or rebuilt master cylinders which the car owner can install or have installed. If you have to "pump" your brakes, but do not lose fluid, you have trouble in the master cylinder.

From the service standpoint, if the master cylinder is in bad order this will be indicated by

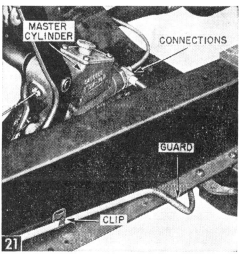

Inspection of hydraulic system should include all connections for leakage, line guards for condition, and line-to-frame clips for security.

111

Looking inside of wheel cylinder boot for leakage.

are held firmly against the frame by clips to prevent vibration. Test the flexible connections by holding tightly by hand one at a time while a helper applies the brakes. Flexible lines will stiffen, but they should not expand.

Look at the lower edge of each brake backing plate. If brake fluid is present, the cylinder of that wheel needs overhauling. Experience indicates that since all wheel cylinders get the same degree of use and abuse, that when one leaks it is good practice to overhaul all. If the brake fluid has not yet reached the bottom of the brake backing plate it is possible that leakage has developed within the wheel, and has not become very serious. To be certain, however, lift the boot (Fig. 22) at the end (both ends on some designs) on the wheel cylinder. This should be dry inside. If it is wet, the cylinder has begun to leak, and it would be well to have the rubber piston cups replaced.

There's an honest difference of opinion between capable mechanics as to whether it pays to rebuild master cylinders and wheel cylinders on the car, or whether new or rebuilt cylinders should be installed. As the cost of labor increases and as machine production gets more efficient, there is a growing trend toward removing the old unit and installing a new one. Automotive wholesale houses are always willing to talk such matters over with garage men or car owners. In that way anyone can decide whether it is better to recondition a brake system with the aid of rebuilding kits or to recondition the system by in-

wear that gives clearance greater than .003 in. between the piston (Fig. 2) and the cylinder in which it slides. A kit to rebuild the master cylinder includes all rubber parts, with the possible addition of a check valve and main spring together with a new piston.

There are two ways of establishing brake pedal free travel. On some types you merely loosen a lock nut, and screw the piston rod in or out in order to establish the 5/16-7/16 inch of freeplay. With the type shown in Fig. 20, loosen the lock nut and turn the eccentric bolt so that the master-cylinder, piston push rod moves in or out as necessary to establish 5/16 to 7/16 inch of freeplay.

If an unaccountable loss of brake fluid is noted, don't rest until you find the leak. Should the rate of fluid loss suddenly increase, you will find yourself with no brakes. The necessity for pumping the pedal to bring the car to a stop is a danger signal that should not be ignored.

Hydraulic leaks can be of two kinds, internal and external. An internal leak may develop in the master cylinder. This may require pumping of the pedal to apply the brakes yet without loss of fluid. The fluid merely works around the piston and back into the reserve chamber. The condition is bad, but not as bad as an external leak. If an external leak is suspected, get the car on a hoist and begin inspecting at the master cylinder (Fig. 21). Raise the rubber boot at the open end of the cylinder to see if fluid is in the boot. If it is, have the cylinder rebuilt or exchanged. If there is leakage where the lines attach, try tightening them. Wipe off the excess fluid with alcohol, and if the connections do not stay tight, have the fittings renewed. Watch out for cracked lines. Go along the lines and inspect the coiled wire guards where the lines pass around the frame. Check, too, to see that the hydraulic lines

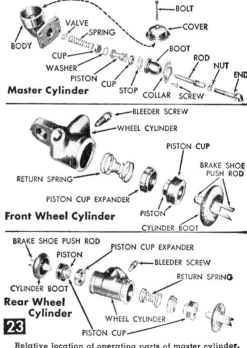

Relative location of operating parts of master cylinder, front wheel cylinder, and rear wheel cylinder as used by Chrysler.

112

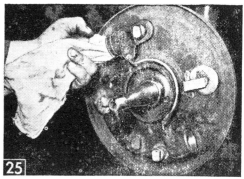

Using electric drill to drive brake cylinder hone.

Wiping out wheel cylinder after honing.

stalling new parts. Where kits are used, it is important to see that the master cylinder or wheel cylinder walls are smooth. If there is just a trace of rust present it can be polished out with steel wool. If scores are present, a specialized brake cylinder hone should be used.

The relative location of the operating parts found in a master cylinder, a front wheel cylinder, and a rear wheel cylinder on current Chrysler products is seen in Fig. 23.

When the cylinders are reconditioned with a hone operated by an electric drill as in Fig. 24, it is important to avoid overdoing the honing. If a master cylinder or wheel cylinder will not clean up before the clearance between the piston and the cylinder exceeds .003 in. then a new cylinder assembly should be installed. When

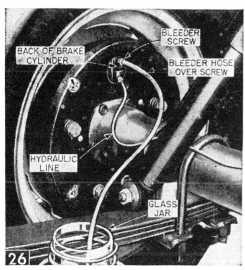

Hook-up for bleeding air from fluid in brake hydraulic system. The bleeder screw is hollow. When the screw is tight, the end seals the system. When the screw is loosened, the system is open allowing fluid and any entrapped air bubbles to pass through the bleeder hose. The hose is used for two reasons—to keep parts clean, and to prevent air from sucking back into the hydraulic system. Air is kept out by keeping the end of the bleeder hose below the level of the brake fluid in the glass jar.

finished, be sure to wipe the cylinder clean of any grit, using a clean, oilless rag (Fig. 25). Any oil is the deadly enemy of the rubber parts that operate the brake system. So as a final step before assembling, take denatured alcohol on a rag and wipe out all parts that contact rubber anywhere in the system. When all parts are mechanically right and thoroughly clean, the rubber pieces should be dipped in brake fluid to aid in their installation.

It will be recognized that as hydraulic fluid from the master cylinder is forced out into the hydraulic lines and wheel cylinders that air takes its place. In fact there is a breather hole in the filler plug on the reserve chamber of the master cylinder. This air may contain grit or moisture. Therefore, it is wise to drain, flush, and refill the hydraulic system. Some authorities have urged that this be done each year. Brake specialists have pressurized tanks for forcing fluid through the system. Any mechanically inclined motorist can accomplish the same result but with greater labor by merely using the master cylinder as a pump. Each wheel cylinder has a bleeder screw. If it is left open and the brake pedal operated, fluid will come out.

To keep from making a mess of things, a rubber tube is slipped over the bleeder screw and placed in a glass jar (Fig. 26). Bleeding is always begun at the wheel farthest from the master cylinder—the right rear wheel. The next wheel to be serviced is the left rear. From there move to the right front, and finish at the left front. On wheels using two cylinders connected in parallel, bleed the one nearest the road surface first and then the remaining one. Where cylinders at a wheel are in series, bleed the one closest to the master cylinder and then the other.

To assure good hydraulic operation if the system is not being flushed with alcohol, the bleed hose and glass jar must be used. Keeping the master cylinder reserve chamber filled at least halfway full, operate the brake pedal slowly while watching for air bubbles coming from the end of the rubber tube submerged in brake fluid in the jar. As soon as no more air bubbles appear, tighten the bleeder valve. Bleed each wheel in this way.

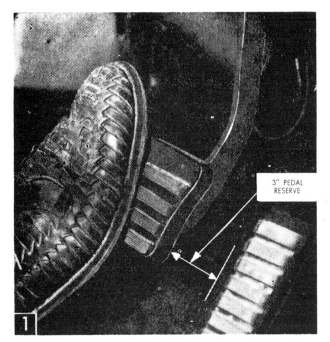

3" PEDAL
RESERVE

Three inches of reserve clearance should be maintained under continued heavy pressure on the brake pedal.

Taking the Mystery Out of Brake Repairs

Pickup-and-delivery parts supply services are now making home brake repairs practical

THERE'S no deep, dark mystery about how a car's brakes are supposed to operate. And it doesn't take a master mechanic to spot the most common brake ailments or to actually make the necessary repairs and adjustments.

Working carefully, you can do a safe, sure job of brake repairing, and count on $4-5 savings for each hour you work.

To determine whether your brakes need servicing, first check out their performance

with this simple road test, performed on a deserted parking lot if possible. While driving in a straight line at 15-20 mph, try a quick stop.

See if any of the tire marks in the gravel are heavier than others or if the rear wheels have swerved out of line. Try the same test again, but ease up on the steering wheel as you stop. If the wheel spins to one side, you know the brakes are not equalized and are dangerous on slippery roads. Now let the car coast and listen to the brakes while they are applied and released slowly. Carefully note any noise or faulty operation and then check the symptoms on Table A for possible causes. We will locate the defect exactly by eliminating the most easily checked and repaired causes first.

Pedal Clearance. Let the car set a few minutes after the road test and then push the brake pedal down hard and hold it there. Then see how much clearance or *reserve* (Fig. 1) you have between the brake pedal and the floorboards. If this clearance is less than 3 in., check the fluid reservoir (Fig. 2) at the master cylinder to make sure the fluid is within ⅜ in. of the threads on the filler neck. This reservoir is usually part of the master cylinder, or else it is a small tank connected to it by a line. If the fluid level is low, refill with a heavy-duty, nationally-available brand that is guaranteed to mix with all other brake fluids. Then repeat the pedal reserve test.

Free Play Test. Next, let's test the brake pedal for *free play*. Apply just enough pressure on the pedal with your fingers to move it. The pedal should move about ½ in. before you feel the resistance of the master cylinder piston. If there is less, the piston is not returning to its normal "brakes-off" position and is blocking the compensating port. Consequently some of the fluid pressure may be retained, preventing the brakes from releas-

114

VENTS

2

Always clean around the master cylinder before opening it and be sure vents in cap are not clogged. Keep reservoir filled to ⅜ in. of threads.

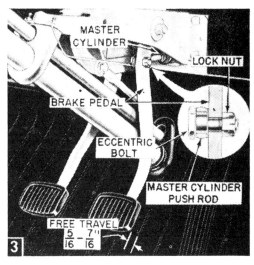

MASTER CYLINDER

BRAKE PEDAL

LOCK NUT

ECCENTRIC BOLT

MASTER CYLINDER PUSH ROD

FREE TRAVEL $\frac{5}{16} - \frac{7}{16}$"

3

After loosening the lock nut, turn the eccentric bolt to provide $\frac{5}{16} - \frac{7}{16}$ in. free play.

ing completely. Adjustment for free play is usually made by loosening the lock nut on the push rod between the brake pedal and the master cylinder. Then adjust the travel of the rod by turning it until the correct amount of free play is obtained. On some Ford cars, the free play is adjusted by turning an eccentric bolt (Fig. 3).

Adjusting the Brakes. If your check this far does not indicate fluid leaks and if no noise was heard while coasting and braking, your next step is to adjust the brakes and repeat the tests. Generally speaking, there are two common methods of adjusting brakes, and you will find that these vary with the year and make of automobile. The most common of these is the *star wheel* system (Fig. 5).

To adjust this type of brake, raise the wheel, remove the oblong rubber dust plug from the back plate and insert a screwdriver or brake adjusting tool (Fig. 6). By working the tool in a prying motion, you will be able to turn the star wheel inside the drum until the shoes are expanded to their limit and the wheel is locked tight. Then, by prying in the opposite direction, back off the star wheel just enough to let the wheel turn freely. Apply and release the brakes several times, and check again for shoe drag by rotating the wheel. If there is any drag, readjust until the wheel turns freely. Be sure to replace the rubber plug.

The second type of adjustment is an *eccentric cam* (Fig. 7). The cam adjustment may be made at the back plate with a wrench or through a hole in the front of the drum using a screwdriver. The adjustment is the same regardless of the method used to turn the cam. Working on one shoe at a time, rotate the cam until the brake shoe is tight against

the drum and the wheel is locked. Now back off the cam just enough to allow the wheel to turn without the shoe dragging. Repeat the operation on the other cam and brake shoe and then check as with the star wheel system.

Hydraulic Line Inspection. Now with the car indoors, continue your inspection by getting under it with a flashlight to inspect the hydraulic lines (Fig. 4). These lines should be firm and dry. Replace a line if there is the slightest trace of brake fluid or oil on the covering or if it shows signs of gumminess and softening.

Although they are less subject to damage or deterioration, the metal lines that connect the master cylinder with the flexible lines should also be checked carefully. Check for leaking connections, dents, loose fastenings at the frame, and for signs of abrasion or wear on the guards where the line bends around

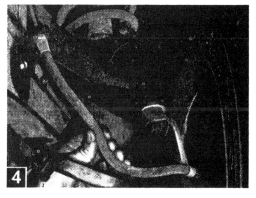

4

Particular attention should be given to the front brake lines where grease from the suspension can contact and deteriorate rubber hoses.

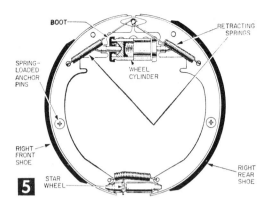

BOOT

RETRACTING SPRINGS

SPRING-LOADED ANCHOR PINS

WHEEL CYLINDER

RIGHT FRONT SHOE

RIGHT REAR SHOE

STAR WHEEL

5

the frame. While you are under the car, check the parking brake cables for wear and the inside of the wheels for bearing grease leaks. Such a leak can affect the operation of your brakes due to grease entering the brake drum and soaking the linings.

Now inspect the master cylinder closely for leakage. Leaks at the brake line connection can often be corrected by tightening, but if the fluid is coming from around the piston rod, the master cylinder is in need of overhauling and must be removed. To remove it, disconnect the brake line, remove the wires from the stoplight switch and unfasten the push rod from the pedal. Then remove the mounting bolts and lift out the cylinder for rebuilding as described later in this article.

Continue your brake check by removing a front and a rear brake drum to inspect the linings and shoe mechanisms. Don't decide whether relining is necessary on the basis of a front or rear wheel alone. It is true that the front linings wear faster, but a poorly adjusted, dragging parking brake can put wear on the rear shoes in a hurry.

In the classified section of your phone book, locate an auto parts dealer who advertises pick up and delivery machine shop service. Go to see him to make certain he has all the parts you may need to complete the brake overhaul and get an estimate of their cost. Also, while you are there, borrow or rent a universal wheel puller (Fig. 9) to remove your rear brake drums. There is seldom a charge for the use of this tool when accompanied by a parts order.

Now block up the car and place a piece of wood under the brake pedal to prevent it from accidentally being pushed while the drums are removed. Remove the hubcap and dust cap from a front wheel and then, without removing the wheel, pull the cotter pin and remove the castle nut from the

TABLE A—WHAT'S THE MATTER WITH YOUR BRAKES?

Here Are the Possible Causes . . .   And Solutions . . .

IF BRAKES PULL CAR TO ONE SIDE:

1. Tires unevenly inflated or worn unevenly	Replace with matched tires on each side and inflate equally
2. Shoes need adjustment	Adjust brakes
3. Back plate or wheel bearings loose	Tighten plate; replace and/or adjust bearings
4. Grease or fluid soaked lining on one wheel, lining charred	Replace linings and repair grease or fluid leak
5. Moisture or mud on shoes	Clean out brake assembly with water if muddy. Drive slowly and maintain light pressure on brakes until friction dries lining. Replace rubber plug in back plate if necessary.
6. Drum scored or out of round	Regrind or replace drums
7. Dissimilar linings on one side of car	Replace with matched linings
8. Weak or loose chassis spring	Tighten or replace worn part
9. Worn king pins	Replace worn parts

IF ONE BRAKE DRAGS:

1. Shoe clearance insufficient	Readjust dragging brake
2. Hydraulic line clogged or crimped	Flush system or replace line
3. Loose wheel bearings	Tighten or replace bearings
4. Weak or broken brake return spring	Replace spring
5. Shoe sticking on anchor pins	Lube anchor pins and other contact points
6. Wheel cylinder pistons sticking	Hone cylinder and replace piston

IF BRAKES ARE HARSH OR GRAB:

1. Linings are wet or damp	Drive car slowly while maintaining light pressure on brake pedal until friction dries linings
2. Back plate loose	Tighten back plate screws
3. Charred, grease soaked or improper linings	Replace linings
4. Drums scored	Regrind or replace drums

IF BRAKES SQUEAK:

1. Loose wheel bearings	Replace and/or adjust bearings
2. Metallic particles or dust imbedded in lining, worn lining	Replace lining
3. Bent back plate	Repair or replace backplate
4. Bent shoes	Check installation and replace shoes

IF BRAKES KNOCK:

1. Roughly finished or warped drum	Replace or regrind drum
2. Secondary shoe clearance insufficient at anchor	Adjust anchor eccentric
3. Adjusting slot in shoe is not square	Repair or replace shoe

IF THERE'S INADEQUATE RESERVE CLEARANCE AT BRAKE PEDAL:

1. Low fluid level in master cylinder	Add fluid
2. Pedal and/or shoes need adjustment	Adjust pedal and shoes
3. Air or fluid vapor trapped in system	Bleed system
4. Fluid leak in system	Repair or replace defective lines or cylinders
5. Worn lining	Replace lining

IF ALL BRAKES DRAG AFTER ADJUSTMENT:

1. Vent in filler cap is clogged	Clean vent
2. Inadequate freeplay at pedal	Adjust master cylinder push rod or brake pedal eccentric bolt
3. Brake lines clogged or crimped	Replace line and/or flush system
4. Rubber pistons swollen	Check and replace brake fluid

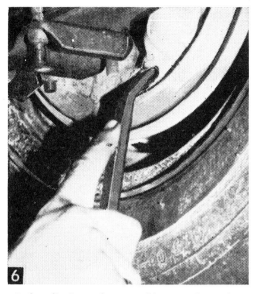

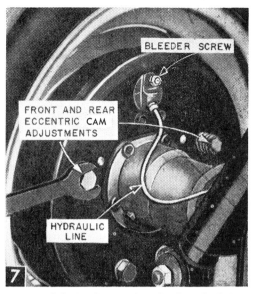

6 Brake adjusting tool or screwdriver may be used to turn star wheel in either direction.

7 Here each brake shoe is adjusted independently by means of eccentric cams.

BLEEDER SCREW

FRONT AND REAR
ECCENTRIC CAM
ADJUSTMENTS

HYDRAULIC
LINE

8 Inexpensive equipment such as a brake spring pliers and a wheel cylinder clamp can speed up brake system overhaul.

Dust cap and castle nut are removed and wheel puller screw is tightened against axle. Light hammering on striking anvils frees drum and wheel.

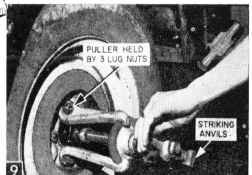

9 PULLER HELD BY 3 LUG NUTS

STRIKING ANVILS.

spindle. Get a good grip on the two sides of the tire, wiggle it a bit, and pull straight back. The tire, wheel, brake drum and wheel bearing should slide off easily as a unit.

To remove a rear brake drum, use a universal wheel puller. After removing dust cap, cotter pin and castle nut, fasten the three arms of the wheel puller under three lug nuts of the wheel and then turn the screw until it is against the axle shaft (Fig. 9). Rap on the striking anvil with a hammer until the drum comes free.

On some models, particularly the Chrysler products, the rear drums are mounted

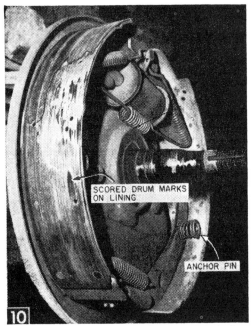

SCORED DRUM MARKS ON LINING

ANCHOR PIN

10

This pair of badly worn brake shoes scored the brake drum beyond repair.

by a method somewhat similar to that on the front wheels. The drum, however, is kept from rotating on the axle by means of slotted keyways in the drum and shaft and a steel key. This type of drum can be removed by hand.

Lining Inspection. As soon as the drum is removed, brush the dust off of all parts and make a close visual inspection of the linings, brake drums and wheel cylinders. If the shoes are to be removed, label each one to show its location (Fig. 5). Don't mark on the linings; when they are replaced, the marks will be lost. It may help you to remember the location of the springs and pins if you make a sketch of the assembly for a front and rear wheel.

If the linings are worn down to within $\frac{1}{32}$

BOOT

11

If no trace of brake fluid leakage is found inside the rubber boot on the wheel cylinder, you can assume the cylinder is in good condition.

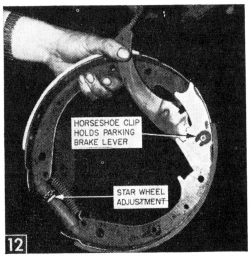

HORSESHOE CLIP HOLDS PARKING BRAKE LEVER

STAR WHEEL ADJUSTMENT

12

After rear brake shoe assembly is removed as a unit, knock out the horseshoe washer and pin with a screwdriver to disconnect parking brake lever.

in. of the rivets you will need new linings. New Ford linings are approximately $\frac{3}{16}$ in. thick, and the factory recommends replacement when they are worn to less than $\frac{3}{32}$ in. Many states have adopted inspection rules requiring replacement of brake linings when they are worn to 40% of their original thickness. For safety's sake, also change linings if they have become coated with brake fluid or grease.

To remove the brake shoes, first unhook the retractor spring (Fig. 5). This spring is most easily removed with a special pliers (Fig. 8) that can be purchased for about $2. You can use an ordinary pliers, but it takes a powerful grip and extra care not to let the spring slip.

Tie a cord around the wheel cylinder or use the special clamp (Fig. 8) to keep the pistons from popping out of the cylinder when the shoes are removed. Then, if the shoes are held to the back plate by a spring-loaded pin, compress the spring, turn it 90° and release it to free the brake shoes.

When disassembling the rear brakes, remove both shoes, the parking lever, the shoe adjusting screw and its lock spring as a unit (Fig. 12). Then disconnect the parking brake lever from the shoes and just let it hang from the cable.

Drum Inspection. If the linings have worn down to the rivets and the drum is scored deeply enough to have made lengthwise marks on the shoes (Fig. 10), have the drum reground at a brake shop. Brake drums should be replaced if there are any signs of cracking, warping or heat discoloration. The number of times a drum can be reground depends on the amount of metal removed during grinding. Since .030 in. is the maximum amount that can be safely removed, drums can seldom be reground a second time.

Check to see if there is a sharp shoulder at the back edge of the braking surface in the drum. This means the drum has been reground at least once and that if it is deeply scored now it is likely the drum must be exchanged. In either case, wire the labeled brake shoes and their drum together so they can be sent to the brake shop as a unit and the shoes fitted to that drum or its replacement.

Now turn up the edge of each of the rubber boots (Fig. 11) on the wheel cylinders to see if fluid has been leaking by the piston. Also check along the back plate for signs of leaking. If there is the slightest amount of leakage, all of the cylinders probably need service.

Your next step is to order the replacement parts from your retail auto parts dealer.

If your car is in need of a complete brake overhaul, order a rebuilding kit for each wheel cylinder and one for the master cylinder, along with a hone for the cylinder bores. Also ask to have the brake shoes relined and, if necessary, have the drums reground. With this, purchase a quart each of heavy-duty brake fluid and a brake line flushing compound. If all of these materials are necessary, you will have spent between $15 and $20 as the total expense for your brake overhaul; a small fraction of the cost of having it done.

Since the replacement parts for rebuilding the cylinders may differ slightly in appearance from the original, check to see that there are instructions for assembling them in each kit. Also see that the brake shoes are still with the correct drums by checking the markings you have made during disassembly.

Then remove the boot and brake shoe push rod from each wheel cylinder (Fig. 13) and gently press against one of the pistons until the opposite piston and its rubber cup are forced out of the other end of the cylinder. Remove the piston spring and push the remaining piston and cup out from the other side. If the brake system has two wheel cylinders (Fig. 16), one end of each cylinder will be closed and the piston must be forced out by applying a light pressure on the brake pedal. On some models there is also an expander (Fig. 14) located between the end of the piston spring and the cup which should also be replaced.

Honing. Chuck the cylinder hone into a ¼-in. electric drill and lubricate the hone by dipping it into a jar of clean brake fluid. Then fit the hone into the wheel cylinder, turn on the drill and move the hone with an even back and forth motion (Fig. 15). Be careful not to let the stones slip out of the cylinder while the drill is running as they are held in spring clips and will fly dangerously when

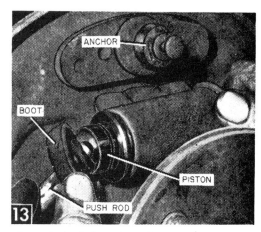

Rear wheel cylinder activates both shoes with equal pressure on two pistons.

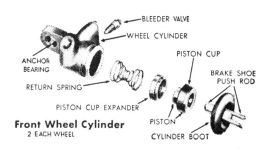

Front Wheel Cylinder
2 EACH WHEEL

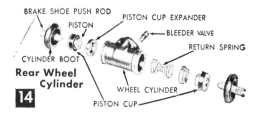

Rear Wheel Cylinder

Wheel cylinders are most easily and economically honed while in place on back plate.

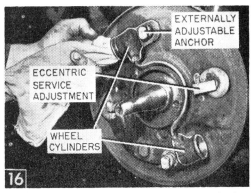

In this example anchored end of shoe at wheel cylinder is externally adjustable in addition to an eccentric cam service adjustment.

placement-type cylinder, unlike piston-type cylinders, does not require honing. In all other ways the service for this master cylinder is the same as that for the piston type.

Check the bore and the valve seat at the end of the bore for rust or corrosion and clean, if necessary, with crocus cloth or a commercial rust remover. Follow the same procedure for honing the master cylinder as was used on the wheel cylinders if the bore is pitted or scratched. Then reassemble the cylinder with the new parts from the kit, following the enclosed instructions.

Install the master cylinder in the car (Fig. 19), connecting the lines and the stoplight switch and being sure the push rod is lined up to work freely before tightening the mounting bolts. Adjust the freeplay (Fig. 3)

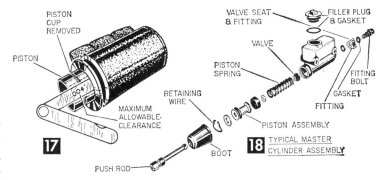

turning free. Also don't overhone the cylinder bore as a few seconds are all that is necessary to clean up most cylinders.

Now inspect the cylinder bore. When it looks bright and free from scratches, wipe it thoroughly with a soft clean cloth (Fig. 16) dampened with brake line cleaner. Then insert one of the new pistons and check the clearance between the piston and the cylinder wall (Fig. 17) with a feeler gage. This clearance must not be more than .004 in. If it's over .004, which is very unlikely, you'll have to get oversize pistons or replace the cylinder housings. Hone all of the wheel cylinders and check each of them in the same way.

Master Cylinder Overhaul. Then mount your master cylinder in a vise and clean the outside of it thoroughly before beginning disassembly. Position the cylinder so the push rod from the pedal is toward you and you will see either a retaining wire (Fig. 18) or a metal collar held with a pair of capscrews. Remove this retainer first so you can take out the piston, piston cups, spring and valve from the cylinder. Lay these parts out in order for reference when assembling the new parts, but do not under any circumstances use them when reassembling the cylinder. The exact number and style of the parts will differ with each make and year of car, but are basically the same as in Fig. 18.

Some Buick cars in the late 1950's have a unique master cylinder in which the piston does not fit against the cylinder walls. This cylinder is serviced by separating the cast housings and removing the retaining wire to expose the long, rod-like piston. This dis-

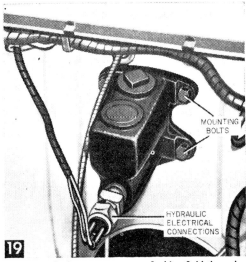

Master cylinder serves to pump flushing fluid through brake lines before wheel cylinder is assembled.

as described on p. 65. If it is necessary to replace any of the hydraulic lines, do so now. No sealer of any kind is necessary or desirable here as the brass fittings will make a very tight seal under moderate pressure.

Brake Line Flushing. Pack each wheel cyl-

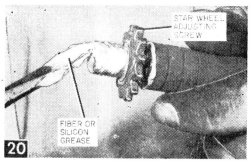

Lubrication of mechanical parts with high temperature grease provides like-new brake operation.

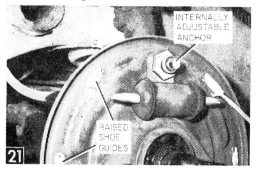

Internally adjustable anchors here, necessitating special gage for adjustment, should not be disturbed during brake overhaul.

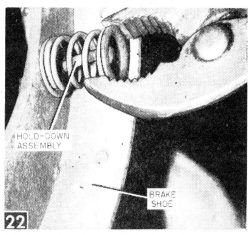

Spring loaded pin assembly holds this brake shoe to back plate.

inder with a clean cloth and fill the master cylinder with the brake line cleaning fluid. Then remove the cloth from one cylinder at a time and flush the brake line by pumping the fluid through it with the brake pedal. Refill the reservoir and continue this until the distinct color of the cleaner can be seen when it is forced out at the wheel cylinders.

Pump the cylinder until the system is empty and then reassemble the wheel cylinders according to the instructions in the kits. Lubricate all the new parts with brake fluid before assembly and insert them from the end of the cylinder in which they will operate. Don't try to push the cups through from one end as the rubber parts may snag on the bleeder or inlet hole and be damaged. If trapped air forces one piston out when you insert the other, open the bleeder valve to relieve the pressure.

If any of the parts become dirty while they are being assembled, rinse them in the brake line cleaning fluid, allow them to dry and then dip them into fresh brake fluid again. *Caution:* do not use the brake fluid that has been used for lubricating these parts or the hone to refill the master cylinder as it will contain grit and air bubbles. Also do not allow any oil or grease to come into contact with the cylinder assembly as it will deteriorate the rubber parts. When the wheel cylinders

have been completely assembled, snap on the boots and push rods and secure them temporarily by tying or using clamps (Fig. 8).

Brake Shoe Assembly. Before installing the brake shoe assembly, coat the threads and contact surfaces (Fig. 20) of the adjusting screw with a high temperature fiber or silicon grease. Also coat the raised shoe guides (Fig. 21) on the back plate with this grease.

Then mount each brake shoe on its anchor pin (Figs. 16 & 21) and set it in the cylinder push rod slots. On Bendix type brakes, screw the adjusting screw all the way in, that is, make it as short as possible and fit it between the lower ends of the shoes. Assemble the hold-down pins (Fig. 23) by placing the plates over the spring and pin, compressing the spring and turning the assembly 90°. On other type brakes, turn the eccentric cam adjustment so its low point will be against the shoe. Finally, secure the entire assembly with the retracting springs.

Be sure to replace the parking brake lever (Fig. 12) on the rear wheel by connecting it to the shoe with the pin and then crimping the horseshoe washer over the pin end (Fig. 24). Repack the front wheels and replace the grease seals in the hubs if necessary. Then fit the drum over the shoe assembly. On brake assemblies where both ends of the shoes fit in slots, it may be necessary to center the shoes somewhat to install the drum. Do this by moving each shoe in the right direction by hitting it with a soft mallet or the heel of your hand.

Be sure to replace the key and lock washer on the rear drum and then draw all of the hubs up tight. Back off the front axle nut to the next cotter pin slot, insert a new pin and replace the dust cover. If the rear brake drum is fastened to the hub with sheet metal nuts, use new ones when reassembling.

Bleeding. Before replacing the wheels,

bleed the entire brake system of air. The principle of operation in a hydraulic system is built around the fact that fluids are not compressible. The presence of even a small quantity of air, which is easily compressible, will seriously affect its efficiency. Your car is equipped with bleeder valves (Fig. 24) which allow this air to escape when they are opened, but it is up to you to see that air is not drawn back into the system.

You can bleed your brakes by having a helper operate the brake pedal while you control the flow of fluid through the bleeder valves. First close all the valves and then fill the master cylinder. Replace the cap and have your helper pump the brake pedal a few times. Then check the level of the fluid again and add more if necessary. Now have him hold a steady pressure on the pedal while you open the bleeder valve with a small wrench (Fig. 24).

Check the color of the fluid that escapes to be sure the cleaner is completely expelled. The fluid will squirt through the valve with a sputtering sound until there is no more air in the line. This may take two or three pumps of the pedal. Your helper should let you know each time the pedal is just about to the floorboard so you can close the valve while there is still pressure in the line. Check the master cylinder reservoir after each wheel is bled and keep it filled to the proper level.

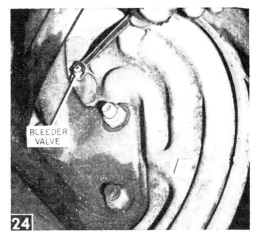

Screw-type bleeder valve releases air and fluid as it is turned counter clockwise. Valve must be closed while brake fluid is still under pressure to prevent air from entering system.

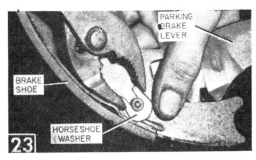

Horseshoe washer is crimped into slot to hold pin connecting parking brake lever to rear shoe.

Bleeding attachments are available which will allow you to do this job by yourself. These will usually have three fittings to adapt to all cars and will have a ball-check valve to prevent air from being drawn into the system when the pedal is released.

When all points have been bled, the pedal action should be firm and should maintain the correct reserve clearance (Fig. 1) under continued pressure. On the second pump of the pedal the reserve should be no greater than on the first pump. If this is not the case, repeat the bleeding operation. If the second bleeding still does not provide the proper pedal action, check for leaks that may have been overlooked during assembly.

The next step is to service-adjust the brakes. Be careful during reassembly and adjustment not to disturb the eccentric anchor adjustments (Fig. 21) that are present on most brake systems. These points are used for major adjustment only. Anchor adjustment is not difficult, but it is rather time-consuming without professional equipment and so should not be attempted unless absolutely necessary.

If the check list on p. 66 indicated that anchor adjustment is required and the symptoms are still present after overhaul, you can make the anchor adjustments provided they are of the externally adjusted type (Fig. 16). Turn each anchor until the wheel is locked and then back it off until the wheel turns freely. Continue the adjustment in this way, alternating between each of the anchors and the star wheel (Fig. 6) or eccentric (Fig. 7), until further adjustment does not make any improvement.

Some brake systems have a small slot in the drum or back plate to allow the clearance to be checked with a feeler gage inserted between the anchor end of the brake shoe and the drum surface. The clearance at this point should be set at about .010 in. by turning the anchor adjustment.

Brake shoes, like most equipment on your car, should be broken in carefully for long, trouble-free use. Allow the shoes about 100 miles of moderate use before attempting mountainous roads or frequent fast stops. After 100 miles make another service-adjustment as before and recheck the lines for leaks.

Then, with these service-adjustments and inspections at 5,000-mile intervals, the brake system overhaul as described will provide safe, carefree service for 30,000 miles.

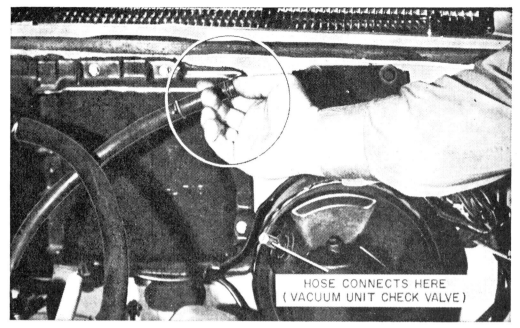

HOSE CONNECTS HERE
(VACUUM UNIT CHECK VALVE)

FIG. 1: Basic power brake booster test is vacuum check made with thumb with engine idling and hose slipped off connector on vacuum check valve (circle).

Power Brakes

How the power assisted braking system operates and what you can do to keep it working right

SO-CALLED power brakes are not really power brakes at all. Power assist from engine vacuum helps you push down the brake pedal of an otherwise ordinary hydraulic brake system. All makes of power brakes or more exactly power boosters used on American cars are similar in operation, maintenance and troubleshooting.

Basically the power booster is a vacuum operated cylinder added between the brake pedal and the hydraulic master cylinder. When you even touch the brake pedal lightly, vacuum sucks a piston forward to push hydraulic fluid from the master cylinder into the brake lines and out to each wheel cylinder (Fig. 7). Without power assist, your foot pedal linkage pushes directly on the piston

FIG. 2: Vacuum check valve (circle) can usually be removed from power cylinder with unit still in place.

HOSE CONNECTS HERE

FIG. 3: Screwdriver or pencil inserted in manifold end of vacuum hose spots brake fluid leak which indicates serious trouble with power brake booster unit.

FIG. 4: Internal air filter for power brake cylinder is exposed for cleaning by dismounting unit from car.

FIG. 5: Flexible hoses can deteriorate and leak hydraulic fluid so should be inspected periodically.

in the master cylinder. (This is what gives non-power brakes much better feel and controlability than power brakes even though it takes more leg power to operate them.)

Most vacuum brake booster units have three major parts: vacuum cylinder, vacuum piston with built-in control valve, and end plate with bracket and lever assembly. Vacuum to power the unit comes from a tube attached to the intake manifold of the engine.

When your foot is off the brake pedal, the vacuum unit is in the released position (Fig. 6). The vacuum port to the engine remains closed, but the atmospheric port is open. Air can pass freely from one side of the piston to the other. With equal pressure on both sides, the return spring holds the piston in the off position. Another port, the compensating port, between the vacuum cylinder and the hydraulic master cylinder is also open. This lets hydraulic fluid from the brake lines return to the master cylinder.

When you touch the brake pedal, the atmospheric port closes and the vacuum port opens. Vacuum from the intake manifold then sucks the piston forward against the pressure of the return spring. This motion pushes the operating rod in the hydraulic

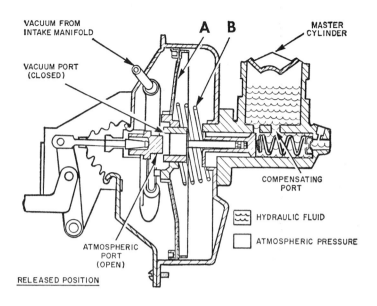

FIG. 6: Diagram shows vacuum power cylinder in released position with air pressure equal on both sides power piston (A) located by return spring (B).

VACUUM FROM INTAKE MANIFOLD

A B

MASTER CYLINDER

VACUUM PORT (CLOSED)

COMPENSATING PORT

HYDRAULIC FLUID

ATMOSPHERIC PRESSURE

ATMOSPHERIC PORT (OPEN)

RELEASED POSITION

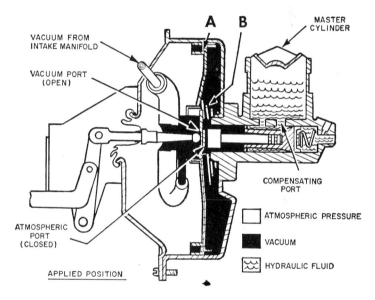

FIG. 7: Power cylinder, brakes fully applied, shows how piston (A) has been sucked forward by engine vacuum compressing spring (B) and forcing piston (C) in hydraulic brake master cylinder to apply brakes.

VACUUM FROM INTAKE MANIFOLD

A B

MASTER CYLINDER

VACUUM PORT (OPEN)

COMPENSATING PORT

ATMOSPHERIC PRESSURE

VACUUM

HYDRAULIC FLUID

ATMOSPHERIC PORT (CLOSED)

APPLIED POSITION

master cylinder to apply the brakes (Fig. 7).

Should the power booster fail, then the operating rod for the power system would move forward to push directly on the operating rod for the master cylinder hydraulic piston. Thus, when you stepped on the brake pedal, you would notice slightly longer pedal travel and increased braking effort, but you could still stop the car.

Trouble shooting power brakes calls for some simple tests you can make yourself. As with power steering systems, you can repair leaks in connections and hoses yourself, or replace the whole vacuum unit with a rebuilt; but very possibly, repairs to this unit may require special tools and skills as well.

Start by testing booster operation. Shut off the engine and pump the brake pedal several times to exhaust all vacuum in the system. Older model power brake systems often incorporate a vacuum reservoir tank, so these may take a few more pumps on the pedal to clear them of vacuum.

Now step on the brake pedal and hold it down firmly while you restart the engine. If the vacuum system is working right, the brake pedal will move forward slightly when

125

the engine starts. No movement and a pedal that feels hard mean the vacuum unit is not working.

The fault may lie in the unit, or it may not be getting any vacuum. Check by removing the vacuum hose from the power cylinder (Fig. 1). Hold your thumb over the open end of the hose; you should be able to feel the suction.

No vacuum at the hose means there is a leak in the system, or the engine is not in good shape. Check the hose for kinks, collapsed areas, or tears. Replace the hose if defective.

If the hose is OK, but you still get no suction check for vacuum at the intake manifold. A vacuum gauge should show 17 to 21 in. with the engine idling. If it does not, check first for manifold leaks. A quick way is to idle the engine after putting oil on the joints at carburetor flange to intake manifold and intake manifold to cylinder block. If there is a leak, vacuum will suck in the oil to seal it temporarily. With proper vacuum, the engine will speed up. Fix the leaky joint by tightening the attachment bolts, or if this does not work by replacing the gasket.

If you find no leaks, lack of manifold vacuum points to the need for an engine tune up or possibly even an overhaul.

If there is vacuum at the hose, but the booster unit does not work, the vacuum booster itself is at fault. Before removing the unit from the car, test the vacuum check valve, a common cause of trouble.

The vacuum check valve (Figs. 1 and 2) is a one-way affair which lets air be sucked out of the vacuum booster into the intake manifold, but doesn't let the vacuum out of the unit when the engine is shut off. To remove it from the cylinder, disconnect the vacuum hose and simply unscrew the valve (Fig. 2). In most systems you can do this without removing the vacuum cylinder from the car.

Check the valve by blowing through it first one way and then the other. No air should come out the end to which the vacuum hose is attached, but you should be able to blow through other end. If the valve is faulty, replace it.

If the valve is in good condition but the unit still does not operate, you must remove the vacuum unit from the car. Further disassembly and inspection should be performed by a serviceman experienced in vacuum unit repair who has the proper tools for the job. He can repair the unit for you, or you can exchange it for a new or rebuilt unit.

You can, however, test your vacuum unit to see if it is causing the brakes to drag. This can wear out one set of linings after another in addition to cutting deeply into your fuel mileage.

First make sure brake shoes are properly adjusted and that wheels turn freely. Raise the front end of the car and start both front wheels spinning. Immediately start the engine and let it idle. Keep your foot off the brake pedal. Each front wheel should coast to a stop and still turn freely. If one or both stops more quickly than it should, or if you can feel a noticeable drag, there is trouble in the vacuum unit. You may have to have it repaired or even replaced.

You can also test the hydraulic brake system through which the power booster works. This is exactly the same as the hydraulic brake system in a car without power brakes.

To test the hydraulic system, release vacuum by applying the pedal several times with the engine off. Then brace your foot on the brake pedal and hold it there for a minute or more. If the pedal holds firm, your hydraulics are in good shape. If it gradually sinks to the floor under continued pressure, then fluid is leaking somewhere. Correct this by inspecting flexible hoses (Fig. 5) and other brake pipes for leaks. Replace faulty hoses or tighten leaky connections. If moderate tightening does not cure the leak, replace the fitting. Leaks at the master cylinder or in the wheel cylinders should be fixed promptly because loss of hydraulic fluid can cause complete brake failure even when the power assist system is working perfectly.

Power booster units all have a filter to clean the air drawn into the system. On some boosters this filter is external and can be removed for cleaning. Check the workshop manual for your car to see if it has this type of filter and how often it should be serviced. Many makes have an internal filter (Fig. 4) which only needs servicing when the booster cylinder is removed from the car.

To clean either type of filter, wash it in alcohol or some other non-oil base solvent. Gasoline or similar solvents should be avoided because they can damage rubber parts in the braking system.

One last check completes the work you can do on your power brake system. Make sure no brake fluid is being sucked through the vacuum line into the intake manifold. To do this, remove the vacuum hose from the intake manifold and run a screwdriver or pencil around the inside of the open end. If it comes out wet with brake fluid, there is a serious leak past the vacuum cylinder piston. The whole unit will have to be rebuilt or replaced to cure this leakage. If it continues, the engine will idle roughly, perform poorly, and hydraulic fluid can form gums which cause sticking valves and may create a variety of other problems.

These simple checks will enable you to tell when your power brake booster is working properly. When it is not, they will help you pinpoint the trouble, and in many cases you can cure it yourself.

DISC BRAKES
OPERATION AND SERVICE

Not only are your discs self-adjusting but they're a snap to re-pad

A FACT is that your brakes fade, or lose effectiveness, as they get hot. Another fact is that disc brakes dissipate heat better than drum brakes. Conclusion: let's have disc brakes. But this simple bit of logic is definitely an oversimplification of the disc brakes versus drum brakes argument. Indeed, drum brakes outperform discs when both are cool:

but drum brakes, except for the most advanced designs, just can't match the relatively fade-free performance of the discs when stopping from high speeds on today's turnpikes.

So, a lot of cars are offering discs. Many European cars have had discs for years, and Chrysler products were offering them more

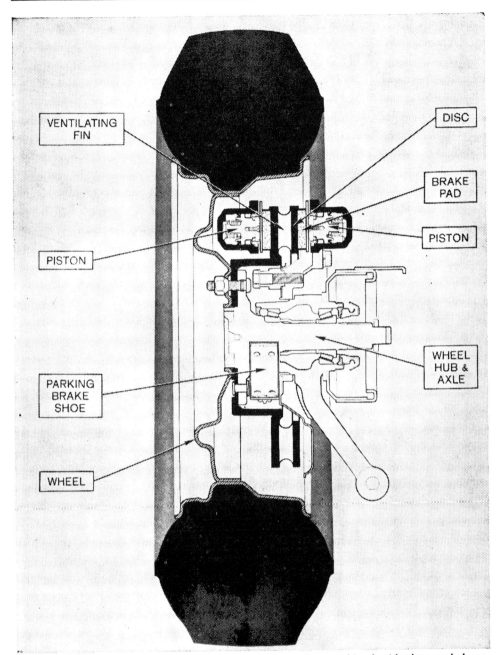

VENTILATING FIN

DISC

BRAKE PAD

PISTON

PISTON

WHEEL HUB & AXLE

PARKING BRAKE SHOE

WHEEL

Cross sectional top view of Corvette rear wheel shows disc combined with shoe and drum.

than a decade ago. But 1965 is definitely the year that the discs have hit any sort of stride. Four-wheel discs are standard on Corvette, and front-wheel discs are standard on Lincoln Continental and Thunderbird, optional on Barracuda, Mustang and Ramblers. And you can buy kits for Corvair, older Corvettes, and even motorcycles.

How They Work. The indication is clear that there's a disc braking system in your automotive future, no matter what kind of car you plan to buy. And if you're among

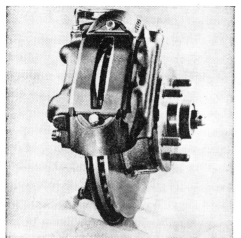

Kelsey-Hayes disc used on Ford and Barracuda. Note cover plate to retain friction pads.

The friction pads are visible with cover removed. Note wear-indicating slots in pads.

Disassembled Corvette rear brake shows disc at the left, conventional brake for parking at the right.

Pad replacement on Kelsey-Hayes system is easy; just pull out.

the *earlybirds* with discs now, your interest should be very keen. Let's take a close look at the various disc systems, show how their components work, and give you a general guide to disc brake service.

Instead of a drum, against which semicircular brake shoes are pushed by wheel cylinders, there's a flat circular disc. This disc rotates with the wheel, just like the brake drum in the other system.

A flat pad, covered with a slab of brake lining, is held a few thousandths of an inch away from the disc by a hydraulic clamping assembly called a caliper. Each wheel on

most systems has a fixed-in-position caliper, (bolted to the steering linkage) which holds a lined pad at each side of the disc. The caliper, with the pad held in position, is poised for action, much like the jaws of a large vise ready to clamp a piece of material in position.

When you step on the brake pedal, the hydraulic fluid pushes out on a piston in the caliper cylinder, which pushes each friction pad against the spinning disc, to stop the car. The caliper with its cylinder is very much like the wheel cylinder in the drum brake system.

The usual American design has two cylinders in each half of the caliper. The imported

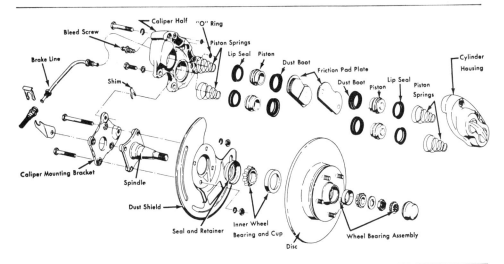

This exploded view of the Rambler disc brake system shows all the components of the caliper assemblies. Pad replacement on the Rambler system requires removal of caliper.

At the right is the Renault floating disc system. Note, in this top view, that the caliper is held to a bracket by king-size cotter pins at both the top and bottom.

cars, except for Renault, have only one in each half. Renault, which uses a *floating* caliper to be discussed, has only a single cylinder in the whole caliper, although it does have a friction pad in each half of the caliper.

The beauty of a disc is that it spins exposed to the air, which means that it dissipates a lot of heat very quickly. Most European discs are exactly that, flat, solid slabs. But many American discs are actually two discs sandwiching a set of radial fins, for even better heat dissipation.

Some disc systems use a metal shield to keep road splash, rocks, etc., off the disc. But the disc is essentially self-cleaning, since centrifugal force spins foreign matter off the disc.

The drum brake system enjoys low pedal pressure because you can take advantage of the wrap-around action of the drum to help wedge the shoes against the drum. This is called the *self-energizing* effect.

The drum brake also can maintain a small amount of pressure in the hydraulic system (called residual pressure), for fast response when you step on the brake pedal.

Disc Design. The disc brake has neither of these factors going for it, so a power booster is a must for a large car. And the disc must be kept very close to the pad, for the same reason.

This means that the disc system must be constantly self-adjusting. As the lining wears, the caliper cylinder piston moves outward, assuming a more extended position. Unlike the drum brake, which has return springs on the shoes to force the piston back all the way, the caliper piston holds its new position. Whatever retracting mechanism is used merely pulls the piston back far enough to provide running clearance between the pad and disc.

In the Ford and Barracuda systems, the caliper cylinder has circular rubber seals in recesses in the cylinder bore itself. As the piston moves outward to apply the brakes, the seals flex outward. When the brake pedal

130

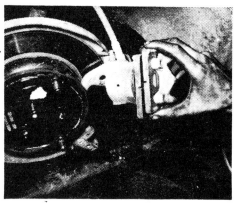

When cotter pin is removed from Renault system, hinge swings down, permitting removal of caliper section. When pads are removed, the caliper piston assembly is exposed (below). See text for tips on reseating piston.

Removal of the caliper section with the friction pads inside is easily accomplished as shown above. Shown below is the Renault friction pad. Note the single slot designed in to indicate degree of wear of the pad.

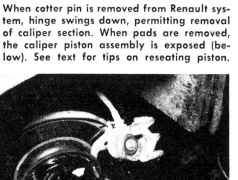

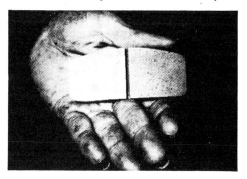

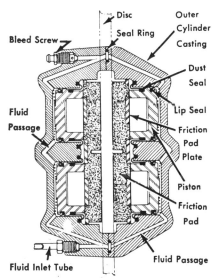

Disc
Seal Ring
Bleed Screw
Outer
Cylinder
Casting
Dust
Seal
Fluid
Passage
Lip Seal
Friction
Pad
Plate
Piston
Friction
Pad
Fluid Inlet Tube
Fluid Passage

This illustration shows a cross sectional view of Rambler caliper and pad assembly.

is released (removing the outward force of hydraulic pressure), the seals flex back to normal shape, pulling the piston with them.

This common design does have exceptions and variations. Some European cars use a mechanical spring and pin arrangement to retract the brake pads, and a sliding rod effect to provide automatic adjustment.

Renault, which uses the flexing seal setup to retract the shoes, has a hollow piston with a sliding rod and circular clip built-in, for its automatic adjuster.

The clip has free play in its groove; this free play is equal to the desired pad-to-disc clearance. The clip bears against the inside bore of the hollow piston with considerable frictional force, but a force somewhat less than the hydraulic pressure developed in the cylinder.

When pad-to-disc clearance exceeds the clearance of the circular clip in its rod, hydraulic pressure forces the piston out further, while the clip, fixed in place except for the

131

free play, holds position.

When the brakes are released, the frictional force of the clip against the inside of the piston prevents the piston from returning to its old position. The new position is the adjusted one, that means that the next position movement will not have to be so long.

And then there's the "differentest" design of all, that used on Rambler and Corvette. It doesn't retract the pads at all, but uses a spring behind the piston to keep the pad lightly dragging against the disc. Reportedly, the drag has a negligible effect on performance, and keeps the disc extra clean and dry.

New Linings. Replacing brake lining pads is the *routine* job on disc brakes, comparable to relining the shoes on drum brakes. But it's usually a lot easier on the discs.

On most American cars, the friction pads are made accessible simply by removing a plate or bolt at the point of the two halves of the caliper. The pads often can be removed by hand, or at worst with a pair of pliers.

There are two exceptions. One is the *floating caliper* design used by Renault of France. All other designs used a fixed caliper, that is, one that is bolted, via an arm, to the steering mechanism at the wheel. The Renault design differs in this sense: the caliper section itself, that is the part that contains the cylinder and piston, is held by hinged arms and king-size cotter pins.

Instead of hydraulic cylinders (single or double) in each half of the caliper, there is only one cylinder, on the hubcap side of the wheel. There is, however, the standard arrangement of two pads, one on each side of the disc. As the one piston moves in toward the disc, the caliper floats outward toward the hubcap, pressing the shoes against the disc.

Replacing linings on the Renault requires removal of the caliper assembly, a simple job. Just remove the cotter pins, unhinge and pull away the caliper and pull out the lined brake pads.

The Rambler system also offers some complications. It uses a fixed caliper, but there's no access plate to the pads. The caliper has to be unbolted at the steering linkage and removed. When removing, be very careful, as there are shims under the bolts. Each bolt has different shims to properly align the caliper around the disc. Take two envelopes,

mark one upper and the other lower, and insert the appropriate bolt and shims in each. Once the caliper is off, the brake pads can be easily removed.

Installing new pads should be a reversal of the removal procedure, but it usually isn't. The worn pads are much, much thinner than the new pads, and the pistons are extended from their cylinders to compensate.

Therefore, they must be pushed back into their bores. Hand pressure, using a pair of screwdrivers, should do the job. Do not attempt to relieve pressure to ease the job by opening the bleeder screw. There is no residual pressure to speak of in the lines of the disc brake system, so there's no pressure to relieve.

It is sound practice, however, to drain most of the brake fluid from the reservoir. If the master cylinder is topped up, and the caliper cylinders are in extended positions to compensate for frictional pad wear, forcing them back will create back pressure that will push hydraulic fluid out of the reservoir. This can create quite a mess.

If a piston doesn't return under hand pressure with screwdrivers, the caliper will have to be serviced. The usual cause of such a condition is a seizure of the piston in its bore.

Disc-Drum Combination. The disc brake is essentially a spot brake with limited friction contact area, an area that is less than a drum brake, and no self-energizing feature as drum brakes. The result is that it does a poor job as an emergency brake.

All American cars, therefore, are using a conventional drum brake at the rear wheels. Even the Corvette, which has four-wheel discs, also has a drum brake at the rear wheels, just for the emergency brake. It sits inside the disc brake assembly, and is adjusted through a screwdriver slot in the rear hub.

The disc brake doesn't represent the millenium in brake system design. It's more exposed to road film and it's more prone to stuck pistons for example. Brake pad life has been extended by improved technology, but it still can be on the short side (most pads have slots in them; when the slots are worn away, it's time to replace the pads).

But as a reasonably economical way to solve the problem of fading brakes on turnpikes, it *is* the better mousetrap.

A flat tire is a flat tire, whether it is a tubeless or a tubed tire. First things first, mechanic pries off wheel disk, loosens wheel lugs before jacking up the car.

How to Repair
Tubeless Tires

to chafe against the inner surface of the tire carcass to cause friction and a build-up of heat. Tubeless tires do not go flat as quickly as tires with tubes, unless cut badly by a large piece of glass or other sharp object. On tubed tires, inner tubes always burst like a child's balloon when punctured, allowing the air to rush out around the valve stem and between the wheel and beads of the tire carcass. Tubeless tires lose air fairly slowly until the puncturing object is removed. Quite often a motorist will not realize he has a puncture in a tubeless tire until he has had a tire re-inflated a couple of times a week at a service station, believing rather that he has some sort of "slow leak" along the rim or in the valve. This, incidentally, was the case with the tire shown in the photos accompanying this article. It was not discovered until the tire was removed for the photo sequence that there were two small punctures caused by the legs of a heavy steel staple of the type used to assemble heavy cardboard cartons.

Even before the advent of the tubeless units, tires were so well built that many motorists drove a car for several years without a flat. For this reason, very few car owners carried a patching kit, unless they were making a trip somewhere in the woods far from a highway where there would be no service stations. It was much

Metal object that punctured tire is removed with diagonal-cutting pliers, spot is marked with crayon or chalk.

THERE no longer is any question as to whether tubeless tires are better than tires with tubes —it is an acknowledged fact that tubeless tires are superior. Today, all American-built passenger cars (and most trucks) are fitted with tubeless tires as original equipment. Also, quite a few foreign-built cars now use the tubeless units.

Tubeless tires run cooler, there being no tube

Wheel and tire are dropped on special machine for fast removal and replacement of tire. Note arrow on sidewall that indicates position of valve stem. This is so tire can be replaced in same position, keeping tire balanced as it was when installed at the factory. Chalk is used for marking here, also.

4

Inner bead of tire is removed using special bar.

put on a special machine (Fig. 3A) and the bead is broken loose with a lever device, or it is positioned under a hydraulic-type tool that loosens the tire on the wheel. A long lever, the end of which is fitted with a roller bearing or a smooth, rounded section, quickly pries the tire off the wheel (see Fig. 4).

Prying open the carcass to permit inspecting the inside is a matter of pressing a lever when a professional does the job, a matter of dirty hands and stained arms for the unequipped motorist. The lever is locked to hold the tire beads apart and the area around the puncture is cleaned and roughened with a wire brush to assure a good adhesion of the patch. Fig. 6 shows a "hot" patch that is vulcanized by heat to assure an air-

easier, and almost as economical, to have a service station, with their special equipment, repair the tubes in tires. Now that tubeless tires are almost standard equipment, the same thing generally holds true. Except that the tire-patching kit carried for tubeless units—when carried—consists of an ice-pick-like tool that forces rubber plugs into punctures up to about 1/8 in. in size.

However, a more positive and permanent patch, with no chance of a "click-click" from a projecting rubber plug is made by vulcanizing a rubber patch inside a tubeless tire. This type of repair can be made by a motorist who wants to take the time (or has to, somewhere on a back road), but it requires considerable care with tire tools not to damage the air-sealing tire beads. Professionals have special equipment that makes the job a matter of minutes and little effort. You can have them do it, or, if you're on good terms with your service shop, do it yourself using their special tools.

Figure 1 shows the first step for repairing any flat tire: removing the wheel disk or hubcap. The wheel lugs then are "broken" loose with a wrench and the car is jacked up. After the tire is removed it is inflated, then dropped into a tank of water. This operation is a real timesaver over what the average motorist would be able to substitute. Not too many would have a container large enough to immerse the tire, and would have to examine the tire surface inch by inch, or use soap and water to find the leak. When the puncturing object is found, it is pulled out with pliers (Fig. 2) and the puncture point is marked with chalk or crayon.

Tire and wheel are then

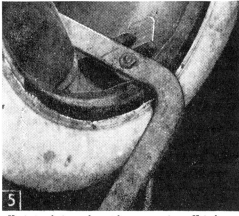

5

Next step is to apply patch over puncture. Note how spreader keeps beads far apart for easy access to inside of tire carcass. Average motorist would have a little trouble here.

tight seal. A special clamp is used to hold the patch firmly in contact with the tire, then a match is used to ignite the back of the patch. Special chemicals produce plenty of heat and smoke (but little flame) to "cook" the patch onto the tire.

The patch is allowed to cool for a few minutes, the clamp and spreader are removed and the tire is dropped back onto the wheel that still is on the special machine. Another lever is used to slide the beads back on the wheel (Fig. 7). The end of this lever is shaped so that it feeds the bead onto the wheel smoothly with no chance of damaging the tire and causing a leak by nicking the bead.

6

Clamp holds patch firmly against tire carcass. Patch then is set afire with match to vulcanize it to carcass.

7 Bar used to replace tire beads on wheel has different shape on end, makes quick work of replacing tire.

8 After both beads are slipped over wheel, clamp is fitted around center of tire to force beads against wheel, then tire is inflated. This clamp is not necessary if tire carcass is not too flexible.

After both beads have been fitted on the wheel, the tire is aligned so that a mark (an arrow in this case) that was made on the sidewall of the tire before it was removed, is opposite the valve. This makes certain that the tire will be balanced as when the car left the factory, or when the tire was installed by a tire shop. A band then is clamped around the tire (Fig. 8) to compress it slightly so the beads are forced out against the wheel. Actually, unless the tire is old and badly worn the band is not necessary. Simply inflating the tire will force the beads against the wheel. A motorist can use a length of clothesline to clamp the tire, a twist in the ends of the line being

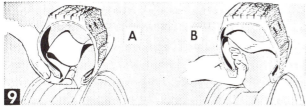

9 How to reposition diaphragm on outer bead edge of tubeless tire. Fingers grasp diaphragm bead as in A, pressure on bead snaps it into place. Cross section "B" shows diaphragm bead properly seated in the bead ledge.

used to insert a short length of pipe or a piece of wood and the line is tightened in the manner of a "Spanish windlass."

Hot-patch kits are available, including a clamp for holding the patch in place, and can be purchased at auto-supply stores and at mail-order houses. Valves are also available from the same sources. If a leak is suspected around the valve of a tubeless tire, paint a soap-and-water solution around the valve stem. The presence of bubbles will show a leak. Various types of valves are used for different makes of cars. Should it be necessary for any reason to remove a valve from the wheel on which a tubeless tire is fitted, the valve must be replaced with a new one, and it must be of the right type. First generation tire valves in second generation tires will only generate danger to tires, drivers and passengers. Some valves are oval shaped, others are round. Be sure to get the right type.

After the location of a puncture is determined, the valve inside, in all cases, is removed so the tire is deflated completely. It is not replaced until the tire is replaced on the wheel and is ready to be inflated. Another complication in tubeless tires occurs when they have an inner diaphragm (see Fig. 9). This diaphragm must be repositioned so it fits snugly against the wheel rim, or its function as a safety "inner tube" is nullified.

While the inside of a tubeless tire is being checked for a puncture, note whether the inner liner, in effect an inner tube cemented solidly to the inner surface of the tire, has bubbles in it. If it has, it means that the liner is separating from the main carcass, and the tire should be replaced. This sort of defect in a tubeless tire makes it worthless for retreading. If you are considering having a tubeless tire retreaded, be sure to examine the inside for these bubbles before sending it out.

If your car has tires with tubes, and you decide to replace them with tubeless units, there are a number of things to be done. First, thoroughly wirebrush the rims so they provide a smooth, clean surface for the tire beads to bear against. A special lubricant is used to assure that the tire beads slide onto the wheel easily. (This lubricant is also usually used when replacing a repaired tubeless tire.) Examine all rivets that penetrate the wheel rim. If any appear loose, use a ball peen hammer to peen it more tightly to make it air tight. Never, under any circumstances, weld the rivet heads.

If wheels are treated as described in this article, there is no reason why tubeless tires cannot be installed on wheels of cars built for quite a few years back. You can determine if tires are available for your car by checking with your local tire dealer. But if your car is a 1955 model or later, you won't have to check. All passenger cars since 1955 have rolled off Detroit lines with tubeless tires.

A Excessive toe-in

B Excessive toe-out

C Excessive camber

D Underinflation

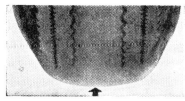

E Overinflation

F Cupping

ABNORMAL TREAD WEAR
(worn areas marked with arrows)

1

The type of tire wear this man finds in the tire will tell him what, if any, front end repairs are needed and whether he has kept the tires properly inflated and has been driving in most economically.

Your Tires Can Tell You

How to enjoy greater driving safety and more economical car operation

IF YOUR tires turn corners with a protesting squeal, if your car has ever gone out of control on a sharp turn, or if your tires show uneven tread wear, you will want to learn some of the reasons and remedies as given in the following account of the story your tires can tell (Fig. 1) through uneven tread wear.

One reason for uneven tire wear is incorrect toe-in, the adjustment of the front wheels so the distance between them is less at the front than at the rear (Fig. 2). This setting is necessary because when the car is in motion, camber (discussed later) plus rolling resistance will cause the wheels to toe out or separate slightly at the front. As a quick check on toe-in, slide your hand from side to side on either front tire. If the tread section feather edges toward the inner side of the tire as in Fig. 1A, there is too much toe-in; excessive toe-out will result in tread feathering toward the outside as in Fig.

1B. If the inaccurate toe-in or toe-out is great, the rubber on both tires will be unevenly worn, but if there is only slight mis-alignment (or if caused by a bent steering arm) only one tire will be affected.

Before checking toe-in, be sure wheels are in straight-ahead position. Then jack each wheel up and mark, with a piece of chalk sandpapered to a knife edge, the actual running center of the tread of each front tire. To do this, support the chalk, with knife edge vertical, on a hub-high box placed about ½ in. from the tire (Fig. 2). Spin the wheel and chalk a line as nearly as possible to the center of the tread. This method offsets possible wheel wobble. Now, with wheels back on the ground measure A and B with a folding rule supported on two hub-high boxes and check against manufacturer's specifications, available at large service stations or car dealers.

Construction of front systems varies with the make of the car, so detailed toe-in correction instructions will not be attempted here. Basically, however, correction is made with wheels straight ahead. Then one of the tie rods, constructed somewhat like a turnbuckle is released. Since the rod has left-hand threads on one end and right-hand threads on the other, the rod is turned to establish the correct toe-in, generally from ¹⁄₁₆ in. to ⅛ in. Before attempting toe-in corrections yourself, be sure you do not have a varying toe-in that cannot be adjusted because of worn and loose parts. When such a condition exists, you have a job for a well-equipped shop. To test for excessive looseness, point wheels straight ahead. Force both front wheels outward and inward by hand. If hand pressure can vary the toe-in ¹⁄₁₆ in. or more look to see which part is allowing this unwanted movement. Don't neglect to retighten anything loosened while the adjustment was being made.

Toe-out is as important on a turn as toe-in is on the straightaway. On a curve, the inner wheel turns more sharply than the outer wheel, as shown in Fig. 3, since it is describing a smaller arc. This, of course, necessitates a compensating toe-out, the amount of compensation being governed by the sharpness of the turn. Front wheel control from toe-in to toe-out is regulated by the steering knuckle arms attached to the front wheel spindles or axles. If these arms are bent, the changeover from toe-in to toe-out will be inaccurate and the tires will give a rubber-wasting squeal on the turns. Correction of this

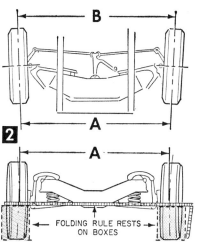

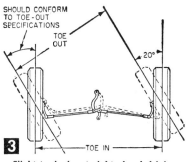

Slight toe-in for straight ahead driving changes to toe-out when rounding a corner. In checking toe-out, one wheel is set to a 20° angle. The other wheel should then conform to toe-out specifications. If it doesn't, steering arms are probably bent.

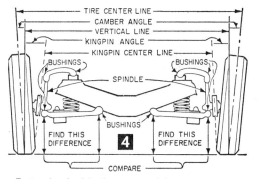

Factors involved in tire wear and front system service. Positions to measure and compare when checking for sagged front springs. Differences between ¼ and ½ in. can usually be corrected with shims while greater sag suggests the need of new springs.

problem is a job for the shop.

Camber is the degree to which a wheel inclines from the vertical as in Fig. 4. Incorrect camber causes uneven tire-to-road contact and camber wear, particularly on the front tires as in Fig. 1C. When camber wear is on the outside of the tread, the tire is tipped too far out at the top—has excessive camber. Cars with worn front systems or sagged springs may develop camber wear on the inside of the tread. Should camber wear occur on a rear tire, it indicates a bent rear axle housing. Don't be misled, however, by a tire that suffered camber wear while on the front of the car and was later transferred to the rear wheel. In any event, improper camber should be corrected at a shop. Neglect is expensive.

To help you know what you're buying when you have camber corrections made, once again look at Fig. 1C, then at Fig. 5. With the car on a level surface, in this instance on a turntable on a level floor, the position of the wheel relative to a vertical line is checked with a spirit level which incorporates a protractor, and the amount of deviation from manufacturer's specifications noted.

Unless front system parts are bent, the correct camber can then be quickly restored with the tool shown in Fig. 6. Here the crowfoot wrench, really the head of an open-end wrench fitted onto an extension and ratchet handle, is turning an eccentric bushing that holds the upper end of the front wheel spindle body. By turning this bushing and checking with the gage, proper camber can be re-established. Then the lock screw is tightened on the bushing and the setting is fixed.

This eccentric bushing also controls caster, the tilt between the vertical part of the spindle and the vertical plane, Fig. 7. You have probably ridden a bicycle "hands off," steering it by leaning to the right or the left. But it was the caster of the front fork that made the bicycle steer. Almost all cars have some degree of caster. As shown in Fig. 7, caster may vary from negative, with the spindle leaning to the front of the car, to positive, with the spindle top inclining toward the back of the car. The latter is the more conventional. Positive caster causes the car to steer in the direction in which it tends to go, which is not necessarily straight ahead. Cross winds or crowned roads may cause a variation in direction.

A car that is easy to steer will turn a corner quietly, straighten itself up after a turn and will tend to run straight on a straight level road. In cars with independently-sprung wheels, the tendency to straighten up after a turn and to steer in a straight line regardless of outside forces such as cross winds or crowned roads is controlled primarily by kingpin angle (Fig. 4). The angle between the centerline of the kingpin and the centerline of the spindle is controlled by the actual spindle forging and will remain constant unless the spindle is damaged. As the wheels are turned from right to left, the spindles seem to rise and fall, with the highest point being reached when the wheels are in the straight ahead position. Because the wheels, and consequently the spindles, cannot rise and fall, the car itself will rise on either a right or left turn. Therefore, the weight of the car will tend to bring the wheels back to the straight ahead position.

If a bent spindle or a faulty camber make these values different on the two sides of your car, the car will pull to one side. Correction of these faults is also a job to be done in the shop. Be sure, however, that the side pull is not due to a dragging brake or a soft tire on the side toward which the car is pulling.

From the above, we can see the importance of camber in helping make the car steer more easily. Any youngster who rolls a hoop knows that when the hoop is rolled straight ahead, it will begin turning in the direction toward which it is tipped. So, high camber tends to make a wheel pull outward. Toe-in offsets this. In other words, our "hoop" by being toed slightly in, goes straight ahead despite its camber.

Should a wheel be driven hard against a curb the wedging effect of the bottom of the wheel against the curb could bend the spindle on which the front wheel is carried (Fig. 4). This would produce excessive camber and cause wear on the outer edge of the tire tread. This usually occurs on the right wheel.

If the car is 40,000 or 50,000 miles old and lubrication has been neglected, you may find wear on the inner edge of the tire tread. An inward tilt at the top of the tire when viewed from the front could be caused by wear in the bushings that support the spindle body. Also, a variation of more than ¼ in. in the height of the front system at comparable points (Fig. 4) would upset camber.

Front system springs become fatigued and sag. And if they sag at different rates, the entire front end is thrown out of alignment. Changing springs or even checking them or shimming them up is a fairly heavy job, and should generally be done by front system service men.

Tire squeals sometimes result from conditions that you can correct. In Fig. 3 you see that on turns the inner tire travels a smaller circle than

5 Spirit level type gage used for checking camber.

Crowfoot-type wrench used with ratchet and extension for turning eccentric bushing that controls caster and camber. The lock screw is released during adjusting, then re-tightened.

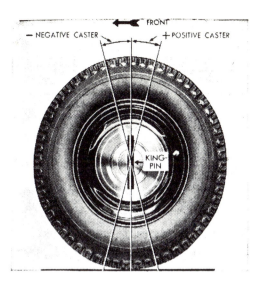

FRONT

— NEGATIVE CASTER +POSITIVE CASTER

KING-PIN

CASTER

Like the crown that holds the front fork of a bicycle, the kingpin of the automobile front system makes steering easier.

the outer tire. Similarly, but to a lesser degree, the inner part of the tread of each tire travels a smaller circle than the outer part of the tread of that tire. Thus, the wider the tread the greater will be the difference in the amount of pavement traveled between the outer and inner edges of the tread.

So slippage is unavoidable, but there are some ways of reducing it.

Tires should be properly inflated, or, possibly two pounds over-inflated to reduce road contact. Because the tread spreads out in an under-inflated tire there is more rapid wear and scuffing near the edges of the tread as in Fig. 1D. In addition, the sidewalls and tread of the under-inflated tire are continually flexing, resulting in high internal temperatures and consequent breakdown of sidewalls.

A rounded, over-inflated tire carries its load in the center of tread rather than spread out over a considerable area of the tread. This, of course, results in rapid center-tread wear as in Fig. 1E. Also, the over-inflated tire is more apt to suffer breaks in the cords from severe impacts and it is more easily cut or punctured.

Worn tires squeal more than new ones. Tires with deep treads have enough flexibility to prevent them from slipping on the pavement between the time they take over the load and the time they break contact with the pavement; therefore they do not squeal as much. As a safety note, a tire in which the tread is creeping has a less secure grip on the pavement than a tire that

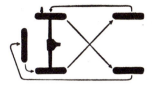

8

Pattern for crossswitching tires every 5,000 miles to even out tire wear.

grips the road firmly.

As the car turns, the center of gravity of the car shifts, putting more weight on the outer tires with more speed resulting in even greater 'centrifugal force. This greater weight spreads the tread, and the wider the tread the greater is the difference in travel between the inner and the outer portions of that tread. This accelerates tire wear. Lower cornering speed will help control this excess wear.

Whether your tires are correctly inflated or not, whether your wheel alignment is perfect or otherwise, and no matter how you drive, it is quite likely that you will eventually find cups, shown in Fig. 1F, developing in your front tires. Some cupping can be due to front end loosening or faulty camber adjustment. This is considered normal and will be reduced by cross-switching, discussed later. These cups do not develop on the rear wheels because the power transmitted through the rear tires and the reversal of load in the tread wears off the tread evenly or smooths it out. What happens to the front tread is much like what happens to pie crust dough under a rolling pin: the dough rolls out ahead of the rolling pin and stays there. Similarly, the rubber of the tire tread rolls out under the weight of the car. But it doesn't roll out very far. And it doesn't stay there.

The extent to which the tire tread rolls ahead of the car weight is influenced by several factors, but the tread rubber does give, and it does snap back. It is this snapping back as the tread loses contact with the pavement that causes these cups.

If an excessive amount of cupping occurs, check the front end bushings; drag link height; camber, and wheels, tires or brake drums for out of balance. If the cupping is neglected for long, the cups will produce a bumping noise in the car and their rate of wear will accelerate.

To keep this type of tire wear to a minimum, cross switch tires every 5,000 miles as shown in Fig. 8. No two tires on a car carry exactly the same kind of load or have exactly the same "luck." Since it equalizes the wear on all five tires, this cross-switching brings about a real economy.

To keep tire squeal and excess wear down to a minimum, check wheel alignment and have necessary adjustments made, maintain full air pressure or two pounds more, and go easy on the turns and braking. It's all good life insurance as well as tire insurance.

Occasionally rub your hand across the tread of each tire. In this way you will get the jump on conditions that if neglected would prove costly if not actually dangerous. Read your tires at every opportunity. They tell an interesting story.

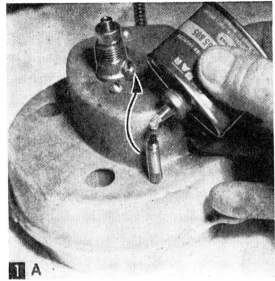

Special lubricants needed: (A) Mopar speedometer lubricant (B) Mallory ignition cam grease (C) penetrating oil (D) speedometer oil (E) graphited lock fluid (F) Door-Ease (G) Lubri-Plate (H) pump oiler with S.A.E. 20 oil. Right, applying speedometer oil to cup removed from back of speedometer head.

How to Do
. . . The Lube Job You Can't Buy

BETTER acceleration, freedom from knocking, improved brakes, better gas mileage and longer engine life, are just a few of the advantages you can enjoy with specialized lubrication. However, specialized lubrication, if applied each time your car needed a general greasing job could, in some instances, actually be harmful. It's not that your professional lube man is out to cheat you. He probably does a good job so far as general greasing goes.

And then it is just possible that some really good lube men aren't

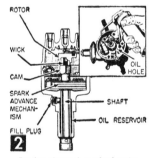

Section through typical automobile distributor showing parts requiring lubrication.

familiar with the five places where the distributor should be lubricated; the internal oiling of a carburetor; or how to lubricate a vital part of the exhaust system to increase engine life and save gas. Some might even revolt at the idea of lubricating your brakes.

The man who wants to take advantage of a really complete lubrication job will, of course, need some special lubricants. These are shown in Fig. 1.

Distributor. Starting with the distributor, which is the key to better engine acceleration and freedom from knocking, first check the schematic drawing of a typical distributor (Fig. 2), showing principal lubrication points. A general chassis

Left, Applying light oil to wick in distributor cam. Right, Using special ignition cam grease on distributor cam surfaces.

lubrication job will usually take care of the distributor shaft. On distributors with a fill plug, the plug is removed at the time of chassis lubrication, and the oil reservoir filled with #20 oil. If there is an oil cup instead of a fill plug, the lube man will generally put in a "squirt" or two of oil. If there is a grease cup, it is usual to turn the cup two turns down, then refill it, and put it back on with one or two turns.

But that's a routine job. When did you last see a lube man lift the distributor cap, remove the rotor, and put two or three drops of S.A.E. 20 oil on the wick? If you simply can't remember ever having seen this—and you probably can't—then open up your distributor, remove the rotor and put in two or three drops of #20 oil as in Fig. 3. If the wick still looks dry put in two or three more. From then on, apply only two or three drops at 5,000 mile intervals.

As the high points of the cam (Fig. 2) strike the fiber rubbing block of the moving point, they tend to wear away the fiber. This results in a retarded spark. And a retarded spark wastes fuel, reduces power, and causes overheating. But don't overdo lubrication of the cam (Fig. 4). Cam lubricant no bigger than the head of a match rubbed uniformly over the face of the cam is all that you need or can use. More lubricant is likely to sling off and get on the points, causing trouble.

Now that we're being "good" to the points by reducing the rate of wear of the rubbing block of the moving arm, it's also a good idea to lubricate the pivot on which the point hinges as in Fig. 5. Unnecessary friction at this location tends to resist the spring pressure that is trying to close the points quickly and firmly. Do not put

more than one drop of oil on the moving point pivot every 1,000 miles.

Actually if you take care of the jobs just mentioned, your distributor will perform better than many on the highway. However, if you wish to go all the way, and have some knack for mechanical work, lift off the plate that carries the contact points. Usually this is held in place by two screws. A little investigating will locate these screws. Usually there will be a notch or two around the edge of the plate (Fig. 6) that will make it certain that you get the plate back in the correct location.

The one pictured in Fig. 6 is from an Auto-Lite distributor. The ball bearings will give longer and smoother performance if they are kept lightly oiled—a drop of S.A.E. 20 oil being applied at 5,000 mile intervals.

The inset in Fig. 2 shows a typical Delco-Remy distributor. Those made some nine or 10 years ago have three balls around the outer edge: a drop of oil on each ball at 5,000 mile intervals is a good idea. Around 1954, these balls were replaced with an oil hole, as shown in Fig. 2: this should receive a drop or two of oil at 1,000 mile intervals. The oil hole in the plate is well marked.

But we're not finished with the distributor yet. While you have the breaker-point plate removed, take a look at the centrifugal weights (Fig. 7) in the body of the distributor. With every change

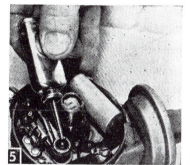
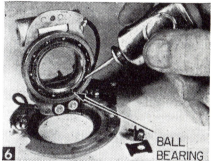

BALL BEARING

Left, Placing a drop of light oil on the pivot bearing of the movable point arm in a distributor. Right, Oiling distributor breaker plate ball bearing.

CENTRIFUGAL WEIGHT PINS

7

Putting Lubri-Plate on centrifugal weight pins of distributor.

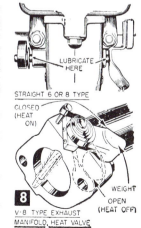

LUBRICATE HERE

STRAIGHT 6 OR 8 TYPE

CLOSED (HEAT ON)

WEIGHT OPEN (HEAT OFF)

8

V-8 TYPE EXHAUST MANIFOLD, HEAT VALVE

in engine speed, these weights move out or in from center to advance or retard the cam relative to the shaft. By applying a small amount of Lubri-Plate to each of these pins, as in Fig. 7, the movement of these weights will be quicker and smoother than if they ran dry. Performing this service at 10,000 mile intervals or whenever the distributor is overhauled is usually sufficient.

Exhaust. The vital exhaust system part requiring lubrication is the exhaust-manifold heat valve that directs exhaust heat to the base of the carburetor. (You will find a complete discussion of this

9

Two screws removed from Carter carburetor to show where oil is applied to accelerator pump shaft.

valve and its servicing in the article beginning on p. 102.)

Whether you own a 6-cylinder car (cylinders in a straight line) or a V-8, it will pay you well to look for a balance weight (Fig. 8) with a coil spring on the exhaust manifold. On any straight engine this will be located directly beneath the carburetor. On any V-8 with a single exhaust it will be at the front of the exhaust manifold opposite to the side on which the tailpipe is located. With dual exhausts, it could be on either side at the forward end of the exhaust manifold.

You should be able to move the balance weight with the tip of your finger. Accelerating the engine briefly but with rather high speed should also cause this weight to move. If the weight is not free to move, you are being cheated. If the heat stays in the full on position, the car will warm up nicely. But on a continued high-speed run you will direct too much heat to the base of your carburetor. This will over expand the incoming fuel and reduce the peak power of your engine. On the other hand, if the valve is stuck in the open position, your engine will be slow to warm up, will waste fuel, and the wasted fuel will wash oil from cylinder walls and cause crankcase dilution that will shorten engine life.

What appears to be a coil spring in Fig. 8 is a bi-metallic spring. As installed, its spring tension lifts the arm with the balance weight on it and closes the valve when the engine is cold. As the engine heats, this coil spring "relaxes" and allows the weight to go to the lower position so that the

Using long spout, pump-type oil can to reach hinge pins located deep in car body.

BENDIX DUO SERVO
VERTICAL ANCHOR
ECCENTRIC ANCHOR

BENDIX
NON-SERVO

LOCKHEED HYDRAULIC

FRONT

REAR

HUCK HYDRAULIC

CABLE AND LEVER OF
MECHANICAL HAND BRAKE

10

VARIOUS TYPES OF BRAKES WITH ARROWS INDICATING POINTS REQUIRING LUBRICATION

valve is open and the heat is off at the carburetor.

Any penetrating oil is helpful in freeing up this valve. Heat and carbon tend to burn the valve causing it to stick in one position or another. Some lubrication specialists use highly-graphited lock oils or powdered graphite applied liberally over the ends of the shaft where they project through the housing to keep this shaft free.

Carburetor. Most motorists and some mechanics are taken by surprise when the need of oiling a carburetor is mentioned. It is true that the external controls should never be oiled, since they will catch dust and sooner or later cause faulty action. But on certain carburetors two screws in the dust cover (Fig. 9) should be taken out whenever the car is lubricated, a drop of S.A.E. 20 engine oil placed in each screw hole. It might be worth your while to wipe your carburetor off carefully and look closely to see if it is of the type that has such a dust cover. This one is plainly stamped "OIL UNDER SCREWS." It isn't necessary to take the cover off. This was just done to show the details of the accelerator pump shaft.

Brakes. Now that we are all set to *GO*, how about being prepared to *STOP*? This is not an article on brakes. But it should be recognized that hydraulic brakes have a great number of mechanical parts. While hydraulic pressure is used to force the brake shoes against the revolving drums, anything that you can do to cut down on friction as the shoes move, will give you softer, faster and more powerful braking action. It goes without saying that lubrication of the brake shoes should be done in such a way as to avoid getting any oil or grease on the brake lining or the brake drum.

It is impossible to give detailed mechanical explanation here on how to remove and replace all of the wheel and brake parts to do the specialized

11

lube job. However, Fig. 10 does show various brake constructions: with a wheel off you can identify yours. Actually you hardly need a diagram because all you need to do is provide lubrication wherever metal slides on metal. You will find, for example, wedges, clamps, or rollers which would move more freely if lubricated. When new, these parts will generally be found to have been lubricated with Lubri-Plate at the factory. Since Lubri-Plate is difficult to apply unless the parts are disassembled, remove them, coat with Lubri-Plate and reassemble. In the event that you haven't the time or the desire to disassemble the brakes and do a thorough Lubri-Plate job, take a highly graphited lock oil and lubricate each frictional surface freely, but wipe it clean afterwards so that none of the oil will drip on the lining. Also lubricate the hand brake and its cables once or twice a year with S.A.E. 20 engine oil.

Body and Chassis. Now that we have a car that starts and runs better, and stops with less effort, how about stopping body squeaks and making door, window, hood, trunk, and control action better? For smoother door locks, give each tumbler a "squirt" of Lock-Ease twice a year. This liquid cleans the lock mechanism and then evaporates, leaving a graphite film that assures smooth action. Using a long spout pump-type lubricator with S.A.E. 20 oil, get into the pins of the door hinges, as in Fig.

Applying light oil to push-button type door lock. Never put oil in lock tumblers.

"Engine room" where all metal-to-metal controls, other than those on carburetor and choke (indicated by arrows), should be lubricated with #20 oil.

11. It's even a good idea to put a drop of oil on the window lift handle where the knob turns. Be sure to wipe excess oil off, so that none gets on the upholstery. If door latches are of the re-

volving type, be sure the bearings are kept oiled. Light oil should also be used on the push button lock as in Fig. 12, but not in the lock tumbler.

Where door strikers slide on each other, use a hard stick-type lubricant such as Door Ease.

The mechanism that raises and lowers the window also deserves attention. This mechanism can be reached by removing the window molding, held in by screws. Then remove the door handles,

Apply #20 oil to all moving parts of the hood hinge.

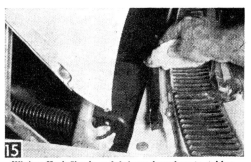

Wiping Hush-Shack, a lubricant harmless to rubber, on all rubber parts under the hood.

usually disassembled by pressing in and removing a clip or pin. Next, remove any screws that are seen around the edge of the door trim panel. After this, the entire panel can generally be pried off. Lubricate the parts as indicated in Fig. 16. When the door is reassembled, lubricate the glass channels with paraffin from a candle that has been whittled down to the thickness of the glass and rubbed up and down each channel, as in Fig. 17.

Now let's raise the hood and see how things look in the "engine room" (Fig. 13). On every metal-to-metal control (except carburetor and choke controls) put a drop of S.A.E. 20 oil. Wherever there is a rubber bushing on a control, use a drop of special lubricant such as Hush-Shack or any oil harmless to rubber. Where a wire control slides within a coiled wire housing, saturate the entire flexible housing with penetrating oil if rusty, and with regular S.A.E. 20 oil if it is not rusty. Use Door Ease on the sliding parts of the hood latch, and #20 oil on the little levers and springs of the hood lock.

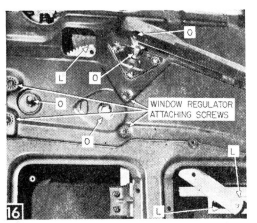

Door with trim and panel removed to show window lift mechanism. Apply Lubri-Plate on L areas and oil on points marked O.

A part under great stress is the hood hinge. To lubricate, move the hood up and down a few inches slowly while applying oil at every frictional point as in Fig. 14. To make hoods, trunk lids and doors operate easily moisten a cloth with special rubber lubricant or brake fluid, and wipe all rubber weather strip or bumper parts (Fig. 15).

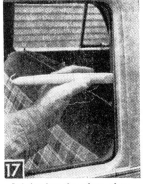

Lubricating the glass channels of the door windows.

All of the foregoing will do much to quiet the car. But if something in the instrument panel sounds like a gremlin scratching a tin ear, it would be a good gamble to remove the speedometer cable at the back of the speedometer by unscrewing the knurled nut seen at the extreme left in Fig. 18. Pull the cable out a foot or two, and apply specialized speedometer cable lubricant to the shaft. Smooth this out on the shaft with your fingers, and work the cable back in the housing. Then reattach the housing to the speedometer.

While you are at it, take a good look at the back of the speedometer housing. Some speedometers have an oil cup where the shaft comes out of the speedometer housing. If there is such a cup, remove it and put a few drops of speedometer oil on the wick (Fig. 1-A), and reinstall the cup. It is important to avoid overdoing this oiling, and to avoid packing the shaft with too much grease, because if any of the lubricant works up inside the speedometer head, it is likely to cause inaccurate readings.

Now perhaps you'd like to know how lubrication can improve visibility. It can. At least once

a year remove the windshield wiper arms. Since they are constantly exposed to dust and moisture, the resulting grime often creates enough friction in the pivots of the arm to prevent the spring (Fig. 19) from exerting enough pressure on the wiper blade against the glass to do a good cleaning job. On curved windshields this spring and hinge action is working continuously. And while specifications do not call for lubrication, experience indicates that action is improved by a drop of oil. Generally these arms can be removed by loosen-

Applying lubricant to the speedometer shaft.

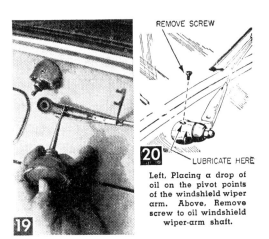

Left, Placing a drop of oil on the pivot points of the windshield wiper arm. Above, Remove screw to oil windshield wiper-arm shaft.

ing a nut on the end of the shaft. Other constructions make it possible to remove the arm by swinging the arm all the way out and pulling straight out on the assembly.

Note too that on some cars there is a Phillips type screw in the wiper arm-shaft housing (Fig. 20). This screw should be removed and the shaft lubricated with two drops of S.A.E. 20 oil at least twice a year. In the event that there is no screw in the shaft housing, it may be possible to get a little lubrication onto the shaft by applying it directly on the shaft while the wiper arm is removed. It's worth the try. And it's not a bad idea while on this part of the job to follow through and put a drop of oil on every frictional point of the levers, and shafts that drive the wiper blades, all the way from the wiper motor right out to the shaft that goes through the body under the windshield.

How to Take Care of Your Clutch

Satin-smooth starts and trouble-free service from the clutch in your car depends on the care you give it

THE majority of passenger cars being sold today have automatic transmissions driving through a torque converter, thus eliminating the need for a clutch, but manually operated friction clutches are still in millions of cars on the road, and sports cars and economy cars, both European and American, couple their engines to the transmissions with friction clutches. Fortunately, these precision mechanisms are built to stand up under an amazing amount of abuse before they fail.

First, let's understand why a clutch is necessary. Unlike a steam engine or an electric motor, a gas engine will not start from rest under load, since its power depends on the number of power strokes per unit time. In other words, it has to be turned up to cranking speed from an outside source (a starter motor) and reach a certain speed, free from load, before the load can be applied. Since the engine must be *kept* turning at an efficient speed—a speed higher than that at which the wheels should turn—the power must be applied to the wheels through a reduction gearing, the ratio of which is variable and under manual or automatic control. Also, suitable reverse gearing must be provided, since a conventional gasoline engine rotates in only one direction. These gear changes must be made while the engine is temporarily disconnected from the drive shaft or transmission. Further, as a matter of convenience, the engine must be enabled to keep running while the car is at rest (as at traffic lights or crossings). All of these functions are taken care of by the clutch.

Automotive engineers do everything they can to reduce friction in an auto's moving parts, yet a car wouldn't budge an inch without it.

If you are driving a car with a friction clutch, knowing more about how it operates will help you use it properly and enable you to recognize trouble symptoms before they become serious.

For it is friction between the clutch parts, under spring pressure, that makes the drive shaft turn with the engine and propel the car. Figure 1, a greatly simplified representation of the clutch, shows the basic operation and construction principles of all friction clutches. Some early clutches were built along very much the same lines as those shown in Fig. 1, but modern high-powered engines demand a more complex and refined mechanism. The basic idea of driving a spring-loaded disc through friction, however, remains unchanged. Notice in particular the effect caused when the driven disc is worn thin. The same thing happens in any conventional clutch, but it is self-compensating for normal wear. Also, the free play in the pedal can be adjusted. Of course,

there may come a time when the friction disc facings are completely worn out and have to be replaced. If sensible operation methods are followed and excessive use avoided, however, there is no reason why the entire clutch should not last for the life of the car.

Figure 2 shows construction details of a conventional single-plate clutch, as used in the 1950-57 Oldsmobile. Almost all clutches are built along these lines, though they may vary from one another in small details. The clutch shown in Fig. 2 is in the engaged position. When pressure on the clutch pedal forces the release-fork rod back against the release fork, it pivots on a ball-socket in the pressure-plate cover and moves the release (throw-out) bearing against the re-

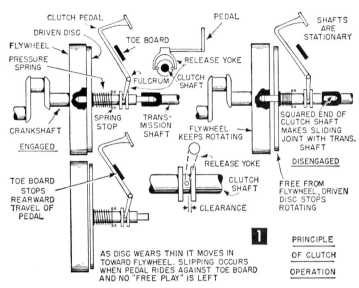

PRINCIPLE OF CLUTCH OPERATION

AS DISC WEARS THIN IT MOVES IN TOWARD FLYWHEEL. SLIPPING OCCURS WHEN PEDAL RIDES AGAINST TOE BOARD AND NO "FREE PLAY" IS LEFT

2) has these weights. As they tend to fly out with increasing force at higher engine speeds, they force the levers to bear more strongly against the pressure plate, increasing the force holding the clutch disc. This arrangement, supplementing the springs when more pressure is needed, allows lighter springs to be used in the pressure plate, reducing the force necessary to operate the clutch pedal at low engine speeds. To illustrate, the total spring pressure may be 1,000 lbs., while at high engine speed (say 4,000 *rpm*) the pressure is increased to nearly 2500 lbs. The spring pressure in this case is more than enough to start the car

lease levers. These levers pull the pressure plate back against spring pressure and allow the clutch-driven plate to rotate freely between the face of the flywheel and the pressure plate. Except for the release bearing and release yoke, the entire clutch assembly rotates with the flywheel and is, from a functional standpoint, actually a part of the flywheel. Powerful springs push the entire assembly together (see Fig. 3) squeezing the friction disc between the pressure plate and flywheel (Fig. 4) when the clutch is engaged. When disengaged, the pressure plate is pulled backward so that the friction plate floats free between the flywheel and pressure plate. Thus, no power is transmitted to the main drive-gear shaft. The three release levers (Fig. 2) are operated when the clutch release bearing is pushed against them by the forked release yoke. When pedal pressure is released, it lets the release bearing slide backward so that the springs in the pressure plate engage the clutch plate.

The release levers on some clutches are fitted with centrifugal weights to increase pressure at high engine speeds. The Oldsmobile clutch (Fig.

in motion, while the effort necessary to operate the pedal is reduced about 50%. Such an arrangement stands up better under the treatment of drivers who race the engine and let in the clutch violently.

Another method of reducing the pressure required to depress the clutch pedal is used on Plymouth cars (see Fig. 5). Here, the pedal is suspended from above and is linked to the clutch release fork in such a manner that it moves part of the linkage to an "over-center" position where a spring assists in depressing the clutch. Adjusting the eyebolt between the spring and linkage permits adjustment of pedal pressure. Generally, the pedal is depressed, the nut on the over-center eyebolt is turned four turns with the fingers, then the clutch pedal is released and one or more turns of the nut is made with a wrench. If you plan to do much work on your car, including clutch adjustments, write to the manufacturer for a price on a service manual. Cost is a few dollars, but it will tell you enough about your car to save hundreds. The Plymouth service manual, for example, will also tell you that if the clutch release-fork rod is adjusted so there is $\frac{3}{16}$-in. play between the fork and the release bearing, the clutch pedal will automatically have the 1 in. required free play.

Most friction discs in clutches are built with a spring-cushioned hub (see Fig. 6). These damper springs take up the shock of engagement and smooth out the torque impulses of the engine before they reach the splined hub and transmission shaft. Observe that the hub floats free in the assembly and is driven through the springs by the friction-faced discs. This type of construction is especially important in cars having

CROSS SECTION, FROM ABOVE, OF CLUTCH ASSEMBLY USED IN 1950-57 OLDSMOBILES flexible engine mounts designed to prevent engine vibration from being transmitted to the chassis of the car (this includes almost every passenger car and truck). What happens is that the engine bounces back and forth in its mounts when the clutch is engaged. Late-model cars have torque rods, or a torque-absorbing thrust face on the rear motor mount, but in an older car with worn mounts, clutch chatter can be a problem. Before blaming your clutch for a chatter problem, however, check your motor mounts. They can be replaced a lot more easily, and for much less money, than can a clutch disc. When motor mounts are in good shape, the cushion springs in the friction disc eliminate chatter by permitting the friction facings to stay in contact during the fore-and-aft oscillations of the engine.

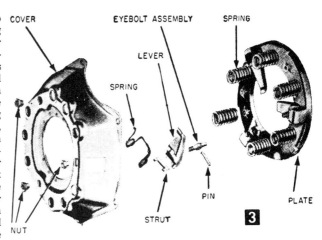

"EXPLODED" VIEW OF REPRESENTATIVE-TYPE PRESSURE-PLATE ASSEMBLY

When a clutch is disengaged, it isn't necessary that the driven disc be separated from the driving members by any great distance. In fact, the distance that separates the parts in a disengaged clutch is almost microscopic—usually about .015 in. You can see, therefore, why it is so important that the working parts be in correct alignment and free from warps or other defects. Any such faults will cause drag, chattering and other troubles. The pressure plate must travel about .090 in. (about 3/32 in.) backward to completely released position. After taking up about 1½ in. of free play, the pedal must be pushed downward about 4½ in. to produce this movement. The standard ratio for this action is 50 to 1.

As you ease back the pedal to let in the clutch, the pressure plate moves forward and pushes the friction disc toward the flywheel. The cushioned facings take up the load and start the car in motion even before the springs have exerted their full force. Thus, they are still under control of the driver and a smooth start is effected. To keep the release bearing out of contact with the release levers, a definite amount of play is provided in the clutch pedal. This play becomes less as the facings wear, since the inner ends of the levers move closer to the release bearing. If neglected, they would finally push against the bearing with sufficient force to let the clutch slip, for the effect is the same as if the bearing were pushed against the levers by the pedal. However, a simple adjustment, which takes only a few minutes, will restore the clearance, which is essential to efficient operation.

Clutch assembly; left to right, flywheel, clutch disk, pressure-plate assembly.

If the pedal shank hits the underside of the floor board (or the overhead bracket, in the case of suspended pedals) about the time the clutch is "engaged," it may not actually be fully engaged, and slipping will result, growing worse as the facings wear. The effect is the same as the notoriously bad habit of "riding the clutch." Just the weight of your foot on the pedal, especially if there is very little free play, exerts a powerful leverage and may reduce the effective spring pressure enough to cause slipping.

Slipping, by far the most common clutch trouble, not only wastes power and causes rapid wear, but also produces other bad effects. Anyone familiar with machinery knows that maladjustment, if neglected, leads to other trouble that aggravates the original condition. Nothing proves this point more than a slipping clutch. Beside the wear just mentioned, destructive heat is generated. This heat may warp or score the parts, burn the facings, or ruin the temper of the springs and weaken them, all of which combine to cause more slipping. The cracked surface of the flywheel face shown in Fig. 7 illustrates this. When the surface is heated by a slipping clutch disc, the cracks expand, presenting dozens of

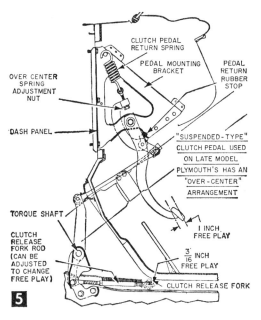

OVER CENTER SPRING ADJUSTMENT NUT

DASH PANEL

CLUTCH PEDAL RETURN SPRING

PEDAL MOUNTING BRACKET

PEDAL RETURN RUBBER STOP

"SUSPENDED-TYPE" CLUTCH PEDAL USED ON LATE MODEL PLYMOUTH'S HAS AN "OVER-CENTER" ARRANGEMENT

TORQUE SHAFT

CLUTCH RELEASE FORK ROD (CAN BE ADJUSTED TO CHANGE FREE PLAY)

1 INCH FREE PLAY

3/16 INCH FREE PLAY

CLUTCH RELEASE FORK

5

tiny but sharp edges that chew up the friction facing in short order. In this case the flywheel must be replaced, or the cracked face must be machined away and a special insert riveted to it with countersunk rivets. If you have this sort of flywheel, check with your jobber or automotive machine shop to see what they can do.

A simple turnbuckle arrangement (see clutch release fork rod in Fig. 5) is the usual provision for pedal adjustment. When checking for free play in a clutch pedal, don't mistake the pull of the pedal return spring for the pressure-plate spring tension. (To make sure you don't, disconnect the spring while making this test). If you listen carefully, you can hear the release bearing when it strikes the release levers. The exact amount of free play may be specified differently by various manufacturers, but a safe amount is 1 or 1½ in. of free travel before the levers and bearing make contact. Normal wear is so gradual that you may not notice it until actual slipping occurs. Warning is given, however, by the fact that complete engagement comes nearer and nearer to the upper limit of pedal travel.

In making adjustments, avoid the opposite extreme—too much free play, for then the pedal can't be pushed down far enough to free the clutch completely and it drags. Since there is then enough contact between the parts to keep the friction disc rotating, the gears clash, making shifting difficult and noisy, and doing the transmission gears no good. While the drag may not be enough to move the car when the transmission is in gear and the pedal is depressed, the friction disc, being held stationary under these conditions, will generate the same ruinous heat and disastrous results as it will when slipping.

However rugged in construction, a clutch was never designed for con-

---

TABLE A—CLUTCH TROUBLE-SHOOTING CHART

POSSIBLE CAUSE	REMEDY
SLIPPING:	
1. Improper pedal adjustment	1. Adjust to provide free pedal travel to 1 to 1½ in.
2. Oil soaked clutch facings, badly worn or damaged facings	2. Replace driven plate
3. Sticking pressure plate	3. Check release levers for free action, also check fit between cover plate indentations and drive bosses on pressure plate
4. Weak pressure springs	4. Replace pressure springs
5. Sticking release sleeve, sticking cross shaft on which release yoke is mounted or retarded return travel of clutch pedal	5. Clean and lubricate bearing surfaces on release sleeve and cross shaft. Check clutch pedal movement and pedal return spring
6. Distorted pressure plate	6. Replace pressure plate
GRABBING:	
1. Defective, worn or glazed clutch facings	1. Replace driven plate
2. Sticking pressure plate	2. Check release levers for free action, also check fit between cover plate indentations and drive bosses on pressure plate
CHATTERING:	
1. Bent or badly worn driven plate	1. Replace driven plate
2. Oily clutch facings or facings which have become flaky from heat	2. Replace driven plate
DRAGGING:	
1. Bent driven plate or oily facings	1. Replace driven plate
2. Excessive free travel of clutch pedal	2. Adjust clutch pedal free travel to 1½ in.
3. Badly worn release levers or other release mechanism parts	3. Replace worn parts
4. Defective or damaged splines in driven plate hub or on transmission clutch shaft	4. Clean and remove burrs or replace parts if defective

tinuous operation, it being assumed that it will stay engaged during most of the car's operating period. Neither the pilot bearing nor the release bearing will stand up under prolonged use, for no method is provided for positive lubrication of these parts in most clutches. (However, some release bearings do have a grease fitting for a gun that can be reached through an opening in the bell housing of the engine.)

To illustrate, the release bearing turns only when you depress the pedal and push it against the rotating release levers to disengage the clutch. It may be either a plain thrust bearing of metal or graphite, or a ball bearing of the thrust type. In any case, if the release levers are in constant contact with this bearing, it will spin all the time the engine is running. Finally, it becomes dried out and damaged and screeches a protest that can be heard for blocks. The same fate is in store for the pilot bearing in the end of the crankshaft (Fig. 2) whenever excessive use of the clutch is practiced. High temperatures prevail in this part of the clutch assembly and the bearing operates only when the speeds of the engine and clutch shaft are not syn-

6

Closeup of clutch plate shows springs that absorb shock between center disk of plate in which is splined hub, and other disk on which is clutch facing.

7

This close-up shows cracks in face of flywheel that have been caused by a slipping clutch. Heat of friction causes these fine cracks to expand, presenting sharp edges to face of clutch, causing rapid wear. This flywheel should be replaced, or face machined and alloy face riveted to it.

lights and crossings with the car in gear and pedal depressed should be avoided. In such instances, it is better to put the transmission in neutral while you are standing. This is a good safety precaution, too, against damage to the gears if you get a bad bump from the rear and your foot slips off the clutch pedal. Further, always make a practice of starting the engine with the gears in neutral.

Other troubles (see Table A) that may cause rough or faulty operation include worn splines in the hub of the clutch disc, broken or weak damper springs, rough, glazed or broken facings, or grease or oil on the surfaces. These are all infrequent. A leaking rear main bearing in the engine sometimes will let oil leak through onto the clutch facings. The solution here is first to replace the bearing before repairing the clutch. Any of the faults mentioned will cause grabbing, drag or chattering. Rarely, will a clutch stick or fail to disengage. Burned grease or gum will make the facings adhere to the flywheel and pressure plate, or, in rare cases, the surface may be worn so smooth that a pneumatic seal is formed between the friction

chronized, as when the engine is running with the clutch released and the transmission is in gear.

If the car is standing still, the bearing will turn around the stationary shaft. Or, if it is rolling very fast under the same conditions, as when coasting, the shaft will be turning faster than the engine, and, again, the bearing will be in operation. The final result of such treatment is that the bearing will become noisy or bind on the shaft end, causing the same effect as though the clutch were dragging.

The idea is to keep your foot off the clutch pedal at all times except when starting, changing gears or stopping. Even prolonged waits at traffic

disc and the flywheel. This can be eliminated by radial slots cut in the facings. Also, there is the remote possibility of breakage in the release linkage or adjacent parts.

Many clutches will last for 100,000 miles or more in the hands of a careful driver, while continuous abuse may necessitate complete replacement after 5,000 miles. In other words, care pays off in long performance.

How important is a clutch? Take a look at your driver's license: if it says "For automatic transmission only," you'd better take a test to prove that you have the skill and know-how to drive with a stick-shift gear box and clutch.— PAUL KRAIT.

Set Your Bearings Straight

Why pay for fewer miles per gallon, worn tires, and front-end repairs, and put up with a lot of shimmy and shake—when you can adjust and lubricate front wheel bearings for $1 or put in new ones for $5

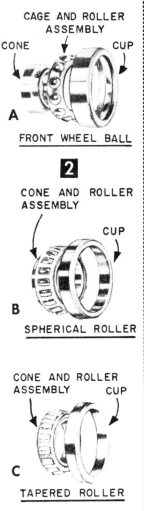

CAGE AND ROLLER ASSEMBLY

CONE   CUP

A

FRONT WHEEL BALL

2

CONE AND ROLLER ASSEMBLY

CUP

B

SPHERICAL ROLLER

CONE AND ROLLER ASSEMBLY   CUP

C

TAPERED ROLLER

WHEN your car begins to roll like it was going uphill through a bucket of glue, wander back and forth across the highway, and eat gasoline like it was going out of style, it's time to have a look at those hard-working bearings whose job it is to keep your ton-and-a-half car rolling effortlessly along in a straight line at 90 *mph* or more.

These periodic inspections and adjustments are your best safeguard against bearing failure when you can least afford it. Only the front wheels need to be inspected because only they are adjustable. Rear wheel bearings are usually not disturbed unless there is some specific reason for removing them, and, once removed, they are replaced.

To Inspect your front wheel bearings, first block the car so it will not roll, and then jack up a front wheel, supporting it so the wheel can be removed. Take off the wheel cover, dust cover, cotter pin, adjusting nut (be careful, it might be a left-hand thread), and flat washer. Then carefully remove the wheel, hub and bearings at one time.

Next, lift out the small bearings at the outer end of the hub and turn the wheel over to remove the rest of the bearing assembly. First pry out the oil seal (Fig. 3A) and lift out the large bearing. Then remove the bearing cups as in Fig. 3B.

When the bearing is removed, note the color and odor of the grease. If it looks burned—almost black—or has an acrid odor, it is a dead giveaway that the bearing has been running hot. If the grease looks and smells normal, clean each part of the bearing assembly as in Fig. 4. Do not dry the bearings by *spinning* them with a blast from an air hose as it will drive grit into the bearings.

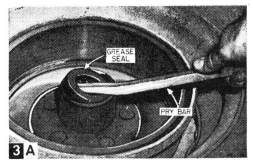

Disassemble bearing by prying out oil seal and then tapping the cup out gently with a long punch while the hub is mounted on wheel. Invert the wheel to remove inner cup.

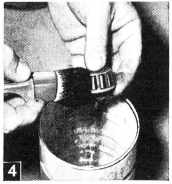

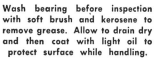

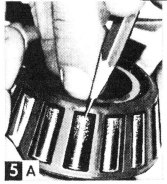

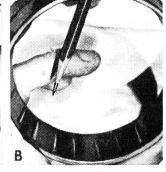

Wash bearing before inspection with soft brush and kerosene to remove grease. Allow to drain dry and then coat with light oil to protect surface while handling.

Severe impact, as when a wheel strikes a hole in the road, will cause *brinnelling* (right), a series of indentations where rollers have slammed into the surface of the cup. *Spalling* (left), a result of excessive clearance or sloppy adjustment, appears as chipping or crumbling on the small ends of roller bearings.

When the bearings and cups are clean and dry, check them for signs of *brinnelling* or *spalling* as in Fig. 5. These are just two of the several ways in which wheel bearings are damaged or worn.

Fractures will appear as fine hairline cracks across the surface of the cup or cone. These are usually a result of forcing bearings onto oversize spindles, forcing cups into warped hubs, or improperly seating the cups.

Corrosion results in pits or pockmarks and appears similar to spalling, but is located at random along the bearings and cups. It is usually an indication that moisture or road chemicals have entered the bearing through a defective seal and have contaminated the bearing grease. It is also possible for corrosion to be caused by handling a bearing when all of the oil has been washed from its surface. Ordinary perspiration is often highly corrosive, so it's good practice to handle clean bearings with a dry, lint-free cloth.

End wear is also similar to spalling, but appears on the large ends of roller bearings. It is generally caused by too-tight bearing adjustments, resulting in insufficient clearance.

Dangerous Dirt: If you find any of these defects, replace the entire bearing assembly. Never replace just one or two parts as the

reason for failure in one part was very likely working on the entire assembly. Also, keep the workbench, tools, lubricant, and your hands free of dirt and grime when working with bearings. Grit is the mortal enemy of free-rolling, long lasting bearings.

When installing replacement bearings, no on-the-spot lubrication is necessary. All new bearings are pre-lubricated to be used just as they come from the box. Old bearings that are in good condition should be repacked (Fig. 6) with special wheel-bearing grease, such as Sears Lithium, or Marfax #2.

Never pack grease into a bearing that already contains some grease. There are two popular types of wheel bearing greases on the market and they are not compatible. One uses lithium (light-yellow in color, similar to petroleum jelly) and the other sodium (dark green) as a base to carry lubricating oil. Mixing these greases may cause the oil to separate from the base and drain past the seal, damaging the brake linings as well as the bearings.

Reassembly: Check the replacement races and bearings against the old parts to be sure you have the right ones. Install the races and large bearing as in Fig. 7A. Then dip the seal in clean oil and start it into the hub by hand, with lip positioned as in Fig. 7B. The

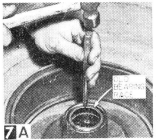

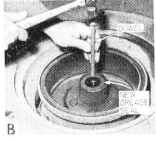

To reassemble wheel bearing, drive in new cup, using the old one as a driver. Tap lightly until you hear the cup seat against shoulder. Next, oil lip of seal, start it into the hub by hand, and drive with wooden driver.

Repacking means to force new grease into thoroughly-cleaned bearing cage with your fingers. Grease must be worked in, not merely spread on the surface. Do not over-lubricate by filling wheel hub or dust cap with grease.

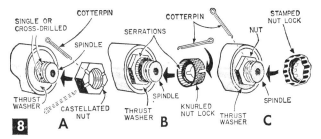

oil will make the seal slide on the spindle easily, preventing damage during reassembly, and will also make it soft and effective as a seal immediately. Never install a seal with just a hammer or use a steel punch which could damage the casing and cause leakage. Under no circumstances ever attempt to reuse a seal. Mount the wheel carefully to avoid tearing the seal on the spindle and install the outer bearing, washer, and adjusting nut.

Adjustment: The most common forms of adjustment are shown in Fig. 8. In all of these the amount of tension applied on the thrust washer by an adjusting nut is set to the manufacturer's specifications, or according to feel for lack of free play and smooth rotation of the wheel. Adjustment by feel, although reasonably accurate and practical, should be done only if a torque wrench is not available.

To adjust a bearing by feel, first seat the bearing assembly by tightening the nut with a 12 to 16-in. long plier-wrench (Fig. 9) until you feel a definite resistance while rotating the wheel. Then loosen the nut and run it up again finger-tight. Continue tightening it with the pliers, rotating the wheel and checking for free play constantly with your other hand. Stop tightening at the point where free play has just been eliminated. Be careful not to overtighten the bearing, mistaking looseness at the backplate or kingpin for free play.

Now spin the wheel, stopping at several points to check for free play, and, if necessary, tighten the nut to eliminate it. Never back off more than one slot on the nut to get to the point where free play is eliminated. If the bearing becomes too tight, back the nut off to finger-tight and start over. On tapered roller bearings (Fig. 2C), line up the nut and cotter pin hole by tightening until the next slot lines up. On ball-bearing assemblies (Fig. 2A),

which are often cross-drilled, back off the nut to align the hole and a slot.

Torque-Wrench Adjustment: When adjusting wheel bearings by feel, it is easy to see that the final adjustment will vary somewhat according to your estimation of free play between the bearings and cups. This variation can be eliminated by following the same procedure as when adjusting bearings by feel, but using the torque wrench (Fig. 1) to measure the tension of the nut on the thrust washer. At a given torque specification, the amount of free play will be correct for the type of bearings being used. Seat ball bearing assemblies at 33 ft.-lbs. of torque and roller bearings at 50 ft.-lbs. Then loosen the nut and retorque it, advancing from one slot in the nut to the next until the torque reading is about 5 ft.-lbs. for ball bearings or 7 ft.-lbs. for roller bearings. If necessary, use the pin slot that lines up just before the specified torque is reached, but do not exceed this.

Special close-tolerance nuts are available in which the cotter pin can be installed without disturbing the setting of the adjusting nut by more than about a thousandth of an inch. These are available at most auto supply stores or can be ordered from J. C. Whitney Co., 1917 Archer Ave., Chicago 16, Ill. These consist of two parts. One has internal threads similar to the original adjusting nut, but with 62 serrations on its outer face. The second piece has serrations to match the first, plus half-round slots to accommodate a cotter pin. In use, the threaded part is run onto the spindle and adjusted with either a torque wrench or pliers. Then the second part is snapped over the serrations and pinned.

Testing and Replacing
WORN SHOCK ABSORBERS

Panic stop like this makes almost any car dip its nose. If the shock absorbers are good, nose will return to level and stay there. If shocks are worn out, car front will bounce up and down through several cycles.

For a total time expenditure of an hour and a half per pair, you can pocket a saving of seven dollars when you replace your car's shocks

TESTING your car's springs and shock absorbers is not difficult. With your car ready for the road but unladen with extra passengers and luggage, it should sit level on flat ground. If it does, your car's springs are okay. There should be no sagging at any of the four corners, the front end should not be lower than the rear end, and vice-versa. All of this presupposes that you have never modified your car's stance with lowering blocks or oversize tires in the rear.

If you wish to make sure that your car's springs retain their factory height control specification, measure vertically from the bottom of the lower control arm, and at the extreme outer end, to the ground at each side of the front. If this measurement differs more than ¼ in., the installation of spring spacers is recommended. No more than two spacers should be used on any spring; to exceed two spacers would allow the front coils to close up on rough roads. The rear springs, too, can be checked for height in a similar manner—by measuring vertically from the left and right ends of lowest point of the rear axle to the ground. Again, if there is more than ¼-in. difference noted, spring spacers should again be employed. We suggest, if you should find the need of spacers, that you take your car to a reliable spring shop where the correct spacers are available. There is the additional possibility that your springs have lost their flexi-

bility, or some of it, and in this case either new springs are indicated or, in the case of leaf springs, re-dishing.

There are several ways to test shock absorbers. Some shop service manuals suggest various hand, bench, or road testing methods, but the average car owner can make a very easy and equally reliable test by hopping on the bumper and forcing the car into a continuous up-and-down motion. Whether you are testing the front or the rear shock absorbers in this manner, the car

Bounce up and down on your car's front bumper; get the nose going up and down through a fair arc. When you hop off, good shock absorbers will snub this action immediately; worn shocks, though, will allow the front end to bounce through several cycles.

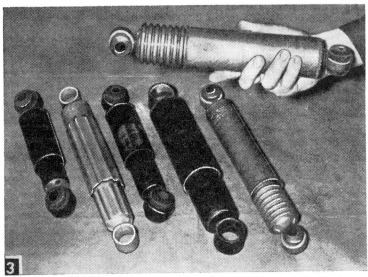

3

A display of top quality shock absorbers: Left to right: Houdaille Standard, Houdaille Golden Glide heavy duty, Gabriel Adjust-O-Matic standard, Gabriel Silver-E heavy duty, Toledo Skyride standard, and Toledo Skyride heavy duty. The best choice for those persons desiring superior roadability and handling qualities on domestic cars is Gabriel Silver-E in front and Gabriel Adjust-O-Matic in the rear. The former give a firm, comfortable ride in front plus top durability; the latter allow choice of soft, medium, or firm quick adjusting by hand for any ride, load, or performance need. All of these are available for nearly all post-war domestic makes and models.

Load Levellers in the rear. These shocks have an additional light coil spring attached and they do wonders for handling and level riding on cars that carry heavy loads and make long trips.

If you prefer the softest possible ride and are inclined to be a conservative driver, standard shocks are your best bet. They can be either factory replacements or replacements purchased from Sears-Roebuck, Montgomery Ward, Western Auto, or selected from any of the numerous quality shocks available. If, on the other hand, you are a spirited driver who wants more firmness and less roll and sway on corners, then heavy-duty shocks are the best for you. Heavy-duty shocks made by Gabriel, Houdaille, Monroe, Toledo, etc. cost upwards of $18 a pair; standard shocks cost somewhat less.

should immediately come to a static position when you hop off the bumper. If the front or rear end, as the case may be, continues to oscillate up-and-down, those shocks are due for replacement.

If you want to subject your car to a more rugged test, seek out the worst railroad crossing in your neighborhood and cross it at various speeds until you find the speed where the jounce and rebound is the worst. Again, if the car continues to bounce up and down once the railroad tracks are crossed, its shock absorbers are just about finished. You can also try several abrupt, panic stops from 30 to 40 *mph*. Naturally the nose will dip on these, but if the up-and-down movements continue this is yet another indication that the shock absorbers have lost their effective snubbing power.

Modern telescopic-type shock absorbers cannot be refilled and they must, therefore, be replaced. Generally the front shock absorbers go first, but in any case, whenever either front or rear shocks are replaced, they should be replaced as a pair in order to maintain left and right stability. It has been my experience that the rear shock absorbers have about twice the life of the front units. As a matter of fact, I have never had to replace rear shock absorbers. On front shocks I get about 25,000 miles per set.

Whether you replace worn-out shocks with factory replacement units depends largely upon how you drive and how heavily you load your car. If you carry heavy loads of passengers and luggage I would suggest that you install Monroe

There are a few distinctive features on shock absorbers of different makes: Houdailles have a vertical steel corrugation claimed to increase strength against torsional stresses and against flying rocks; Gabriel Adjust-O-Matics can be hand-adjusted to give a soft, medium, or firm ride control; Toledos have a horizontal ribbing of heavy molded rubber around the bottom end to resist grease and also to act as a stone shield. Our purpose, though, is not to make like a TV

4

Before installing new shock absorbers make sure that those you have just purchased are the right length both when expanded and compressed. Here, the new shock absorber is compressed when compared to the old shock; this can lead you to believe the new shock is the wrong size. Shocks, when compared, must be compared in the same condition—that is, both must either be compressed or expanded.

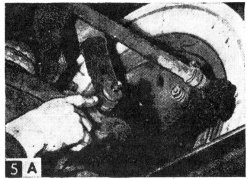

Removal of a telescoping shock absorber from an independent front coil spring suspension: First, a socket wrench is applied to the top shock absorber lug nut which is removed enabling the top end of the shock to come free. The bottom lug nut is then removed, freeing the bottom end of the shock (A). The large flat washer should be retained for reinstallation later (B). The front shock absorber is pulled free of the top and bottom lugs (C).

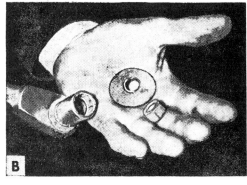

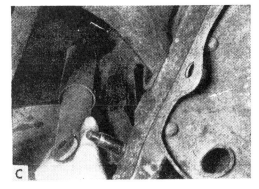

commercial and extol the virtues of the various makes of shock absorbers. If you are really in doubt about the type of shock absorber you want, go to any large and reliable auto supply store and ask to see the types carried in stock. You will find many types from which to choose; the merchant concerned will be able to advise you on those types best suited to your car. Probably the most important thing is to make certain that you purchase the correct size for your make and model; I've known do-it-yourselfers who, upon removing the old shocks, found that the replacements they had just purchased were either too long or too short and they had to call for help in taxiing back to the supplier for the right size of shocks for their car.

The most important thing about changing shock absorbers is to securely block your car so that it cannot possibly roll in either direction. Hide the ignition key and block the end that stays on the ground. You would do well, if there are children around, to roll all the windows up on your car and then to lock all the doors to prevent any tampering with the clutch or brakes. You don't want to find yourself pinned beneath two tons of steel for want of foresight.

Some front shock absorbers are inside of the coil springs, others are angularly displaced outboard of the front coils. Removal is simple and consists mainly of removing the top nut and lifting off the washers and rubber bushings from the top lug. The latter is either attached to the car's

frame or it extends vertically through a web-like plate that is attached to the top of the coil spring. The bolt that secures the bottom of the shock absorber through the mounting plate on the lower A-frame arm is then removed. Some bottom mounting plates must themselves be removed from the lower A-frame in order to allow removal of the shock absorber. Some makes use a saucer-shaped washer of generous size to hold the bottom end of the shock absorber to the A-frame or the bottom of the coil spring.

Take note of the order in which washers, rubber grommets or bushings, and various small parts are removed so that the same order can be retained when you install the new units. Make a rough diagram of the order to aid your memory.

To install the new shocks, first fit them in place loosely securing top ends first. In some cases the top of the shock has an integral steel ring inside of which there are rubber bushings. You should always receive new bushings with a new set of shocks. Before replacing the new shocks, squirt a bit of brake fluid on the rubber bushings to make them seat more easily. Now, on the bottom end of the new shock install the mounting plate (if that web-like piece comes free upon removal or has to be removed), the bushing, the washer, the lock washer if any, and the locking nut—in that order—and tighten securely.

In some cases, especially where the shock absorber is mounted inside of the coil spring, it will be necessary then to replace the bolts which

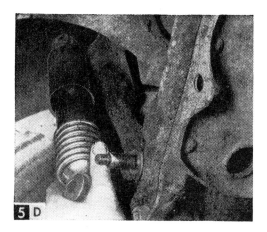

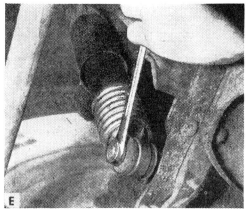

The new shock absorber is placed on the top and bottom lug bolts for attaching (D), then the bottom lug nut is secured after first placing the flat washer in place (E), and the new front shock absorber is secured after replacing the top lug washers and nut.

the car—the mounting bolts extend through and into the trunk compartment or, in the case of many station wagons, into the spare wheel bin beneath the rear floor. Washers, lock washers, and nuts secure the top ends and the removal of these is generally easier than to loosen the top ends of the front shocks due to more space.

The removal of any shock absorber, front or rear, is made easier if you take a few moments to inspect the means by which those used on your car are mounted. Sometimes, in order to reach the upper mountings in front, it is necessary to remove the front wheels. The same is true of the rear shock absorbers.

Just as it is possible to buy a new car with faulty shock absorbers, so it is possible, though unlikely, that you will purchase a set that is not quite up to snuff. Before installing new shock absorbers, hold them close to the ear and pull hard on each end of the shock unit. A good shock will, when tested in this manner, emit an audible sucking noise when the fluid is forced through the piston port under pressure and against resistance. Test the shock unit, again, by collapsing it while you listen for the gurgle that indicates a serviceable unit.

Once your new shocks are installed, bounce on the bumper again, get the car moving up and down, then hop off abruptly. New units will im-

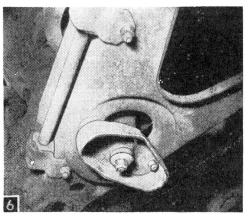

Here, the front shock absorber bottom mounting is through a web plate in the lower A-frame arm.

hold the bottom end mounting plate against the lower A-frame arm. Once the bottom end is secured, the washers and nut are replaced on the top mounting bracket. With a torque wrench, torque the upper pivot or mounting bolt to 67 to 75 lbs. and the lower bolt to around 35 to 45 lbs.

Rear shock absorbers, generally, install much as do the front units. There are some variations depending, again, on whether the rear shocks attach on the bottom ends to a web plate mounted to the side of the leaf springs, to a bracket on the top or bottom of the leaf springs, or to a bracket on the ends of the axle housing. Coil springs in the rear are coming into vogue and in a few cases the shock absorbers mount inside of the coils; this is rarely found, however.

Generally, the rear shock absorbers are canted outward in order to achieve greater stability and, therefore, lugs or brackets are employed to secure the bottom ends. Most rear shock absorbers mount, at the top ends, through the steel floor of

mediately render the car motionless. Try the car out over the same course on which you discovered the old shocks to be faulty. Make some quick stops and note how the new units stop the vertical jounce and rebound.

The tools you will need for replacing shocks are the open-end or box-end wrenches generally found in the kit of the average do-it-yourselfer. A large screwdriver is sometimes handy for prying loose a stubborn lug bolt once the nut is removed, and a torque wrench is desirable, but I'll bet a buck that more shock absorbers have been installed with a simple wrench than with the torque type.

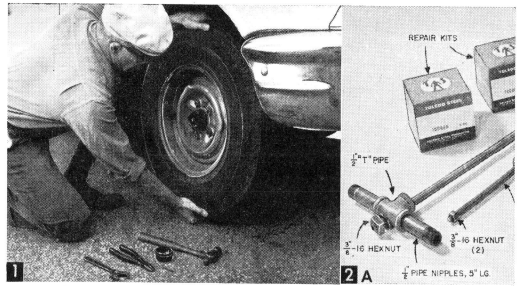

1

2 A

REPAIR KITS

½" T" PIPE

⅜"-16 HEXNUT

⅜"-16 HEXNUT
(2)

¼" PIPE NIPPLES, 5" LG.

Servicing Front Suspension

THE replacement of ball joints on Chevrolet and Ford cars is not a difficult job and can be performed without special tools by anyone accustomed to handling tools and making minor repairs to his car.

The only items needed in addition to regular tools are a spring compressor and two guide bolts (Fig. 2A) that you can make, a jack, and the replacement ball joint assemblies for the model car you're working on.

The ball joint as used in the front suspension is really a king-size tie rod end with certain modifications. The ball joints allow the knuckle and spindle assembly to turn and also permit vertical motion previously provided by the knuckle support pins. The use of ball joints results in a reduction from nine parts to three, easier steering, better handling characteristics and the elimination of three lubrication points at each side.

Front suspension ball joints, however, (particularly the lower joints) are subject to wear because each front wheel supports approximately 900 pounds of car weight. When wear does take place, front wheel alignment cannot be maintained, resulting in wander and poor wheel tracking. The upper suspension ball joint's only function is to hold the upper end of the spindle assembly in alignment and is spring loaded in order to dampen

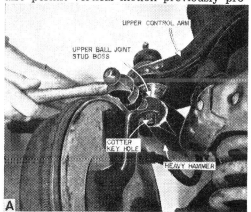

UPPER CONTROL ARM

UPPER BALL JOINT
STUD BOSS

COTTER
KEY HOLE

HEAVY HAMMER

A

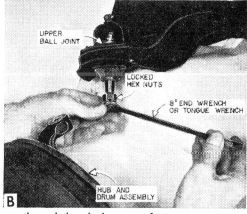

UPPER
BALL JOINT

LOCKED
HEX NUTS

8" END WRENCH
OR TONGUE WRENCH

HUB AND
DRUM ASSEMBLY

B

FIG. 3: With jack under lower control arm, remove cotter pin and hex nut from stud. Then free joint assembly by striking the stud boss, backing up the joint with a hammer or other heavy object. To determine condition of upper ball joint, lock two hex nuts

on the stud, then check amount of torque necessary to turn ball in its sprocket. Normally between 2 and 8, though 14 ft. lbs., torque is permissible. If torque wrench is not available, pressure applied with finger tips at extreme end of 8-in. end wrench will do.

157

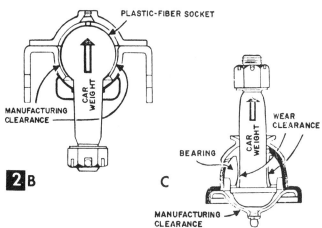

Ball Joints

How to restore your Ford or Chevy's handling to like-new smoothness for as little as $15

the gyroscopic action of the wheel.

The 1955 Chevrolet-type lower ball joint (Fig. 2B) is typical of the inverted-stud, weight-carrying lower joint. Buick, Pontiac, Oldsmobile and Cadillac also use the inverted-stud design. The upright-stud lower ball joint (Fig. 2C) is typical of the joint used in Ford and Chrysler products.

Checking for Wear. Illustrations in this article show the installation of new lower ball joints in a 1957 Chevrolet. Except for a slight difference in the ball joint kit for 1955-1957 and 1958-1962 however, the procedure is essentially the same for all Chevrolets.

The first step is to lift one front wheel. The upper control arm spindle and wheel assembly will drop until it contacts the rubber upper frame bumper (Fig. 4). The coil spring force keeps the lower control arm and ball joint socket tight against the ball stud.

Carefully adjust the front wheel bearings to eliminate play, then grasp the wheel at top and bottom (Fig. 1) and check for looseness.

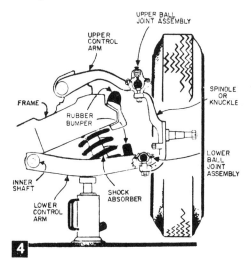

FIG. 5: Before beginning work on the ball joints, lift front of car and place blocks under frame. A concrete block and short pieces of 2x4 are satisfactory substitutes for frame stands. When using bumper jack, lift and block one side of car at a time.

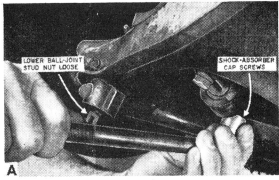

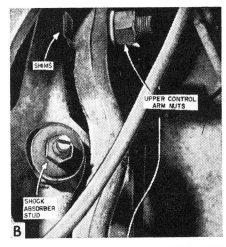

FIG. 6: Remove cotter key and loosen lower ball joint stud nut in same way as you loosened nut on upper stud. Then free shock absorber by removing two 5/16-in. bolts at bottom and a 3/8-in. nut from stud at top. Remove shock absorbers through lower control arm center hole.

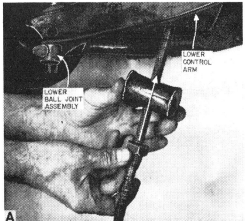

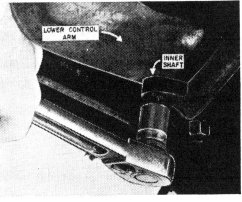

FIG. 8: Remove the four nuts and lockwashers from lower control arm shaft and remove arm by backing off nut on compressor to release spring tension.

FIG. 7: Spring compressor is now dropped through opening left by shock absorber and crossbar is installed on lower end. Turn lower nut up until upper control arm is clear of rubber bumper. Strike the stud boss to break the taper loose, remove stud nut, and pull the spindle down until it swings clear of the ball joint stud. Move hub and drum assembly back out of the way, being careful not to kink brake hose.

Any motion in excess of 1/8 in. indicates wear at the *lower* ball joint.

The *upper* joint is checked as in Figs. 3 through 7. In this particular instance the upper ball joint was found to be all right, the stud was replaced in the spindle, the nut tightened securely and the cotter key installed. If the upper joints are found to be worn (loose) and are replaced, the lower joints must also be replaced.

In the event the upper joint is found to be worn, it is only necessary to complete the removal of the upper control arm by removing two nuts (Fig. 6B). Be sure to note the number and position of the shims between the inner shaft and frame and replace in the same positions.

Servicing Lower Ball Joints. After making up the spring compressor and guide bolts as in Fig. 2, follow the correct procedure for servicing the lower ball joints as in Figs. 5 through 13. The author used an old brass hammer head as a crossbar on the compressor (Fig. 7A) although the 1/2-in. pipe nipples

FIG. 9: Ball joint rivets are removed by first drilling away heads with ⅜-in. drill. Remainder of rivet head is cut away with chisel and shanks driven out with punch. Holes are then enlarged to ²¹⁄₆₄ in. to take replacement bolts-supplied with Kit.

and tee will work just as well. Use *Redi-bolt* threaded stock.

On Ford cars, the upright stud ball joint used (Fig. 2C) requires a different procedure as follows: 1) Remove shock absorber by unbolting from frame at upper end and removing two cap screws that retain mounting plate to lower control arm. 2) Detach stabilizer from lower arm. 3) Loosen lower ball joint stud nut one or two turns (Fig. 3A) and loosen stud by striking boss as in Fig. 7B. 4) Place

FIG. 10: With lower control arm in vise, install kit parts. Use longer bolts in top face and two shorter bolts in sides. Wrench torques nuts to 20 to 25 ft. lbs.

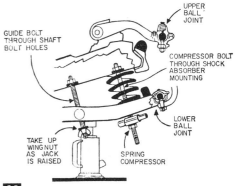

11 REINSTALLING SPRING AND LOWER CONTROL ARM

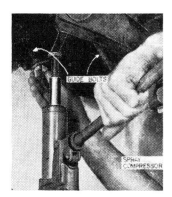
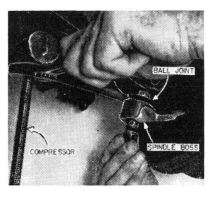

FIG. 12: To reassemble, install guide bolts (Fig. 2) in place of two lower control arm shaft bolts, running guide through shaft and frame holes. With coil spring properly seated, lift outer end of control arm, and install compressor crossbar. Raise outer and shaft ends of control arm alternately with jack while taking up on nuts. When shaft is in place, install two shaft bolts, remove guides, and install two remaining shaft bolts. FIG. 13: Compress spring by tightening nut until spindle boss comes into position. Stud is then dropped through boss by releasing compressor. Install nut and cotter key, replace wheel and one side is complete.

jack under outer end of lower control arm (Fig. 4), and raise until upper arm rebound bumper is clear of frame. 5) Remove nut, lift spindle off the stud, and move spindle and drum out of the way. 6) Unbolt old ball joint and install new joint. 7) Assembly is essentially the reverse of the disassembly.

In all cases, installation is identical for each front wheel. If you find that ball joint studs cannot be freed by using two hammers (Fig. 7B), apply heat with a propane torch and hammer.

Power Steering

Here is how your power steering unit works and what you can do to keep it working right

FIG. 1: Clean hydraulic lines to check for fluid leaks with dyed fluid to distinguish between freshly leaked hydraulic fluid and old oil.

UNDERSTANDING your power steering is easy and important when pinpointing trouble. Fixing it, though, may be another matter. You can easily make some repairs, but if the trouble is in the power steering unit itself most repairs are best left to an expert who knows what he's doing and has the special tools and gauges. However, if you watch the repair being done and know your power steering, you should get a more careful and less expensive job.

All power steering systems have these three components: (1) a pump which supplies oil under pressure to provide the power and (2) a control valve assembly to meter the amount of fluid delivered to (3) the cylinder and piston assembly that does the work (Figs. 2 and 5).

Systems differ in design and location of control valves and cylinder and piston assemblies. The two basic categories are those where the power is applied to the steering gear and those where it's applied to the linkage. Geartype units are built into the steering gear box with opposed power pistons working on a crank attached to the pitman arm shaft (Fig. 5). Some use a single power piston working on the pitman arm shaft through a

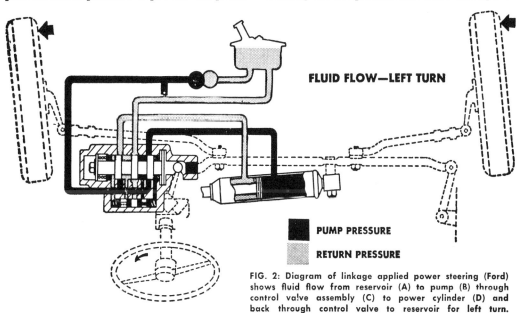

FLUID FLOW—LEFT TURN

PUMP PRESSURE

RETURN PRESSURE

FIG. 2: Diagram of linkage applied power steering (Ford) shows fluid flow from reservoir (A) to pump (B) through control valve assembly (C) to power cylinder (D) and back through control valve to reservoir for left turn.

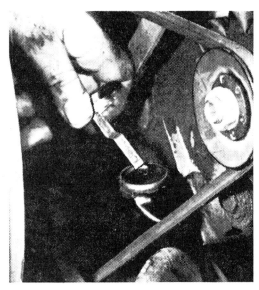

FIG. 3: Reservoir cover has built-in dip stick for checking fluid level often required at 1000 mile intervals.

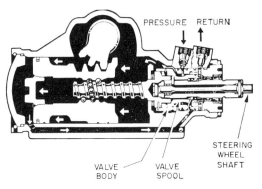

FIG. 5: Gear applied power steering unit (Buick) shows how hydraulic pressure (arrows) pushes on piston (A) with integral rack gear turning sector gear mounted on pitman shaft (B) to aid on left turn.

power rack. Both of these gear-type units have the shaft from the steering wheel passing through the control valve assembly.

Linkage-type power steering (Fig. 2) mounts the cylinder and piston assembly between one of the steering rods and the vehicle chassis or frame.

Here is what happens when you turn the wheel on a power steering equipped car. The pump, belt driven by the engine, draws hydraulic fluid from a reservoir and sends it out under pressure. Inside the pump, flow-control and pressure relief valves govern the amount of pressure in the system. The harder you turn the steering wheel, the more

hydraulic pressure is applied to help you turn it.

Two hydraulic lines connect the pump to the control valve. One is a flow line, the other a return line, or both may be flow lines depending on front wheel position. The control valve, like a traffic cop, directs fluid under pressure to the power cylinder.

With the wheels straight ahead, a centering spring holds the control valve spool in the neutral position. Fluid from the pump bypasses the valve, enters the power cylinder and returns to the reservoir. Pressure is equal on both sides of the piston.

When you turn left, twisting the steering wheel makes the valve spool move to the right overcoming the control valve centering spring (Figs. 2 and 5). Hydraulic fluid, under pressure from the pump, flows through the line to the right side of the power cylinder. Fluid on the left side of the cylinder is forced back through the return line as the piston moves to the left to assist your turn. On a right turn the process is reversed.

Spotting Power Steering Troubles. Leaking fluid, hard steering, binding or poor recovery, excessive free play, noise, steering chater, rattles and complete loss of power assist are all trouble symptoms. Fluid loss and hard steering are the most common.

When you notice one of these symptoms, there is usually no need to replace any of the complete power steering assemblies, let alone the entire system. Never let yourself be talked into such replacement until you are absolutely certain you need it.

Fluid leaks show up as a few drops or even a puddle on the garage floor. Ignore this warning and you're in for hard steering and

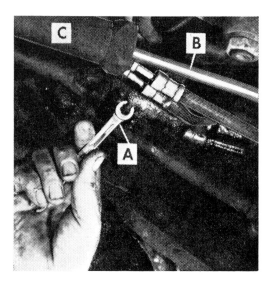

FIG. 4: If possible use special tubing fitting wrench (A) instead of open end to avoid damage when tightening leaky hydraulic line fitting. If piston rod (B) is scored or damaged, power cylinder (C) will have to be replaced

the expense of replacing fluid.

To find the leak, get under the car. If you can get it up on a hoist, it's much easier. Clean off the pump, control valve, power cylinder, and all the flexible lines and fittings (Fig. 1). Drain the pump reservoir catching the fluid in a clean container. Add ½-teaspoon of premixed red oil-soluble analine dye to each pint of fluid. Auto supply stores carry this dye. Then refill the pump reservoir with dyed fluid. Start the engine and turn the steering wheel from one side stop to the other at least ten times to circulate the dye through the system. Get an assistant to turn the wheel from one stop to the other and hold it at each stop for 10-15 seconds while you look for leaks in the system.

If a tubing fitting leaks, try tightening it. Use special tubing fitting wrench (Fig. 4) in preference to an open end wrench. If this does not help, replace it with a new fitting of the same size and type. If the leak is in one of the fluid lines, replace the line.

Leaks can occur at six places on the power steering pump and reservoir unit: cover joint, cover center stud, reservoir body to pump housing joint, between pump body valves, carrier shaft, and relief valve retainer. Fix any of these leaks by removing the pump and reservoir units from the car and replacing the leaking gasket or seal. Individual gaskets and rebuild kits are available from auto supply stores and mail order houses.

Control valve leaks point to a badly worn or damaged valve. Rebuild the valve with a complete rebuild kit to solve this problem.

Leaks at the power cylinder usually call for rebuilding with a kit. If the piston rod (Fig. 4B) is scored, you may have to replace the entire cylinder assembly. If the piston rod is not scored, installing the rebuild kit should fix the leak.

Hard steering is often caused by troubles outside the power steering system. Check first for soft tires, front end out of alignment, and worn steering linkage. Sometimes all you need is a lube job or air in the tires.

Check the power steering system for these easily spotted faults: low fluid level (Fig. 3), which should be checked about every 1000 miles anyway, loose or slipping drive belt on the pump (Fig. 7). Top up the fluid or tighten the belt until you can deflect it only about

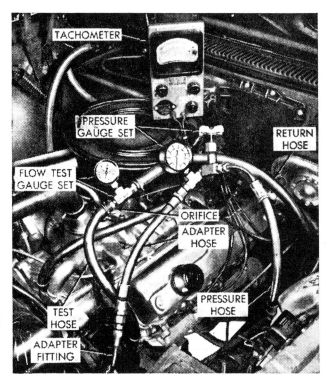

FIG. 6: Pressure test set up shows test lines and flow gauges required plus tachmometer to measure pump speed.

½ in. If the belt appears glazed, oil soaked, or cracked, replace it.

Now try the steering again. If it is still hard, you need professional help with test

FIG. 7: Drive belt on power steering pump should have only about ½-in. deflection between pulleys.

instruments. A pressure test is not expensive, but it calls for two pressure gauges and a tachometer (Fig. 6). It definitely will not pay you to buy these instruments just to make an occasional check on your system.

Before the test, run the engine for several minutes to warm up the hydraulic fluid. Test lines connect pump outlet with the pressure hose and return hose with pump reservoir. Turn the wheels full right and full left to check the pressure at each stop. Normal pressure is 700-850 *psi*. If pressure is normal, the trouble is probably in the control valve. Often all you need is an adjustment to the centering spring.

If the pressure is low, you have pump trouble. Fix it by removing the pump and rebuilding it using a complete seal kit.

Binding or poor recovery are usually caused by mechanical problems. Front end alignment, gear shaft out of adjustment, tight or worn steering linkage are probable causes.

Excessive free play in the steering may be caused by a bent gear shaft or worn steering linkage. Have these mechanical faults corrected at once for safety.

Noise in the power steering is caused by a loose and squeaking belt, kinked or twisted hydraulic lines, or air in the system. Fix it by tightening or replacing the belt, or aligning the hoses.

Bleed air out of the system whenever a line has been disconnected, a component replaced, or the reservoir has been emptied to change the fluid (usually recommended at about 25,000-mile intervals). Make sure the reservoir is full. Jack up the car so the front wheels clear the ground. With the transmission in neutral, the rear wheels blocked, and the engine running, depress the accelerator until the engine races at a speed equal to about 35 *mph*. Slowly turn the steering wheel all the way left, then all the way right. Lower the car to the ground and again turn the wheels slowly all the way left, then right. Recheck the reservoir, add fluid if needed and the job is done.

Complete loss of power steering doesn't happen often and will show up on the pressure test. If the pump is all right, test the power cylinder by disconnecting the piston rod from its bracket in the power cylinder and pushing the piston in and out by hand. If it offers no resistance, replace the entire cylinder. If the cylinder checks out then the centering spring in the control valve needs adjusting.

Even though you may not be able to make all these repairs and adjustments yourself, you should be able to pinpoint the trouble for your mechanic. Making these checks will insure you against work you don't need or missing a possible cause of trouble. And since most power steering troubles are caused by simple hydraulic leaks at hoses or fittings, you can save money by fixing these yourself.

Spring Care in the Fall

For really safe driving, it's not enough that your car's brakes and steering are in top working order—its springs have to be too

Tightening the U-bolt nuts on a rear leaf spring, using a socket wrench of the correct handle length.

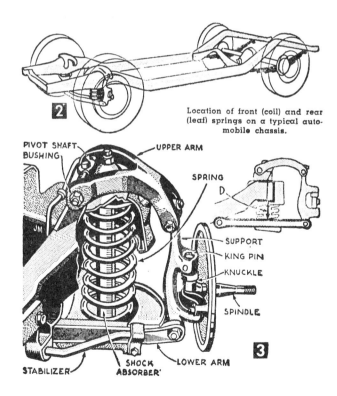

Location of front (coil) and rear (leaf) springs on a typical automobile chassis.

THOSE icy streets right around the weatherman's corner mean it's a mighty good time for a car checkup, particularly of your brakes and steering. But let's not forget those good-and-faithful servants—the *springs* on your car. A bum spring can turn a simple skid into disaster, since the spring suspensions control the alignment of both the front and rear axles. Wear on the front spring suspension parts causes steering misalignments you can't afford to have in icy weather (or any other time for that matter). Wheels out of alignment due to sagged spring suspensions also cause expensive tire wear and require expensive replacement of front spring control arms and bushings. So let's give those springs a real going over.

Starting with the front coil springs (Fig. 2), the first thing to look for are any signs of cracks on the coil spring surfaces; these signify a progressive fracture's on

Here is a typical front coil spring suspension. As shown in the detail, control arm-to-frame distance (D) should be equal on both right and left front wheels.

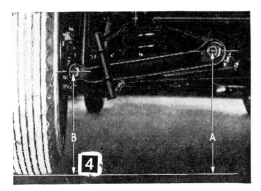

Check coil springs for sag by comparing measurements A and B with car maker's specifications.

the way, and the coil should probably be replaced. Next, look for sagging by checking the measurements shown in Fig. 4 against the manufacturer's specifications (your dealer can supply these or they may be obtained from the manufacturer's manual). You won't have correct steering alignment unless the height of these front coil springs on both sides meets the manufacturer's "specs." When you check for sagging be sure the car is on a smooth, level floor and rock it several times from side to side to allow it to settle; this should shake loose any binding that might affect the dimensions. Also check control-arm-to-frame distances (D in Fig. 3) to make sure they are the same on both right and left front wheels. Those bushings on the control arms (Fig. 3) may also show some signs of wear, which can cause steering misalignments.

If these checks you have just made, plus the common signs of excessive or uneven tire wear, rough riding or some trouble with steering—all factors which call for an examination of the spring suspensions—show you some repairs are necessary, what should you do? The replacement of worn front spring suspension *bushings* nearly always makes it necessary to make an accurate correction of front wheel factors, including caster, camber, toe-in and toe-out. This is a complex job that should be done by a service station using special equipment. You can, however, shim up sagged front coil springs, or even replace them, without having to readjust the steering alignment.

Since coil springs cannot be "preset" (as adjacent coils contact each other) they often take some permanent set during the first 5,000 or 10,000 miles of use. As the coil spring is mounted at the middle of the A-bar (Fig. 3), a $\frac{1}{4}$ in. set of the 11-ft. (before coiling) spring rod means a $\frac{1}{2}$ in. sag of the car body on that side. In such cases, a special "shim" (supplied by manufacturer) is usually placed between the spring and its top seat (Fig. 5). Many car manufacturers allow the use of 2 shims, but recommend replacing the coil spring if more than 2 shims are needed to restore the spring to its original height. Instructions for Chevrolet, for instance, are that

a $\frac{1}{16}$ in. thick shim can be added but more than 2 shims should definitely *not* be used because additional shims cause spring coils to bottom before the lower support arm movement is stopped by the rubber bumper. On the other hand, Buick specifies that, when the trim dimension is too low, you can correct by installing special $\frac{1}{8}$ in. shims, but when more than 3 shims are required, you should replace the spring instead.

Coil spring suspensions are used at the car's front because they permit a wide range of spring action, while still maintaining accurate caster or "slant" (Fig. 6) of the front wheel king pins nec-

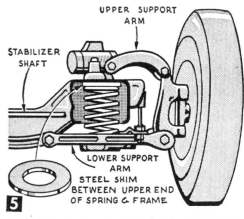

Method of shimming up sagging coil spring. Manufacturers usually okay the use of 2 shims, specify spring replacement if it will take more than 2 shims to do the job.

essary for steering. Since each coil spring front suspension has more points of motion and resultant wear (as compared with the 2 points on the leaf springs used on older car models and on the front axles of trucks) it is important that these points get regular and adequate lubrication, either at a service station, or by doing it yourself. The weight of the car body must be jacked up off the spring suspension, while lubricant is forced in (Fig. 7). This is necessary, because the spring suspension bearings have only a very limited, oscillating motion (say $\frac{1}{10}$ of a turn or less), as contrasted to the complete rotation of, say, engine or wheel bearings. This not only concentrates the wear but means that the actual "wear points" are held together by the weight of the car so that the lubricant cannot be forced in—unless the car body weight is jacked up off the springs.

So, when lubricating the front spring suspensions, use a bumper jack to raise the front end of the car if you are doing it yourself or make sure the service station attendant jacks up the weight of the car off the springs. Since coil springs act in torsion or twisting, rather than by bending, the greatest stresses occur at the surface and so the surfaces of coil spring bars are finished by grinding and should be protected against rust by paint during the life of the car. Check to see that the paint coat is adequate.

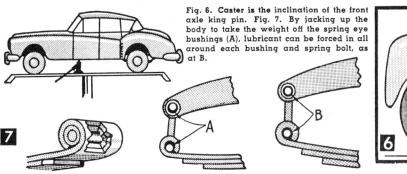

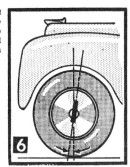

Fig. 6. Caster is the inclination of the front axle king pin. Fig. 7. By jacking up the body to take the weight off the spring eye bushings (A), lubricant can be forced in all around each bushing and spring bolt, as at B.

For several years, the trend has been towards the almost universal use of airplane-type direct action shock absorbers, mounted *within* the coil spring for compactness and protection against flying stones (Fig. 3). Such airplane-type shock absorbers are not designed for refilling or repair and should be replaced when they become worn. To check whether the shock absorbers require replacement, grasp one end of a bumper and jounce the car up and down. If the shock absorbers are in good condition, the car will settle to a normal position immediately upon releasing the bumper. If the car continues to bounce, or stays in an up or down position, remove the shock absorber for further checking. This is not a difficult job. For instance, on late model Fords (Fig. 3) it requires (working from the top down) removal of a lock nut, washer and rubber bushing assembly from the top of the frame spring dome, and the cap screws which attach the plate to the lower suspension arm. Shock is then pulled through the bottom.

To check a shock absorber, after it has been removed from the car, clamp the lower end in a vise in a near vertical position and pump a few times to expel any air. A good shock absorber will have a steady "drag" in both directions when operated by hand. If it is very hard or impossible to operate, or if it pulls apart without any drag, it should be replaced.

Now let's check the *rear* leaf type spring suspensions. Here the problem is a bit different. While the regular lubrication of *front* wheel spring suspensions is recommended, you must deliberately avoid lubricating part or all of the *rear* spring suspension on many modern cars. Here's why. The bushing of the front spring suspensions are of metal to hold the front wheels in exact driving and steering alignments. But rubber bushings are now usually fitted into the eyes of the rear leaf springs positioning the rear axles, because they have to prevent the transmission of sound from the road to the car, and also because they eliminate the need for lubrication.

These rubber bushings are tightly fitted against the metal spring eye and against the metal shackle bolt, and no motion or wear is intended to occur at these points. All relative motion between shackle bolt and spring eye should occur in the flexing of the rubber itself. Thus, if you lubricate the rubber bushing, the inner and outer surface will slip on the metal, causing rapid wear and noise. Instead, when leaf springs are replaced, the inexpensive rubber bushings should also be replaced, due to fatigue wear in the rubber.

While the springs of earlier model cars had metal-to-metal contact between adjacent leaves (as used for truck springs), the spring leaves on nearly all modern cars are insulated from each other by waxed fabric liners, rubber spring buttons (Fig. 10), or a viscous grease lubricant held in place between the leaves by steel spring covers. The waxed fabric liners (you'll find them between the spring leaves of Cadillac, Packard, Lincoln, Chrysler, Mercury and some others) or the square waxed fabric pads on 1949-50 Fords should definitely *not* be lubricated, since oil will deteriorate the wax and fabric. Instead, when the waxed fabric liners are worn, they can be replaced. You don't have to take the spring apart, since nearly all motion and wear occurs near the tips of the leaves. Just jack up the car weight off the springs and separate the tips of the leaves with a

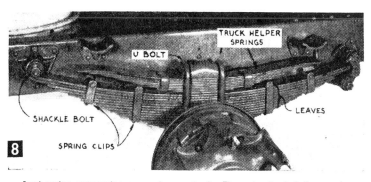

Leaf spring suspension as used on a truck. The extra truck helper springs shown here should contact the pads when the truck is at 40% of full load.

hardwood wedge, so that you can cut off a 4 in. piece of worn lining, using a hacksaw blade ground down to a ¼ in. width. The 1¾ in. waxed fabric squares for Fords, or on some other cars the rubber buttons fitted into depressions in the ends of the tips of the leaves, are easily replaced by prying apart the leaves.

According to the manufacturer's recommendations, these rear spring buttons should not be lubricated.

Many modern cars have steel covers on the rear springs, to keep dirt out. What kind of care should these get? A special lubricant which retains its consistency even in unusual temperatures and gives the proper control of inter-leaf friction and spring action is required. These steel spring covers should be refilled every 5,000 to 10,000 miles, and it's a job you can do if you have the special lubricant fitting (to be clamped on to the spring cover). If the spring shackle bolts have lubricating fittings, these bolts should also be lubricated. But not if they are of the rubber-bushed type.

Since it is impossible to check springs having steel spring covers for broken leaves (except by noting the sag), keep the U-bolt nuts firmly tightened (Fig. 1) so that by holding the middle of the spring firmly against the axle pad, as in a vise, no bending, and consequently no breakage will occur at the tie bolt hole in the middle of the spring. Check U-bolt nuts with a socket wrench for tightness, using a wrench with a 3 ft. long handle for the ½ in. U-bolts on passenger cars (or a wrench with 4 ft. handle for the ¾ in. U-bolt nuts on light trucks). After installing new spring leaves or replacing a spring, retighten the U-bolt nuts after the springs have been bedded down by a couple of hundred miles of driving. With center U-bolt nuts really tight, center breakage of leaf springs will hardly ever occur. Center or tie bolt should be equally distant between the two U-bolts.

You can also check the spring leaves for sideways displacement or "fanning out" (due to

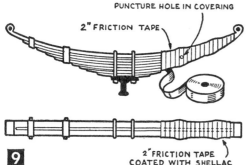

PUNCTURE HOLE IN COVERING

2" FRICTION TAPE

2" FRICTION TAPE COATED WITH SHELLAC

Spring covers like these are easy to make, keep winter road salts out of springs. Wire on top of the spring leaves ensures space for lubricant.

broken or missing spring clips), small checks or cracks along edges of leaves (which would result in progressive fractures) and sagging or broken leaves (where there is no steel cover). Incidentally the spring leaves can be covered as shown in Fig. 9. Check the spring clips (Fig. 8) for free fit between clips and edges of leaves. There should also be $\frac{1}{16}$ in. clearance between the surface of the main leaf and the bolt which holds the clip nearest the end of spring, to allow "twist" of main leaf when one wheel drops into a rut. Check spring eyes for a free but not a sloppy fit. Check shackle bolts for wear and for lubrication—if of metal-bushed type. Center or tie-bolt should not only be equally distant between the two U-bolts but also should not be bent, loose or broken.

Many rear shock absorbers have a "stone shield" or plate welded to the lower end of the inner cylinder. When installing a replacement, if one is needed, be sure to position such shock absorbers with shield facing toward front of car.

Specialists in spring service work sometimes use a "trick" method when one or more leaves (but not the main leaf) are broken. First, the weight of the car or truck body is jacked up off the spring and supported securely. Then the head of the center or tie-bolt is cut off with a cold chisel. Next the U-bolts are removed and a longer center bolt (having much longer threads) is installed. Now by tightening the nut on the center bolt, the leaves are pulled together enough to allow the U-bolts to be replaced and tightened.

Since several thousand different car and truck springs are now in use, if you should order any replacement parts, supply all possible information you have, such as the catalog and part number (when available), make of car or truck, year and model of car, serial number and body style, and whether springs are for right or left and for front or rear. For your guidance, spring lengths are measured along the curvature of the main leaf, from the center of one eye to the center of the other.

How to Select the Right Anti-Freeze

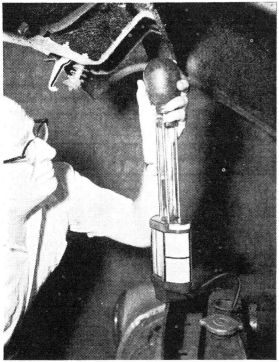

When using a hydrometer, read the amount of freeze protection at the mark indicated by the liquid level on the float.

Some Are Anti-Freezes in *Name* Only

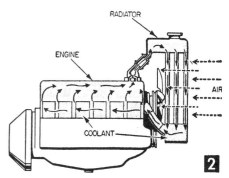

Simplified drawing of automobile cooling system. Heat represented by the solid arrows is absorbed by the coolant in the engine block and carried into the radiator. Here the air does the actual cooling to the point where the coolant in the bottom tank of the radiator is ready to be re-circulated by the belt-driven water pump in order to pick up more heat from the engine. Engine temperature is controlled by the thermostat at the water outlet of the engine block, which is open for greatest cooling, closed for fastest warmup.

YOU are driving an air-cooled car, although a liquid called the *coolant* carries the engine heat to the radiator so that the air can carry the heat away (Fig. 2). Since engine life and efficiency are very directly dependent upon controlled temperature, the cooling system must not overcool nor freeze on a zero day, yet it must keep the engine from overheating when outside temperatures are well above 100°F.

A car radiator can throw off enough heat to keep a six-room house comfortably warm on a zero day. The coolant carrying this amount of heat may circulate at a rate of anywhere between 4,000 and 10,000 gallons an hour. This coolant moves up and around the cylinders (Fig. 2). In many engines the coolant is directed against the valve seat where temperatures of burning gases may go as high as 2000°F. To prevent avoidable wear from extreme temperatures and uneven expansion, the coolant must be capable of absorbing heat quickly. This means that the cooling system must be clean (free from rust, scale, dirt, oil or sediment) and must be free of leaks.

Check by the methods described below for these factors each fall before installing anti-freeze.

Checking for Leaks. Leaks often occur at the hose connections between the engine and the radiator and between the engine and the heater (Fig. 3). If a hose is either soft and mushy or hard and brittle, replace it; otherwise, tightening the clamps will usually cure the leak. If there are traces of rust near any of the headbolts, remove the bolts (after the coolant has been drained) and wire-brush the threads clean. Then apply a film of non-hardening gasket cement to the threads and pull the bolts up to uniform tightness, using a torque wrench, if possible, to make sure the bolts are tightened uniformly. Refer to the engine or wrench manufacturer's specifications for the correct torque in foot-pounds, which may vary between 50 foot-pounds and 65 foot-pounds, depending on the size of the headbolt.

If an expansion plug in the block is rusted, remove it by driving a sharp centerpunch through the plug about ¾ in. near its center and giving

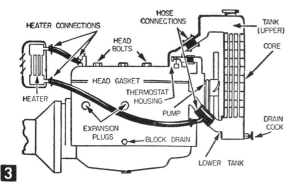

3 Schematic diagram of cooling system showing where leaks most often develop.

4 With clean head gasket laid on a sheet of paper, apply a thin film of gasket cement to both surfaces and allow to become tacky before installing.

with water and remove the fan belt. Carefully block all four wheels or set the emergency brake, then put the car into automatic drive. With a conventional transmission, shift into "high" and apply the load by slipping the clutch. Have an assistant start the engine and very quickly, before it has warmed up (which might create steam bubbles), accelerate it very briefly to rather high speed. If there is an exhaust gas leak into the coolant, you will see bubbles in the cooling system water in a matter of seconds. If bubbles appear, a new head gasket is in order (Fig. 4). Before installing the gasket, be sure that head and block mating surfaces are clean.

The presence of a white deposit (lime) on the radiator core (Fig. 5) is a warning that water has leaked out and evaporated. The use of an acid and rust inhibitor and also a cooling system sealer when conditioning a cooling system for summer will probably take care of this type of leaking. The inhibitor controls the rusting of the engine block and stops the corrosion of the radiator core; the sealer, except in extreme cases, makes the system watertight.

It is not necessary to add inhibitor when putting in fresh anti-freeze, since any first-class anti-freeze liquid contains its own. However, inhibitor is likely to lose its effectiveness after one season of use, and fresh inhibitor should be added to anti-freeze before draining it out if you intend to use it again the next season. Use of the same anti-freeze for more than one season is generally discouraged because of the slight savings possible and the corrosion or freezing of the cooling system that can result if the anti-freeze has turned acid or lost its ability to protect against freezing.

If there is any sign of leaking around the water pump, install a new or rebuilt pump, cementing the gasket in place (Fig. 7).

While the thermostat plays no part in the tightness of the system, it is a good idea to check its operation at this time. There are three kinds of thermostats: the bellows

the punch a sharp tap sideways with a hammer. Scrape clean the recess in which plug fits, using a screwdriver blade. Then drive a new plug into place, after first applying a thin film of gasket cement to both the plug and the surface upon which it rests. Strike the domed side (which should always face *out*) a sharp blow with a machinist's hammer to cause plug to expand and form a tight fit in the block.

You will need a new cylinder head gasket (Fig. 4), if there is any sign of water in the crankcase oil. To check for leakage of exhaust gas into the coolant—and consequently the possibility of the leakage of coolant down into the engine—first remove the top hose from the engine and take out the thermostat. Then fill the engine

TABLE A. QUICKIE COOLING-SYSTEM SERVICE
(Draining and cleaning)

1. Take off radiator cap
2. Open all drains
3. Remove heater hose. Drain heater separately
4. Reconnect upper heater hose
5. Plug lower heater hose opening
6. Take out thermostat and reinstall housing and hose
7. Run water from garden hose through cooling system
8. With water running (drains open) run engine till water runs clear. Turn off engine
9. Check thermostat (see text)
10. Remove and inspect radiator hose inside and out
11. Replace hose or install new hose; tighten connections
12. Torque headbolts uniformly to car manufacturer's specifications
13. Fill cooling system (water in summer, anti-freeze in winter)
14. Examine for leaks especially at radiator, hose connections, gaskets, core plugs and thermostat housing
15. Put in a good cooling system sealer
16. Loosen fan belt
17. Spin fan and check for mechanical condition
18. Check belt for wear, hardness and cracks. Replace if any are found
19. Adjust for 1/2-in. of play under light thumb-pressure midway between two pulleys
20. Flush air passages of radiator core gently with water from hose and brush out leaves, bugs, and such
21. Replace stuck, damaged or rusty drains
22. Put in rust inhibitor in summer. Be sure your winter anti-freeze contains inhibitor

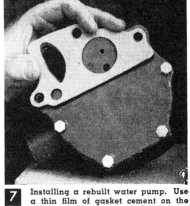

5 White blotches of lime indicate the presence of water leaks in this radiator. The actual location of the leak will be at the top of the white area.

  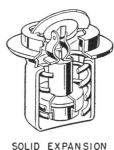

6 BELLOWS   BI-METALLIC   SOLID EXPANSION

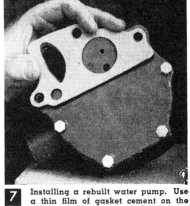

8 Removing thermostat from its housing in order to test its opening point.

type (Fig. 8), and the bi-metallic and solid-expansion types (Fig. 6). Whatever the construction, those intended for use with alcohol-type anti-freeze should open when the temperature is between 140° and 160° F. For use with ethylene glycol (permanent) anti-freeze solutions, the opening point should be somewhat above 160° F. Engines generally operate between 140 and 180°F.

To check the thermostat, wash any dirt from it with soap and water or radiator cleaner and suspend it in a pan of water. Begin warming the water and, with the aid of a thermometer which goes as high as 212° F., note the temperature at which the thermostat opens. If it does not vary more than 5 or 10° from the temperature stamped on the valve, the thermostat may be used again.

The cooling system is pressurized by means of a special cap that seals off the overflow tube. As the system warms up, the expansion creates pressure which helps prevent excessive loss due to the boiling of volatile type anti-freeze solutions. If engine oil should work into the cooling system, the seals in the pressure cap will be ruined, and a new cap must be installed. When installing a new cap be very sure that the surfaces in the filler neck of the radiator are clean and smooth where the seals meet them. If necessary, polish the radiator neck with No. 320A abrasive paper or steel wool (Fig. 9).

A simple and effective test for checking tightness of the cooling system can be made with a 3-ft. length of $\frac{5}{16}$ in. soft rubber tubing forced over the lower end of the overflow tube, which goes into the cooling system at the filler neck. If a pressure cap is used on the radiator, place a paper match in the neck to keep the lower seal from being airtight. The upper seal of the radiator cap must be a perfect fit. Now suck on the rubber tube and then plug the tube with the tip of your tongue. The tube, due to the vacuum created in an airtight cooling system, should hold itself to your tongue. If air cannot enter the cooling system, coolant cannot escape.

Choosing the Coolant. The primary job of any coolant is the absorption of engine heat. Water alone, or mixtures of water and standard brands of anti-freeze, absorb heat readily. Using more anti-freeze than is required for the lowest temperatures expected in your locality causes the coolant to remove heat slowly. Petroleum base coolants also have this fault. The result of using a too-strong concentration of anti-freeze or a

9 Cleaning off the contact surfaces before installing a new radiator pressure cap.

A coolant containing ethylene glycol and water would boil above this temperature. A coolant composed of denatured alcohol or methanol and water would boil below 212° F. at sea level. All three of these products, however, serve well as anti-freeze materials under normal driving conditions and without excessive loss. Petroleum-base coolants and those composed of alcohol present a fire hazard when boiling occurs.

2. FREEZING. Expensive damage may be caused by expansion when water freezes. Coolants of anti-freeze and water may form a harmless slush if chilled only a few degrees below their protection point. The slush may circulate while the system warms above the thaw point.

3. MECHANICAL DAMAGE. Water alone rusts iron where air is present, and impurities in hard water increase this form of damage. The regular use of rust inhibitor or of anti-freeze containing an inhibitor cuts down or eliminates this trouble. Petroleum-base coolants damage natural rubber hose connections and lead to their breakage, whereas mixtures of anti-freeze and water or water alone will not do so. Salt solutions which are sometimes used for anti-freeze purposes are very destructive to metal parts, and when spilled, may possibly short out the electrical system.

4. SURGING. A hard, fast run followed by a sudden stop may induce boiling. This kind of boiling is due to the heat stored in the engine and the sudden stoppage of air and coolant movement. This after-boil or surging may cause the loss of coolant through the overflow tube. If you cannot idle fast for a few moments after a hard run, connect a surge or overflow tank to the overflow line from the radiator to hold coolant that could be lost.

5. EXPANSION. Heating causes the expansion of any coolant. If your radiator tank does not have a mark which indicates the point past which it should not be filled, make it a rule never to fill past the middle of the top tank.

6. FOAMING. Inhibitors that reduce foaming are a part of many standard anti-freeze materials. Foreign matter suspended in the cooling system may cause foaming, with its resulting loss of liquid. Leakage of the water pump may cause air to be drawn in which, injected into the coolant, causes foaming.

7. EVAPORATION. Experience indicates that very little coolant is lost by evaporation. For this reason it may be unfair to classify methanol and alcohol-type anti-freezes as volatile—they are very satisfactory in this respect.

petroleum-base coolant may be damage of the overheated engine wall, even though high temperature is not indicated by the temperature gage. You can test your anti-freeze for its protection against freezing by using a hydrometer that is correct for its specific gravity (Fig. 1). Modern hydrometers are marked according to the brand of the anti-freeze used or the material of which the anti-freeze is made. The response of the float in the hydrometer is very sensitive. To prevent sticking and improve visibility, clean glass tube and float after each use by rinsing with soap or detergent solution. When making the reading, shake the hydrometer slightly to be sure that the float is free. Then hold it in a vertical position so that the float does not stick to the glass tube. Make an accurate reading at eye-level and interpret the value of the reading on the correct scale.

Since some anti-freeze solutions are *lighter* than water and others are *heavier,* it is impossible to obtain a correct hydrometer reading on a solution made by mixing different anti-freeze materials. In such a case, draw off a sample of the solution and place it in a deep freeze. By using a thermometer or setting the freezer adjustment at various temperatures you can determine the lowest temperature at which the unknown anti-freeze will furnish protection.

Study the eight problems that follow. These are faced by any coolant, and may help in the selection of the best coolant for your car, according to your needs.

1. BOILING. Water boils at 212° F. at sea level.

TABLE B. COOLING SYSTEM COSTS

If you are doing your own work, here are the approximate costs of some of the materials which you may need. Obtain from local car dealer or automotive supply house.

Radiator cleaner	$ 1.25—$ 2.50
Radiator rust inhibitor	.60— .75
Radiator sealer	.75— 1.75
Radiator (complete)	50.00— 90.00
Radiator core (installed)	35.00— 50.00
Radiator repairs	9.00— 18.00
Radiator hose	1.00— 3.00
Radiator hose clamp	.30— .50
Thermostat	2.80— 3.25
Pressure cap	1.10— 1.50
Water pump (new)	10.00— 28.00
Water pump (rebuilt)	7.00— 18.00
Draincock	.50— .85
Gasket cement	.39— .79
Anti-freeze (per gallon)	1.60— 3.25
Expansion plug, each	.10— .15

A New Way to Flush Your Car's Cooling System

Thermostat must be removed to permit reverse flow of water during flushing.

THE makers of permanent antifreeze know that the success of their products depend on a thoroughly flushed and clean engine cooling system.

That's why the manufacturer of *Telar*, a new combination antifreeze and summer coolant, has come up with this method of flushing your car's waterjacket and radiator. In addition to doing a better job of cleaning, this procedure can be completed in less than 15 minutes without putting your car on a lift.

First, open all the drain cocks on the radiator and engine block, and then open the valve to drain the heater core. As soon as the water level is low enough, disconnect the thermostat housing from the block and remove the thermostat (Fig. 1). Disconnect the upper hose from the radiator, and then reassemble the housing. When the system is completely drained, plug the upper radiator neck with a stopper (Fig. 2) and close the radiator drain cock.

Next, remove the radiator cap and insert a water hose into the filler neck. Run the water at a moderate speed while watching the water being forced out of the hose that has been disconnected from the radiator neck. Be sure to deflect this flow to keep the engine ignition system dry (Fig. 3).

In about five minutes this reverse flow of water should become completely clear, in-

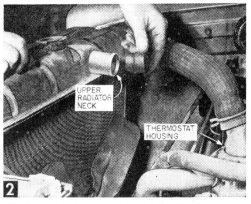

To force cleaning water through block, plug upper radiator neck with cork or rubber stopper.

dicating that the entire system has been flushed.

Now remove the stopper and reconnect the upper radiator hose. Install the correct thermostat for the time of year and fill the system with coolant and water mixed according to the maufacturer's instructions.

When water flows clean from disconnected upper hose (usually less than five minutes), cooling system is clean and ready for refill with coolant-water mixture.

Temperature-corrected hydrometer helps good summer maintenance. Hold it vertical for accurate reading.

Summer Care for Winter Starts

In the summertime, your battery may be quietly suffering.
If you learn how to recognize and treat the symptoms now,
chances are good you'll avoid those cold weather stalls

WHEN YOU TURN the key of the car on the first cold morning in winter and discover that the battery has turned up its toes, the reason isn't just the sudden freeze; it's the battery maintenance you didn't do in the summer. The time when a battery is functioning the best is just when it may be deteriorating the most—quietly, so you don't notice it.

The reason is simple. *Cold* is a battery's obvious enemy. When the temperature is low enough to put frost on the ground, even a brand-new, fully charged battery is operating at about half its peak efficiency. But *heat* is its undercover enemy. Neglect in warm weather can drag down the other 50% of its efficiency to the point where there's nothing left when you need it.

Fortunately, many battery troubles can be stopped before they reach this stage. Even when the battery is suffering in silence, the symptoms of galloping deterioration are there to see if you look for them. Usually they can be successfully treated if you catch them in time—and that means during the summertime.

Watch the Water. The weapon that hot weather uses to assault the battery is evaporation. This attacks the heart of the little black box—its electrolyte, the combination of water and sulphuric acid that's the "chemical" part of its "electro-chemical" power. As the water evaporates, the proportion of acid in the mixture rises—and so does the rate of corrosion and wear. Rule number one for summer battery care is this: the hotter the weather gets, the more often you should check the water. Every two weeks is about right for mid-summer. Take off the caps and check the level in each cell. In summer, it ought to be kept about ⅜ inch above the plates—a quarter-inch higher than you usually need to keep it in winter. When it's below this level, raise it to the right point with distilled water or clean rain water.

If the level in one cell falls consistently lower than the rest, look for leaks or cracks in its container. And if you find them, have the container replaced.

Check the Gravity. When the water level in the battery seems to drop at a rate that's fast even for hot weather, you begin to suspect that it's getting too much charge from the generator. Over-charging is most often the fault of the voltage regulator, and it's not specifically caused by hot weather. But in an over-charged battery, the proportion of acid to water stays high even when you're careful to keep the water level up. When this occurs in combination with the quick evaporation of summertime, it's deadly.

The instrument that clues you in to this unhealthy state of affairs is the hydrometer, which measures the "specific gravity" of the electrolyte.

The standard analysis of a hydrometer reading goes like this:

Below 1.225—battery needs re-charging
1.270—1.300—battery is okay
Above 1.300—battery is over-charged

But even a slight amount of over-charge can cause a damaging concentration of acid. In hot weather, when evaporation is making trouble in the same direction, a reading that stays between 1.270 and 1.280 is better than one that's always nudging the high side of the safe limits.

Even though you can almost always get a hydrometer reading at a service station, it's a handy gadget to own, and at $4 or $5, a good investment. But if you buy one, be sure you know whether or not it's "temperature corrected." When air temperature goes above 80°, an uncorrected hydrometer gives a lower-than-true reading that has to be adjusted by arithmetic.

In any case, an over-charged battery calls for quick attention to the voltage regulator. Take the problem to a pro. Adjusting the regulator is no task for even a talented amateur.

Keep It Clean. Winter or summer, a major cause of battery breakdown is corrosion. You can't change the acid nature of a battery, but you can clean up its external effects. Here are the steps to a safe, thorough job:

1. When you remove the battery for cleaning, always disconnect the ground cable first. This lessens the chance of getting a bad burn.

2. Before you take it out, notice where the plus and minus terminals are located, so you can put it back in the same position.

3. If the battery is badly corroded, wash it

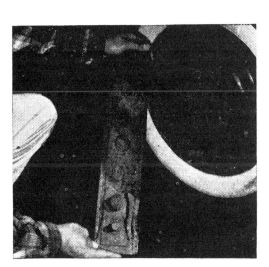

The case of the battered battery: warping, cracking can be caused by excess heat, too-tight hold-downs.

Loose battery terminals should not be pounded with hammer. When they're on right, they're tight.

down with a garden hose and a broom. Then scrub it clean with a solution of baking soda and water, which neutralizes the acid. Let the solution dry on the battery.

4. With the baking soda solution and a wire-brush, clean the battery box in the car.

5. Clean both battery cables at *both* ends, particularly the insulated cable, where it's attached to the starter or starter solenoid. But be sure also to clean the metal mesh cable where it grounds to the frame. At the battery terminal ends, scrape the inner surfaces of the terminal clips with a pocket knife or a round file. Scrape until the metal is bright. Then scrape lightly over the battery posts. Remove, clean, and replace the tensioning bolts of both terminals.

6. Clean the hold-down assembly—frame and tie bolts—with soda and water, and then wire-brush the whole works. A spray job with silver paint will go a long way toward delaying the next clean-up. A light coating of vaseline will do the same thing for a shorter time. Applying both can't hurt.

7. When you put the battery back in the car, slide the top-frame down over it and snug down the tie bolts. *Snug* down. Don't crank. Wing nuts should be finger tight; the hex-head type should be run down just enough to hold the battery in place without jiggling. A too-tight hold-down often cracks the battery on top. A too-loose one allows it to bounce and crack on the bottom. Just *snug.*

8. Give the battery posts a thin coating of vaseline. Do the same with the cable terminals, then replace them on the battery. Remember these points. Replace the hot lead first, the ground cable last. Be sure to connect positive to positive, negative to negative. If the cable won't reach or the terminal won't fit the post, you're not doing it right: reverse them. *Don't pound the terminals on the posts with a hammer.* A tap or two with a screwdriver is permissible, but that's about all. Tighten the tensioning bolts, give them another coating of vaseline, and quit.

Taking these precautions will pay off in the long run, especially when that long run is going to be during the wintertime when you need and want a frisky, efficiently operating battery. Just remember the main points. Check the water approximately every two weeks in the summertime. If you find leaks or cracks in the cell's container, have it replaced.

If the water level is dropping at a too-fast rate, chances are the battery is getting too much charge from the generator. Check the specific gravity and if your voltage regulator needs adjusting, take your problem to a pro. Make sure your battery is kept clean. Corrosion is one of the causes of battery breakdown.

Take these precautions in summertime, and you'll rarely hear the low, defeated growl of a dying battery in winter. What's more, you may also outwit the battery manufacturers. Most of them "expect" a battery to be good for about two years. Maybe you'll make it five.

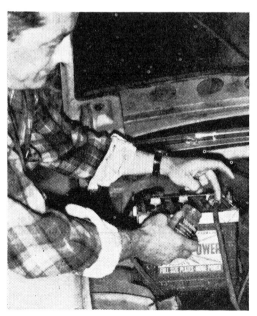

Hold-down assembly has been spray-painted to retard sulphation. Wing nuts are finger tight.

The final touch is thin coating of vaseline. Cruder lubricants should never be put on battery terminals.

Use the Right Thermostat

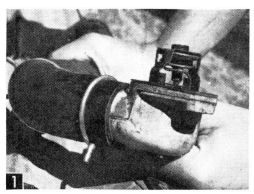

A thermostat may be found in one of several spots, but wherever it is, remove it and check it if your engine starts suffering chills or running a fever.

THE engine in your car is designed to operate at its greatest efficiency when it's relatively hot. If your engine is water-cooled, there's a thermostat in the cooling system to make it heat up quickly and to the right temperature.

A Small, Stopper-Like Device (Fig. 1), the thermostat keeps the liquid in the cooling system from passing through the radiator until the engine warms up. There may be one in your car, or there may be two, but if your machine is newer than a Stutz Runabout, it's sure to have either a bi-metal coil or bellows-type thermostat (Fig. 2) somewhere in the cooling system.

In-line engines, even late-model versions like the Dodge Slant Six, use one thermostat. Some V-8s with two hoses from radiator to cylinders use two thermostats—one for each bank of cylinders. The thermostat may be mounted in any one of several spots (Fig. 3): in the block, at the radiator hose elbow, in a secondary hose connection, or even in the radiator. Instead of playing "find-the-thermostat," check your owner's manual or a nearby garage. In most cars, the thermostat —wherever it is—can be removed by loosening two bolts.

If your engine refuses to heat quickly on cold mornings or to cool quickly on hot days, the thermostat may be at fault. If it is misaligned, or the valve inside it is stuck open, it will allow water to circulate freely through the radiator even when the engine temperature is below normal, and the engine may never heat. If the valve spring is worn or stuck closed, it will force the water in the cooling system to bypass the radiator—even

when it's boiling—and the engine may never get a chance to cool. The remedy is a new thermostat.

Getting the Right One. All thermostats are not the same. Every auto manufacturer specifies the best type and the proper heat range for his car, and in some cases may even specify one thermostat for use with water and another for use with a permanent-type antifreeze.

Be sure to buy the right thermostat for your car. If you bought the car second-hand, don't go by the one now in the cooling system: it could be wrong. Check a factory manual for the right model, heat range, and size.

If no factory guide is available, you will be safe if you buy a thermostat designed to begin opening at 166° to 175°F and to be wide open at 194°—for use with permanent antifreeze. A thermostat used with alcohol antifreeze should start opening at 148° to 155° and be fully open at 178°. You'll find some variation here when the wide-open point has been adjusted to increase the efficiency of a hot-water car heater. A thermostat for water may be in either range if the cooling system

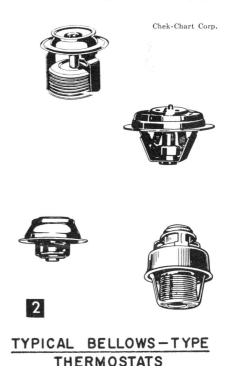

TYPICAL BELLOWS—TYPE THERMOSTATS

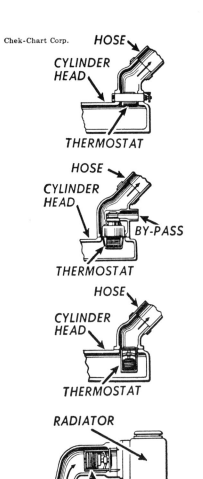

FOUR TYPICAL
THERMOSTAT INSTALLATIONS

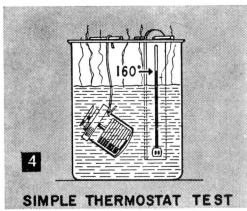

SIMPLE THERMOSTAT TEST

Use sealing compound, and replace a damaged gasket.

has been pressurized.

Remove the Thermostat, if you think there may be something wrong with it, and check for corrosion and for worn or broken springs. If you can't see anything wrong, test it before you decide whether to discard it or to put it back in.

Many thermostats have their temperature ranges stamped on the casing. The lower temperature is the one at which the thermostat is supposed to begin opening, and the higher temperature the point at which it should be fully open.

To test the thermostat, heat water on the stove to a temperature 10° below the point at which it should begin opening. Suspend the thermostat in the water for a couple of minutes (Fig. 4): if it starts to open, discard it. If it remains closed, heat the water to a point 25° above the opening temperature, and suspend the thermostat in the water again. At this point, it should open fully; if it doesn't, discard it.

It will probably be necessary to remove one or more radiator hoses to remove the thermostat. Check the hoses for breaks and splits while they are off the car, and when you put them back on be sure to clean the connections. Before you replace an engine-mounted thermostat coat the elbow or housing with sealing compound (Fig. 5). If the gasket is torn or chipped, replace it. Tighten the hose clamps, start the engine, and check for leaks.

How to Clean Upholstery

With a little knowledge of fabrics and cleaning agents, you can add beauty, value and comfort to your car with minimum effort

THE beautiful outside appearance of a carefully washed and waxed automobile is meaningless if the interior does not receive the same care. Car carpeting and upholstery should be given periodic attention. Dust and dirt accumulations on the upholstery and carpeting should be removed every few weeks. If the car receives hard use, it should be cleaned oftener. This does not mean that any handy means of cleaning should be used.

It would be harmful to use a whisk broom on upholstery having a raised tapestry pattern. The stiff bristles would damage the fine threads which compose the raised pattern. To remove dust from such fabrics, use a vacuum cleaner. On other types of upholstery, a whisk broom may be safely used. Go over the material with a vacuum cleaner after the brush has loosened dirt that remains in the tiny pores of the weave. Dust and dirt hinder the cleaning powers of the agents

used. The better the job of dirt and dust removal, the easier and better the job with cleaning agents will be. There are three basic kinds of cleaners readily available: synthetic detergents, neutral soap, and volatile cleaners.

Broadcloth and Flatcloth. Avoid using any solutions containing water on broadcloth no matter how efficiently they remove signs of soiling or stains. Broadcloth finishes are produced by a process employing multiple pressings and other operations which result in the fine finish of this fabric. Water causes the nap to curl and become rough. The result is an unsightly appearance and restoration of the original finish is impossible.

The use of a volatile cleaner is recommended on both flatcloth and broadcloth upholstery. Naphtha or gasoline may be used, but make sure that no coloring or tetraethyl lead is contained in the solvent. Since naphtha and gasoline are dangerous as a fire hazard, they should only be used as a last resort when

Fig. 1. Use a volatile cleaner on broadcloth. Avoid using colored gasoline or naphtha.

Fig. 2. Genuine and imitation leathers are best kept clean by using a neutral soap.

a safer type of cleaner such as carbon tetrachloride is not available. Make sure there is plenty of ventilation when using any type of volatile cleaner since the fumes are toxic in large amounts. Also, remember to wear rubber gloves to protect the skin if it is sensitive to irritation.

After all dust and dirt has been removed from the material, wet a cloth with the volatile cleaner (Fig. 1). Spread the cloth open and permit the cleaner to evaporate so that the cloth is just damp. Apply the cloth to the upholstery with a very light pressure and rub over a small area at a time. Change to a clean portion of the cloth every few strokes.

If the material is to be gone over again, give it time to dry thoroughly. This will prevent the solvent from penetrating to the padding underneath. Avoid soaking or heavily wetting the upholstery with any volatile cleaner.

Upholstery on doors is treated in the same way. Remove all seats that can be easily taken out of the car for cleaning or they can be cleaned inside the car using the same procedure. For best results, all the upholstery should be dry before using.

Leather, genuine or imitation, requires the use of neutral soap which is obtainable at almost any drugstore. Never use volatile cleaners, household detergents or soaps, furniture polishes, oils or bleaches. These may mar the finish of the leather permanently.

There is a natural tendency for leather to show signs of wrinkling; it may also bear the marks from the animal's encounters with barb-wire and other scars. Such marks do not impair its durability or quality. But wrinkles and scars are natural collectors of dirt and dust, and if this condition continues, the dirt becomes a hard and abrasive grit. Under pressure, this grit will cut into the finish and will be the cause of color bleeding and cracking in pressure areas.

To restore the original bright color, use lukewarm water and a neutral soap. Work up a heavy suds and apply *only* the suds (Fig. 2) to the leather. Next, go over the leather again, but this time, use only a damp, clean cloth. Then, wipe the leather with a soft, dry cloth. This same treatment can be used in the treatment of imitation leathers.

Synthetic Fabrics such as nylon, viscose, orlon, rayon and the related synthetics are easily cleaned by foam-type cleaners in pressurized containers.

After brushing to remove free dirt, release about a cupful of foam from the container on the bristles of a *soft* brush (Fig. 3). Rub briskly over a small area at a time. Overlap the applications of foam to prevent streaks. Be sure to wipe each area after cleaning with a damp cloth to remove dirt-laden foam.

Synthetic upholstery may also be cleaned with a good household detergent where foam-type cleaners are not desired. This process is equally simple.

Stir enough detergent into a pail of lukewarm water to work up a thick and heavy suds. Dampen a cloth or sponge. Again, use the suds only. Use light or medium pressure and overlap new areas (Fig. 4). Wipe off dirt-soaked detergent suds with a second damp cloth. Then, use a dry, clean cloth to wipe off excess moisture.

Should a second treatment be immediately necessary because of stubborn soiled areas, do not allow the upholstery to become completely dry before recleaning. Repeat treatment when the upholstery has reached a faintly damp stage.

Ceilings and Floors. Ceilings should be cleaned in the same way as the rest of the upholstery (Fig. 5). Use the cleaning agent recommended to the type of material.

Floor carpets are best maintained by frequent and thorough brushing and the use of a vacuum cleaner. If this does not remove the dirt, use a foam-type cleaner to do the job. Do not apply the foam cleaner to more than one square foot of carpet at a time. Use a vacuum cleaner to remove the foam from each processed section. After cleaning, the carpet may be fluffed by working a soft bristle brush gently over the nap. Make sure the carpet is completely dry before using and open the windows to prevent mildewing.

If a carpet has been badly stained and must be removed for cleaning, care must be taken to prevent damage. Carpets are cemented or

Fig. 3. Clean upholstery made of synthetic fibers with foam type cleaner and soft brush.

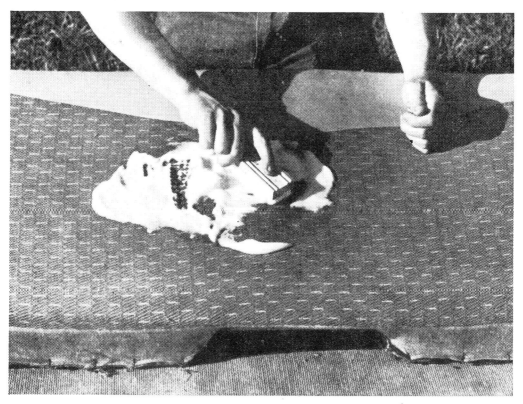

Fig. 4. Work cleaner over small-overlapping areas with light or medium pressure.

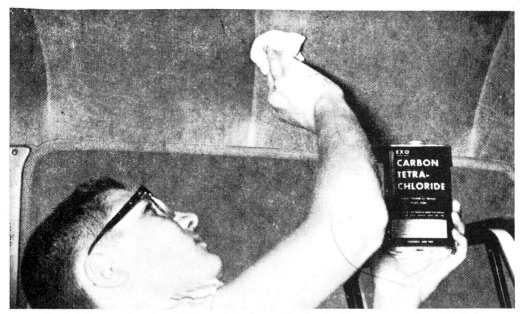

Fig. 5. Ceilings are best cleaned with a volatile cleaner after first brushing to remove all possible dust.

held in place with metal molding, or both. First, remove screws and molding. Then, turn back a corner of the carpet. Use a wide-blade putty knife to separate the carpet from the cement. Do not pull or jerk the carpet. Avoid getting any of the cement on the face of the carpet. Once removed, use a volatile cleaner to remove oil or grease spots. Then clean with foam as outlined earlier.

STAIN REMOVAL

Different kinds of stains require different treatments and the use of the wrong treatment may cause even worse damage than the stain itself. However, the removal of the most common stains is well within the ability of the average person. It should be remembered that the sooner after occurrence the stain is treated, the better will be the results.

Battery Acid. Saturate affected area with common household ammonia. Allow it to remain on the stain about one minute to neutralize the acid. Rub the spot with a clean cloth wet with cold water. Blot with dry cloth and repeat wet rag application. Action must be immediate to limit destructive action of the acid on the fabric.

Blood. Never try to remove blood with hot water or with soap and water. The action may set the stain and make removal almost impossible. With a clean cloth wet with *cold* water, rub the blood stain to remove as much of it as possible. As the wet cloth absorbs the stain, fold it to present a clean portion to the stain. Failure to do so will work the stain in a diluted form back into the material. If done soon after the stain's occurrence, this procedure should remove all of it. Should the stain be obstinate after this treatment, apply a bit of household ammonia. Let stand a minute

or two, then rub the stain with a clean cloth saturated with cold water. Should the water and ammonia treatment fail to have the desired effect, another remedy must be used. Make a thick paste of corn starch and cold water and apply it to the stain. After the paste has dried, remove it to determine if the paste has absorbed the stain. If not, several applications may be necessary.

Candy. Non-chocolate candy stains are best removed by applying a cloth soaked in very hot water to the stain. Rub gently and allow to dry. Should some sign of stain remain, remove by applying a cloth wet with volatile cleaner. For chocolate candy, the same treatment is recommended except that lukewarm water instead of very hot water should be used.

Chewing Gum. Apply an ice cube to the gum to harden it. Scrape off hardened particles with a dull knife or edge of a spoon. If all the gum cannot be removed, moisten it with a volatile cleaner. While the gum is moist, remove it by separating it from the material with a dull knife or spoon.

Fruit, Liquor or Wine. Apply very hot water with a clean rag, and wet thoroughly. Rub briskly with hot water soaked cloth. If the stain persists, scrape with a dull knife or spoon while wet, and allow to dry. If signs of the stain remain, then rub lightly with a cloth dampened with a volatile cleaner. Never use soap and water since such treatment may permanently set the stain. Also, never use heat to dry the treated area.

Enamel, Lacquer or Paint. Wet a clean cloth in turpentine. Rub over the stain to remove as much as possible. If the stain is stubborn, saturate with a mixture of one part

182

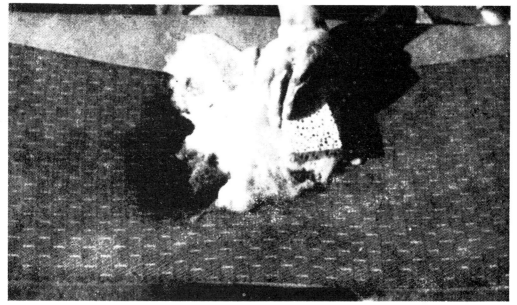

Fig. 6. Try removing mildew stains by first rubbing with suds; old stains may require oxalic acid solution.

denatured alcohol and one part benzine. Apply dull knife or spoon to stain and scrape away as much as possible. Repeat if necessary. Apply a final saturation of the mixture and follow immediately with a vigorous rubbing with a cloth soaked with lukewarm soapsuds. Rinse by sponging with cold water.

Tar. Moisten the tar slightly with a volatile cleaner. Use a dull knife to scrape away as much as you can. Rub the spot gently with a cloth dampened with a volatile cleaner until it disappears.

Grease or Oil. Remove as much of the grease or oil as is possible with a dull knife blade or kitchen spatula. Rub lightly with a cloth wet with a volatile cleaner over the affected area. Rub from the outer edges of the stain toward the center to reduce the possibility of spreading the stain. Keep applying cleaner on fresh cloths as needed. Confine oil or grease to as small an area as possible by pouring a small quantity of the cleaner directly on the stain. Keep doing this until no more grease or oil can be blotted up. This method also aids in the preventing of a ring formation. If repeated treatments with the solvent still leave a dirty stain, rub the area with lukewarm soapsuds. Rinse with cold water applied with a clean cloth. Always rub from the outside to the center of the stain.

Ice Cream. Wet the stain with very hot water applied with a clean cloth. Scrape wet area to remove as much of the stain as possible. Rub vigorously with very hot water again. If the stain is stubborn, rub it with a cloth wet with warm neutral soap suds. Rinse by rubbing with a cloth wet with cold water, and allow to dry. If faint signs still remain, rub with a cloth dampened with a volatile cleaner.

Mildew. Rub mildew vigorously with warm soap suds (Fig. 6) and rinse by rubbing with a cloth dipped in cold water. Old mildew stains are harder to remove. The only treatment recommended for treating discolorations caused by old mildew growths is the use of oxalic acid. Wet the mildew with a 10% oxalic acid solution. Let it soak a minute or so. Next, use a blotter or absorbent cloth to blot up acid. Rinse with either hot or cold water. Repeat this sequence as often as is necessary.

Shoe Polish. White shoe polish should be allowed to dry completely. With a brush, go over the dry stain briskly until it disappears. Should it persist, moisten it with cold water. Allow to dry, then brush vigorously until it vanishes. Wax or paste type shoe polishes need to be rubbed gently with a cloth dampened with a volatile cleaner. Rub from the outside of the stain to the center, changing to a clean portion of the cloth frequently.

Lipstick. Different brands of lipstick are made of varying components which make stains difficult to remove. Use a spoon or dull knife to scrape away as much as possible. Rub lightly with a cloth dampened with a volatile cleaner. Repeat several times. Should some stain remain after repeated treatments, it is recommended that no more be done to it. Other measures might do more harm than good.

Ink. Apply Ink Eradicator Solution Number One. Use an eye dropper for the purpose. Blot up excess with a blotter. Keep repeating until as much of the stain as possible is removed. Then, rinse with a cloth dipped in cold water.

Basic Tool Kit for the Weekend Mechanic

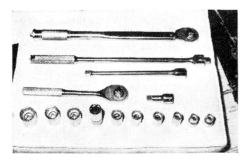

A good tool kit starts off with a ½-inch socket set that includes a torque wrench. (The torque handle is shown at the top.)

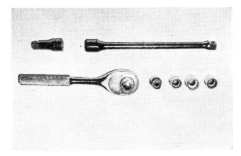

A ⅜-inch drive socket set with short and long extensions and ratchet is also a must; socket dimensions are listed in the table.

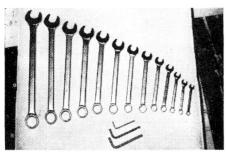

A complete set of combination box and open end wrenches from ¼-inch to 1-inch is shown with an assortment of Allen key wrenches.

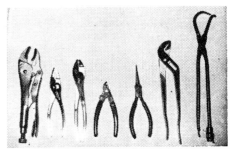

Assorted pliers from left to right: vise grip, general, hose clamp, wire stripper, needle nose, water pump, and brake spring.

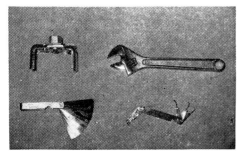

At lower left are feeler gauges; lower right, spark plug gauges; upper left, oil filter wrench; top right, adjustable wrench.

This compression gauge reads to 300 psi; the hard rubber tip is designed to fit and seal spark plug hole with no pressure loss.

Maintaining and troubleshooting your automobile requires more than just the know-how; without the right tools your hands are tied. This basic toolbox outfitting will enable you to tackle any of the ordinary problems you'll run into.

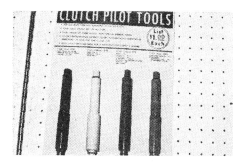

These light duty wooden clutch pilot tools are ideal for the weekend mechanic; they're not used frequently and they're inexpensive.

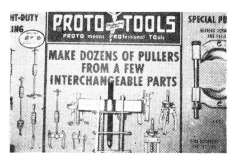

The advanced weekender who may be pulling timing gears *needs* a general gear puller; but it's always good to have one around.

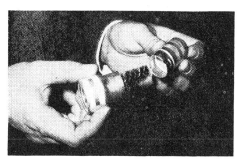

A specially designed wire brush makes cleaning battery posts and terminals so easy you'll have no excuse to neglect the job.

Induction ammeters indicate current by holding them over the circuit to be tested; not too accurate but good troubleshooters.

BASIC TOOL KIT

Half-Inch Drive Socket Set consisting of short and medium extensions, ratchet, breaker bar and the following sockets: $7/16$, $1/2$, $9/16$, $5/8$, $11/16$, $3/4$, $13/16$ (deep spark plug socket), $7/8$ and 1 inch.

Three-Eighths-Inch Drive Socket Set consisting of short and long extensions, ratchet and the following sockets: $1/4$, $5/16$, $3/8$, $7/16$, and $1/2$-inch.

Combination box and open-end wrenches in the following sizes (those with asterisks indicate duplicates should be purchased): $1/4$, $5/16$, $3/8$,* $7/16$,* $1/2$,* $9/16$,* $5/8$,* $11/16$,* $3/4$, $13/16$, $7/8$ and 1 inch.

Sets of feeler and spark plug gap gauges

Assorted screwdrivers in the three popular style heads

Pliers (needle-nose, brake return spring, water pump, spring clamp, vise-grip and general)

Nut cracker

Hacksaw

Torque wrench (range to 150 ft. lbs.)

Compression gauge (range to 300 psi)

Vacuum gauge (pressure gauge range to 9 psi)

Assorted Allen wrenches

Valve spring compressor

Test lamp

Clutch aligning tool

Oil filter wrench

Battery post-cable terminal wire brush assembly

Wire cutter and stripper (best purchased as part of crimp-type terminals' kit)

Battery and anti-freeze hydrometers

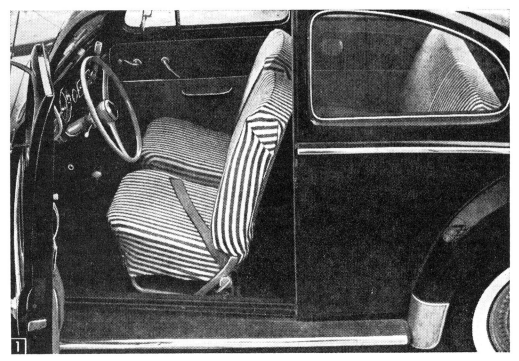

Besides brightening interior, covers protect the seats from stains and the passengers from heat and cold.

Comfort Condition Seat Covers

By tailoring to fit accurately, you can save more than half of what a ready-made set will cost

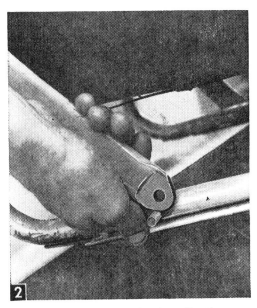

Separate the front seat sections by pulling the arms away from the dowels and sliding them toward the rear so they won't rip the vinyl cover.

VINYL or leather covered seats in big and small cars have the uncomfortable habit of retaining heat in hot weather. During a cold spell they take a while to warm up. You can eliminate these discomforts and have the added advantage of washability with a set of terrycloth or denim seat covers that make driving more comfortable.

Even if you're not handy with a needle and thread you can make covers for the front and back seats of your car by following the procedures used to tailor the set for the Volkswagen in Fig. 1. The tools you need for this job are straight pins, sewing needles, black basting thread, pinking shears, and a sewing

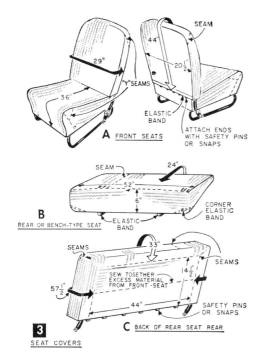

A FRONT SEATS

B REAR OR BENCH-TYPE SEAT

3 SEAT COVERS

C BACK OF REAR SEAT REAR

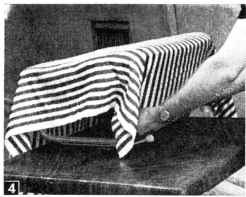

Lay the material over the seat for general measurement and alignment.

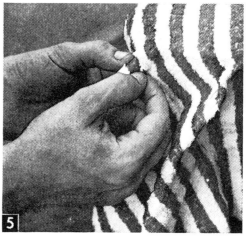

Pin the corners with straight pins so a Y-shaped seam is formed to ensure a tight fit.

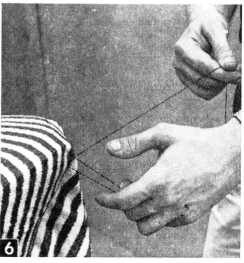

Use a thread that shows up against the material and baste loosely just over the pins.

machine equipped with a medium needle.

The front and back covers for the VW (Fig. 3) require 7 yds. of 36-in.-wide terrycloth and about 8½ ft. of ½-in. elastic, used to hold the material on the seats. Measure your seats as in Fig. 3 to determine how much terrycloth or denim you need for your seat covers.

Start to Work on the front seats (Fig. 3). To make the job as easy as possible, unbolt the assembly from the floor, or with the VW, slide the seat forward off the floor runners. With the front seats out, remove the back rest by pulling the vertical support arms from the dowels in the runners (Fig. 2). These arms are held by pincer action and you might need some help to free them.

With the bottom and back separated, spread the terrycloth or denim material over the bottom (Fig. 4). The 36-in. wide material is enough to cover the width of a bucket seat, but you have to sew two pieces together for models that have a bench-type front seat. Let the excess material hang over the back of the seat.

Allow a 2 in. overhang in the front and pin the front corners so a Y-shaped seam is formed (Fig. 5), then pull the material taut and pin a straight, vertical seam in the back corners. Baste all seams with black thread (Fig. 6), or use another color that shows up against the material. Leave a 2-in. overhang when cutting the material off from the back of the seat with pinking shears.

Carefully remove the stitched cover and machine sew all the basted seams. Hem the

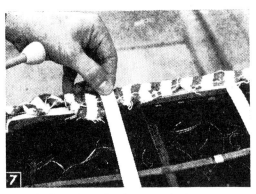

Stretch three elastic bands across the bottom, sewing the back end and using safety pins or snaps to hold them to the front of the seat.

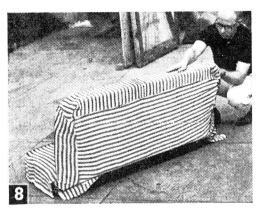

Completed terrycloth covers on the back seat are held in place with elastic bands and pins to ensure a custom fit and facilitate removal.

bottom to give the cover a more tailored look. Trim away the "ears" that will form bulges at the corners, and turn the cover inside out to hide the trimmed edges of the seams. Place the cover on the seat to make sure it fits straight and taut.

Finish the cover by attaching three strips of 8-in.-long elastic under the seat as in Fig. 7. These strips must run parallel from front to rear; sew them in front and fasten them to the back with safety pins. With this hookup you can remove the covers for washing.

Fold the Material over the back rest. Starting with the front, fold over the top, and trim off at the lower edge in the back. Pull the material taut and pin the edges together. Adjust the material so one side seam meets cloth-to-cloth, and cut off the excess material from the other side. This cut-off will later be used for the rear seat.

Follow the basting procedure as in Fig. 6, sew, then check for fit. Sew an unstretched strip of ½ x 12-in. plastic at the meeting edges of the terrycloth. Begin at the ends of the elastic and hand sew toward the center.

This should give proper tautness and added strength to the fabric when the ends are attached.

Be Careful not to scuff the upholstery below the rear side windows when you remove the bottom of the rear seat. With the front seats out you have more room to work. Lift the seat up so it clears the brackets and pull it forward.

A single length of terrycloth is not wide enough to cover the entire width of the seat, so you'll have to sew two pieces together. Seam these pieces together, being careful in the case of striped cloth to match the stripes so they blend and the seam is straight.

Use the excess material that was cut off the front seats to cover the lower front of the rear seat as in Fig. 3B. Cut it to the required width and pin it to the edge of the seamed cover. Let the irregular shaped end hang free, because this will be hidden under the seat. Stretch the material taut, baste and sew.

Attach two parallel strips of 8-in.-long elastic from the front to rear near the sides where they can be slipped off when you want to remove the covers. Attach a third strip of elastic in the center for wider seats. Also sew two 6-in.-long elastic strips underneath the corners (Fig. 3). Elastic on this seat can be sewn at both ends.

Use the remaining material for the back rest. Cut a 14½-in.-wide band and use this for the back section as in Figs. 3B and 8. Sew the two pieces together so they cover the width of the seat, then pin the front and back sections together. Baste all the way around and remove for sewing. Trim away the excess material, then use safety pins or snaps to hold the fabric together at the bottom of the seat.

Vacuum Gage Checks for Clogged Muffler

• If your car has lost some top speed and runs a bit hot, be sure to check for a clogged muffler. To do this, attach a vacuum gage (about $5 from mail-order houses or auto accessory stores) to the intake manifold, as at the vacuum windshield fitting. Then start the engine and watch the gage. In a well running engine the vacuum may be between 15 and 21 in., but it should be steady. Now increase engine speed to what you estimate would be about 50 *mph* on the highway. To the extent that the exhaust system is clogged and resistance increases, the vacuum reading will drop off. A badly clogged muffler may send the vacuum indication down to four or five points on the gage—or even to two. To check the reading, drop the exhaust pipe from the engine manifold and repeat the test. If the vacuum reading stays up as your speed increases, you can be certain that the muffler and possibly the exhaust pipe are clogged and should be replaced.—M. A. Tidd.

188

Left, using suction cup fitting, unique new tool pops out shallow dent where metal is merely sprung, but not creased or bent. Right, typical crease caused by car bumper. Fit piece of sandpaper in flat file and rub it over crease to outline area of dent.

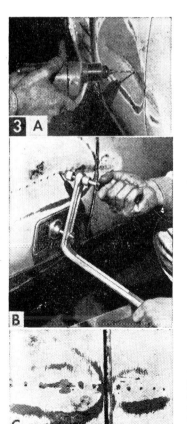

New Ways to Remove Car Dents and Scratches

THE local body shop might sock you $30 to $35 for a "crease" job and, if you have ever removed a car's inside panel in order to pound out a dent, you would probably agree it's worth it.

Now, thanks to development of a new dent-removing tool, you can do an efficient job yourself (Figs. 1, 2, 3) without disturbing the paneling and for less than half the normal cost. Tool, attachments, flat sandpaper file, fiber glass body filler and hardener make up a kit called the Spaulding Dent Remover, now available for under $15 in Sears Roebuck, Western Tire Auto Stores and similar outlets.

The Crease or Small Dent commonly caused by bumpers of other cars maneuvering in and out of tight parking areas is often deceptive to the eye so the first step is to define it.

Three steps to dent removal. Top, drilling ⅛-in. diameter holes about an inch apart across deepest part of crease. Center, applying gradual pressure with new dent-removing tool to pull out dent with sheet metal screw, a process repeated in each hole. Bottom, after lifting out panel and checking with sandpaper file for low spots, this pattern will appear if panel is properly straightened.

4

Grind out whole area with disc sander after removing crease. Slightly low spots (white areas in center) will be leveled with fiber glass body filler.

Go over the area with the flat sandpaper file as in Fig. 2 to outline the damaged section. Run your fingers over it to locate the deepest part of the depression, then drill small holes through the metal from one end of the crease to the other as in Fig. 3A. Don't let the thought of actually drilling holes into your car disturb you. They serve a double purpose, allowing you to pull out the dent and giving a firmer hold to the filler as it becomes almost as hard as the body itself. When done, you won't be able to locate the dent or holes.

Chuck a sheet metal screw from the kit in the screwdriver attachment, secure through long end of dent-removing tool and turn screw into an end hole as in Fig. 3B, until it has a firm bite. Apply gradual pressure with the tool until you feel the dent come out in much the same way as you feel a nail give when you pull it out of a board with a hammer. *Don't pry too hard,* or you may ripple the metal. Lift each section a bit at a time, then repeat the process with each succeeding hole until you reach the other side of the dent.

Unless the crease is very severe, one lift on each hole should do the job. If it doesn't, repeat the process until panel regains its original shape. When the dent feels smooth, go over it again with the sandpaper file. If the panel is sufficiently straight to proceed, it will produce a file mark pattern similar to that in Fig. 3C.

After smoothing with a rotary sanding pad on your electric drill, the area should appear like that in Fig. 4. If any low spots are still in evidence, remove with the dent puller. This can usually be done without drilling additional holes.

To fill drill holes and any depressions remaining, scoop out a gob of fiber glass body filler the size of a golf ball onto a polyethylene mixing dish and add a few drops of the

catalyst from the tube of hardener as shown in Fig. 5, following directions carefully. These materials are included in the kit. Mix thoroughly and apply a ¼-in.-thick layer all over area, with a flexible plastic spreader as in Fig. 6. Use enough pressure to force some filler through the holes, where it will mushroom slightly and, when dry, doubly insure the permanence of the patch.

Once the fiber glass has thoroughly set, sand off the excess, smooth out the whole area with rotary sander (Fig. 7.) or sandpaper file and the repaired section is ready to prime and paint. Up to this point, it took us 45 minutes to do the job.

Large, Shallow Dents. Where the metal is sprung rather than creased, as often happens in door panels, use the suction cup attachment with the dent remover. Screw cup to hole in end of the longer arm and fit the pivot pad in slot of the same arm near the bend. Wash the damaged panel with water and moisten the suction cup.

Clamp cup to center of the dent and place pivot pad against panel below. Apply gradual pressure as in Fig. 1 until the dent pops out. To remove suction cup, slide it off panel edge.

5

6

Left, add catalyst to filler in plastic dish and mix well with putty knife. Normal mix will set for sanding in 15 to 20 minutes. Adding more hardener will speed setting, as does warm temperature. Above, use flexible spreader to apply filler, forcing some through holes to anchor it securely. Apply too much rather than too little; it's easier to grind off excess than add another layer.

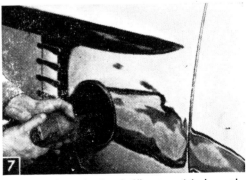

7

Sanding down hardened filler to original panel shape. Since fiber glass dust is irritating and hard to remove, wear long sleeves; if your skin is sensitive, wear gloves.

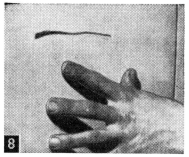
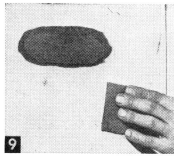

Left, this 6-in. scrape is typical of scratches caused by garage doors, bicycle fenders, car doors opened in parking lots, which can be repaired easily—if care and patience are your watchwords. Right, sand out scratch to bare metal, also enough of surrounding paint to leave extremely fine feathered edges.

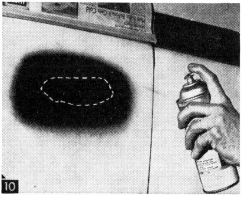

Carefully build up sanded area with primer in series of light coats extending well beyond edge indicated by dotted line. Avoid temptation to rush job with thick applications and let each coat dry thoroughly.

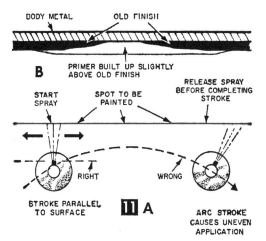

Nicks, Chips and Scratches. The paint on your car is pretty tough stuff to hold up the way it does, considering the beating it takes. Unfortunately, the paint hasn't been made that will deflect flying stones, Junior's bicycle

fenders and other things that cause most of those unsightly little scrapes on your car. If you don't cover them before winter weather sets in, they will be an open invitation to body-rotting rust.

With the recent introduction of touch-up paints and primer in high-pressure Aerosol spray cans, you can make those rough spots in the finish vanish with so little effort that your biggest problem is to avoid a temptation to rush the job because it seems so easy.

Treatment is generally the same, whether the trouble spots are small scrapes as shown in Fig. 8 or larger exposed areas which started out small and increased as surrounding paint peeled away.

Sand area around the spot with 320 (fine) paper down to the bright, bare metal as in Fig. 9, leaving such a fine feathered edge all around that you can hardly tell where the bare metal ends and the finish begins. Half the success of the job depends on how smoothly you do this step.

You can follow the steps from here on to repaint a dented area repaired as previously described.

After sanding, rub the existing finish around the spot with a cleaning compound until you have a clean area at least 6 inches beyond the part you plan to paint. This is particularly important if your car has a light-colored finish, since any dirt left on the old finish will bleed through new paint and leave a "bullseye." Rub out the cleaner, sponge off the residue with clean water and wipe thoroughly dry.

Using primer-surfacer from a push-button pressure-can as in Fig. 10, build up the area with several thin coats, letting each dry before applying the next. Remember to keep the can moving steadily and in a line parallel to the work while spraying as in Fig. 11A, and stop the spray each time before reaching the end of your sweeping motion. Guard against the natural tendency for your hand to arch the stroke or turn the can. Extend the primer beyond the feathered edges and build it up until primer is slightly higher than the existing paint as in Fig. 11B—about .005 in.

When thoroughly dry, sand the built-up primer with 320 paper until smooth and even with the existing paint as in Fig. 12. If you're working on a large flat surface, you'll find it easier to get the necessary smoothness by

12

Smoothing primer surfacer calls for a very light touch to avoid sanding through to the metal or leaving finger ridges.

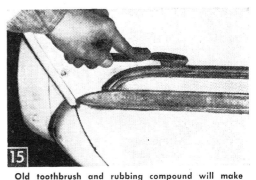

15

Old toothbrush and rubbing compound will make short work of stains along edges of chrome trim.

FIG. 13—PITFALLS TO AVOID IN SPRAY TOUCH-UP WORK

PROBLEM	CAUSE	REMEDY
Paint runs.	Coats are too heavy	Move can faster.
Paint is ripply.	Can too close; air blast is moving paint.	Hold can farther from work.
Paint is fuzzy; looks like it is full of lint. (Occurs only with lacquer.)	Can is too far from work; paint is partially dry when it hits work surface.	Hold can closer.
Paint peels.	Improper or insufficient sanding; not using primer.	Sand to bare metal and use primer.
Raised area around perimeter of spot painted.	Edge was not properly feathered or primer was not sanded down smoothly.	Finer feather; more complete sanding after priming.

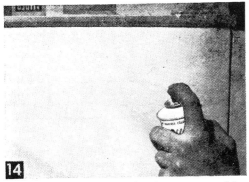

14

Spray finish according to directions on can and in several coats, each so light that it is hardly visible.

using a rubber-faced sanding block.

Do the sanding either wet or dry. When through, sponge the entire area again with clean water.

You can buy the push-button spray paint in lacquer or enamel form, and the primer, in auto supply houses and many hardware stores. If your car is a 1956 or later model, you will have no trouble duplicating its original factory color, but some finishes on earlier models may be difficult to match. To be sure, test it first with a little spot under the hood or some other obscure part of the body. Then study the chart in Fig. 13 to check on causes of paint failure and how to avoid them.

Apply the finish in the same way as the primer with several light coats as in Fig. 14 but extend the coats slightly beyond the primer edge. If the area is large, a light mist sprayed just after the finish from a can of leveler (thinner) will help smooth out any lumps. After the leveler has dried, give the spot a very light finish coat.

If you are using enamel, keep the car indoors at least overnight and wait at least two weeks before applying some rubbing compound and rubbing out the new paint.

If your finish is lacquer, it will dry almost instantly and you can then apply the rubbing-out process.

Chrome Trim Stains. While you have the rubbing compound out, take advantage of the opportunity to rid your car of blemishes that frequently appear along edges of the chrome.

Substitute an old toothbrush for your rubbing rags to get well down into cracks between car body and trim as shown in Fig. 15.